Collins

Cambridge International AS & A Level Drama

STUDENT'S BOOK

Series editor: Emma Hollis
Authors: Holly Barradell, Rebekah Beattie, Gail Deal, Mike Gould and Emma Hollis

William Collins' dream of knowledge for all began with the publication of his first book in 1819.

A self-educated mill worker, he not only enriched millions of lives, but also founded a flourishing publishing house. Today, staying true to this spirit, Collins books are packed with inspiration, innovation and practical expertise. They place you at the centre of a world of possibility and give you exactly what you need to explore it.

Collins. Freedom to teach.

Published by Collins
An imprint of HarperCollins*Publishers*
The News Building
1 London Bridge Street
London
SE1 9GF

Browse the complete Collins catalogue at
www.collins.co.uk

10 9 8 7 6 5 4 3 2 1

© HarperCollins*Publishers* Limited 2020

ISBN 978-0-00-832614-2

British Library Cataloguing-in-Publication Data

A catalogue record for this publication is available from the British Library.

Authors: Holly Barradell, Rebekah Beattie, Gail Deal, Mike Gould, Emma Hollis
Series editor: Emma Hollis
Product manager: Catherine Martin
Content editor: Alexandra Wells
Development editor: Sonya Newland
Copyeditor: Catherine Dakin
Proofreader: Nikky Twyman
Text permissions researcher: Rachel Thorne
Cover designer: Gordon MacGilp
Cover illustrator: Ann Paganuzzi
Typesetter: Ken Vail Graphic Design
Production controller: Lyndsey Rogers
Printed and bound by: CPI Group (UK) Ltd, Croydon CR0 4YY

The publishers gratefully acknowledge the permission granted to reproduce the copyright material in this book. Every effort has been made to trace copyright holders and to obtain their permission for the use of copyright material. The publishers will gladly receive any information enabling them to rectify any error or omission at the first opportunity.

With thanks to the following teachers for reviewing sections of the book as it was developed:
Alistar Boucher, Ackworth School, Ackworth, Pontefract, West Yorkshire, UK; and
Ann-marie Cubbin, The ABC International School, Ho CHi Minh City, Saigon, Vietnam.

This book refers to the Cambridge International AS & AL Drama syllabus 9482 for examination from 2021. You should always refer to the appropriate syllabus document for the year of your examination to confirm the details and for more information. The syllabus document is available on the Cambridge International website at www.cambridgeinternational.org.

Exam-style questions and sample answers have been written by the authors. In examinations, the way marks are awarded may be different. References to assessment and/or assessment preparation are the publisher's interpretation of the syllabus requirements and may not fully reflect the approach of Cambridge Assessment International Education.

Cambridge International recommends that teachers consider using a range of teaching and learning resources in preparing learners for assessment, based on their own professional judgement of their students' needs.

Third-party websites and resources referred to in this publication have not been endorsed by Cambridge Assessment International Education.

Contents

Contents

Introduction

Drama is a vibrant and dynamic art form. At Advanced Level, students are offered the opportunity to consider the nature of theatrical text as well the various aspects of theatre-making. The Cambridge International syllabus is designed to develop rich knowledge and understanding and build essential skills in performance, directing, designing and devising. There are many opportunities to consider the journey made by a text as you move it from the page to the stage.

This book is structured to support the process of building skills and knowledge with in-depth, up-to-date coverage of each area of the syllabus and a stimulating range of international texts to analyse, respond to and inspire your own work. Throughout the book, you will work with an exciting range of texts from different cultures and time periods, chosen to expand your understanding and enjoyment of studying Drama and Theatre. We aim to encourage and support you to develop specific areas of interest and a lifelong love of the theatre.

In **Chapter 1** the key concepts and frameworks of drama studies are introduced. You will explore the building blocks of drama by considering the importance of style, genre, form and context. In this chapter, a spotlight is placed on Noh and Kabuki and examples of political, symbolist and physical theatre.

In **Chapter 2** you will build on this work by exploring the skills required to stage a text. Here, two classical texts, Shakespeare's *A Midsummer Night's Dream* and Goldoni's *A Servant to Two Masters*, are used to help you consider how a play's context influences its themes and ideas. You will explore the extent to which a director's interpretation is influenced by their audience.

In **Chapter 3** you will consider the process and nature of devising theatre. In this chapter, a range of types of stimuli for devising, including visual imagery and literary texts, are explored. Through a range of spotlights, you will explore a number of theatre practitioners who have developed a distinctive style of devising.

In **Chapter 4** you will focus on design and cover the key features of a broad range of design and production elements including costume, set, lighting and sound. The aim of this chapter is to develop your design skills and technical understanding with illustrative examples drawn from a range of theatrical genres, texts and practitioners.

In **Chapter 5** you will return to text, but with a specific focus on the skills required to engage and write analytically about both extracts from a text and the whole text in performance. To demonstrate your skills, in this chapter you will draw on both a contemporary and a classical text: *The Jungle* by Joe Robertson and Joe Murphy, and *The Cherry Orchard* by Anton Chekhov. Through this work, you will consolidate your understanding of the key features of dramatic text.

Finally, in **Chapter 6** you will focus on your role as a theatre researcher as you begin to choose a topic for an investigation. With reference to a range of dynamic case studies, the skills required to plan a project, choose appropriate research methods and structure a research plan are modelled.

Please note: exam-style questions and sample answers have been written by the authors. In examinations, the way marks are awarded may be different. References to assessment and/or assessment preparation are the publisher's interpretation of the syllabus requirements and may not fully reflect the approach of Cambridge Assessment International Education. The Cambridge International syllabus clearly lists the set texts, practitioners, traditions and styles you need to study for your examination. Please go to www.cambridgeinternational.org for full syllabus details.

Cambridge International recommends that teachers consider using a range of teaching and learning resources in preparing learners for assessment, based on their own professional judgement of their students' needs.

My co-authors and I hope that you will find this book to be a valuable aid in supporting you as you address the demands of Advanced Level study. Whether you are working with your peers or engaging in an individual investigation of text or performance, we wish you many hours of stimulation and enjoyment.

Emma Hollis, August 2019

HOW TO USE THIS BOOK

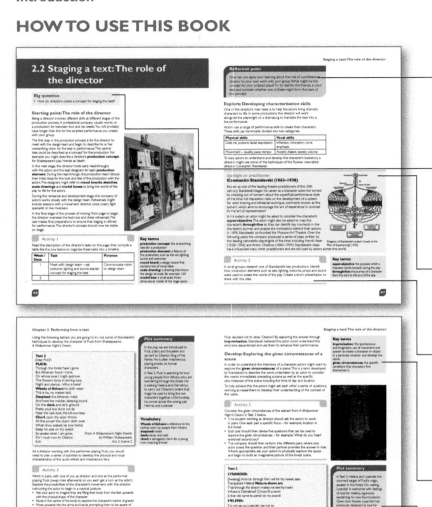

- *Reflection* points help you to evaluate and reflect on your own performance or contributions, and apply your learning to your own set texts, performances or devising work.

- A *Big question* provides a clear focus for your learning in each unit and can be revisited at the end of the learning sequence.

- *Spotlight* sections provide detailed information on specific practitioners and theatre traditions.

- A wealth of activities encourage you to develop, explore and apply ideas for performance. Analysis and writing skills are also developed throughout the book.

- *Key terms* are defined on the page where they occur and collated into a full Glossary of key terms at the end of the book.

- *Plot summary* boxes help you situate the various play extracts within the plot of the full play.

- Any culturally specific words, phrases or references in the texts have been glossed in a Vocabulary box to support your understanding.

- *Thinking more deeply* sections ask you to explore an idea in greater depth, to develop a more sophisticated skill or to extend your learning.

Chapter 1
Introduction to theatre

In this chapter, you will explore a brief history of the development of theatre across the world. You will be introduced to the key characteristics of particular practitioners and examine the role that they have played in developing theatre as an art form. You will also consider the extent to which practitioners develop work within a variety of local and national contexts.

1.1 Introduction to theatre from around the world

Big question

- How has theatre developed in different parts of the world?

Starting point: Early theatre

The word 'theatre' derives from the ancient Greek word 'theatron', meaning 'viewing or seeing place'. In the ancient societies of Rome and Greece, an audience of people – from all sections of society – would gather to see actors tell a story.

The earliest theatres were usually semi-circular and carved into large open spaces. In these **amphitheatres**, actors would perform plays written to both entertain and educate. It was here that the core principles of drama were established. The philosopher Aristotle (384–322 BCE) established six elements that he considered to be the defining features of a play:

- plot (the story)
- character (the people in the play through whom the drama is presented)
- thought (or intent – the purpose of the play)
- diction (choice of words and phrases)
- music or song
- spectacle (the combination of a range of art forms, such as music, drama and dance).

In ancient Greece, from around 600–400 BCE, theatre largely consisted of **tragedies**. In these plays, the **protagonist** (a high-status hero) usually experiences a dilemma. They are often confronted by an **antagonist** (anti-hero), who presents a moral message or lesson. In classical tragedies, the hero usually experiences a fall from power, often towards death.

By dramatising these stories, early playwrights intended to create a sense of **catharsis** in the audience. That is, the audience would release powerful emotions and thereby experience relief from them. Playwrights also had a moral purpose, hoping that by watching characters face difficult dilemmas and suffer the consequences of their actions, the audience would avoid making the same mistakes.

Activity 1

Working on your own, research the plays of some of the ancient Greek **tragedians**. Copy and complete this table to help you organise your notes.

Playwright	Key plays	Distinctive features of the drama
Sophocles	*Oedipus Rex*	Fall of the tragic hero
Aeschylus		

Key terms

amphitheatre: a large semi-circular auditorium set in an outside space

tragedy: a form of drama based on human suffering that provokes a mix of sympathy and horror from the audience at the inevitable downfall, usually death, of the protagonist

protagonist: the main character in a drama, who often engages with the antagonist to create tension and conflict

antagonist: the opponent of the hero or main character of a drama; someone who competes with another character in a play (usually the protagonist)

catharsis: the feeling of release felt by the audience at the end of a tragedy; a sense of being set free from the emotions of the play

tragedians: playwrights who write tragedies or actors who perform them

As theatre developed, a second genre emerged – comedy. Comedies usually include **archetypal** characters who make some kind of error or create mild mischief that does not cause pain to others. They experience confusion and mishap before the play reaches a happy ending. In ancient Greece, comedies were often staged as part of competitions in tribute to Dionysus, where they would include music and dancing. A third form, **satyr plays**, took heroic elements but subjected them to farcical situations.

Explore: The development of theatre around the world

Other countries and cultures began to develop their own founding principles of drama as an art form with a social and cultural purpose. In China in around CE 200, for example, shadow puppet shows became one of the earliest examples of how theatre was used not only as a form of storytelling, but also as political commentary and **propaganda** (see page 12).

In India, around CE 300–500, a form of drama known as Sanskrit developed (named for the language in which it was performed). Sanskrit drama used archetypal characters, including those of high status and those intended to entertain (clowns). Like the commedia dell'arte theatre of 16th-century Europe (see pages 52–59), Sanskrit actors usually specialised in playing a certain type of character. In Sanskrit plays, there is evidence of a type of actor training, as well as of the use of **props** and costumes.

Many of the theatrical forms that have developed since the early centuries CE are used to reflect on the moral problems in society. The development of theatrical form and genres was therefore shaped by the work of diverse theatre-makers from different parts of the world.

Key terms

archetypal: typical of a certain kind of person or thing

satyr play: a rude, energetic and boisterous drama that followed on from or commented on heroic tragedies, placing the protagonists in ridiculous situations; the 'satyrs' who appeared in these plays were legendary half-human, half-animal creatures

propaganda: information used to promote a cause or present a message, and which may be biased or misleading

props: short for 'properties'; anything used in a dramatic production that is not costume or set; props may be personal (such as a pocket watch) or belong to a room or space, such as a chair that a character uses in a physical way

Activity 2

In small groups, pick an ancient theatrical form. Find out about its key features and then write a 10-minute presentation to share this information with the class. Focus on the aspects of the form that have influenced the development of modern theatre. Use visual aids if you can.

Develop: The rise of the theatre practitioner

A theatre practitioner may be a director, **dramaturg**, actor or designer (or combine different aspects). During the European Renaissance of the 16th century, the role of the actor-manager emerged as a way of coordinating the organisational tasks involved in bringing a play to the stage. The earliest actor-managers did not have the same status as a modern theatre practitioner, however, who is defined through the creation of a distinctive body of work. In theatre history, the late 19th century was key in the emergence of the theatre practitioner. Away from Europe, theatre practitioners emerged as companies of actors started to develop recognisable styles and ideas. As transport links and opportunities for travel have improved, practitioners have become truly international and have sought new forms of non-verbal communication to engage with audiences.

Key terms

dramaturg: someone who interprets, edits and adapts a play text to match a director's vision

physicality: the way in which something is expressed by the position or movement of the body

poor theatre: a style of theatre which aimed to strip theatre of all non-essentials (for example, a set, lighting, sound, elaborate costume) to focus on the skill of the actors

Spotlight on practitioner:
Jerzy Grotowski (1933–99)

Grotowski was born in Poland. He studied acting in Poland and Russia and made his directorial debut in 1957 with a production of Eugène Ionesco's play *The Chairs* (see pages 175–179). Two years later, Grotowski founded a theatre workshop that provided him with a base for experimentation with the actor's **physicality**. During the 1960s and 1970s, Grotowski toured his work around Europe and the United States, to critical acclaim. He used the term '**poor theatre**' to describe the 'co-creation' of the theatrical event by performers and spectators that he felt would be 'therapeutic' – to support the mental health of the audience. In the 1970s, Grotowski spent time exploring 'paratheatrical' techniques based on the use of communal activities and long interactive exchanges between actors and audience. For example, the audience might be asked to chant with the actors or simply observe an actor for a long period of silence. Grotowski was particularly interested in the role of an actor's breath in creating pace and atmosphere in performance.

Activity 3

In pairs, undertake some research into the techniques Grotowski developed that informed his production style. Make some notes on what his productions looked and felt like in performance.

Apply: Investigating practitioners

Several modern practitioners have been influenced by Grotowski's work. Today, theatre-makers use projection, live film and digital displays to reflect the external world of the spectator in a different way. For example, the work of the theatre company Frantic Assembly (see page 91) seeks to communicate directly with the audience using physical methods, which could be said to draw directly on Grotowski's interest in the relationship between actor and audience.

Consider the following example of a modern production, which used digital technology to communicate key themes.

Case study:
All About Eve, Ivo van Hove, National Theatre (2019)

The National Theatre's 2019 production of *All About Eve* (based on the 1950 Joseph L. Mankiewicz film) was set backstage in a theatre. The director used live film feed to capture the main character's vanities and anxieties about getting old, and the camera is both visible and hidden. The audience is asked to watch both the theatrical telling of the story and the documentary being played out on the screens above. The filmed action also takes place in two cramped spaces representing rooms, such as bathrooms and kitchens. By doing so, the director suggests that the smallest but most significant events in life take place in these rooms. To show the petty jealousies and desperate ambition in the world of the theatre, he used techniques such as repeated sequences (for example, a young fan entering the star's dressing room at the beginning and end of the play) and the symbolic use of colour, especially red, to represent passion and danger.

All About Eve, Ivo van Hove, National Theatre (2019)

Activity 4

Choose a practitioner from the list below, then copy and complete the table to deepen your investigation into the non-verbal techniques of a theatre practitioner.

- Ivo van Hove
- Tadeusz Kantor
- Ariane Mnouchkine
- Peter Stein

The first row has been completed for you using the example of the French-Canadian director Robert Lepage.

Theatre method	How it is used by the practitioner to communicate with an audience	Example and impact
Performance style	Highly physical, often including choral movement and speech; sometimes spiritual	*Geometry of Miracles* (1998). Chorus represents a car crash that involves a key character – very moving and shocking.
Ensemble style		
Set		
Lighting		
Sound		
Costume		

Reflection point

Write a short action plan that enables you to explore the practitioner who will be the focus of your devising work. List particular things you need to do, such as source photos of productions, to identify the key features of their style.

1.2 Genre case study: Political drama

Big question

- What are the key features of political drama?

Starting point: What is political drama?

Political drama may be part of a campaign or movement, or designed to further a particular cause. The political **satires** of ancient Greek theatre were intended to communicate key social messages and either maintain or disrupt the status quo. Political messages might include those that promote one side or another in a war or one powerful individual over another. Whatever the message intended by the playwright, political theatre exercises one of the key principles of democracy – freedom of speech.

Spotlight on theatre tradition:
Agit-prop theatre of Soviet Russia

In Soviet Russia during the early 20th century, agit-prop (from 'agitation propaganda') theatre was developed as a way of communicating messages that reinforced government authority. Agit-prop theatre is characterised by archetypal heroes and villains. Plays had simple plots in which enemies of the state were exposed and defeated, or in which the uneducated were brought to a state of enlightenment. After the Russian monarchy was overthrown in 1917, a group of performers travelled the country putting on short plays and distributing leaflets to the rural poor. At about the same time, a network of literacy centres was established to ensure that Russian peasants learned to read and write, which would allow them to spread the government's political message. Agit-prop theatre was later adopted by different groups to create political or social agitation or to communicate protest messages.

An agit-prop poster. The text says: 'Want it? Join / 1. You want to overcome cold? 2. You want to overcome hunger? / 3. You want to eat? 4. You want to drink? / Hasten to join shock brigades of exemplary labour!'

Agit-prop theatre inspired the politicised theatre of Bertolt Brecht in Germany in the 1920s (see page 15). In turn, the hallmarks of Brecht's style can be seen in the work of the British playwrights from the 1960s onwards. David Hare, Howard Brenton and David Edgar produced plays in major national venues in key cities, which drew attention to perceived problems with institutions such as the Church or government. Other playwrights, including John McGrath, encouraged a counter-cultural movement by performing in small venues in local communities. The name of McGrath's 7:84 Theatre Company is a direct reference to the inequality of wealth distribution (it was claimed that 7 per cent of the population owned 84 per cent of the country's wealth). A group of female playwrights including Caryl Churchill and Timberlake Wertenbaker has written specifically about the socio-political issues facing women.

Explore: Fugard's depiction of protest in South Africa

Britain was not the only country embracing political theatre in the 1960s and 1970s. In apartheid-era South Africa (1948 to the early 1990s), playwright Athol Fugard addressed the difficulties experienced by black people in his country during this time.

Key context

Fugard is known for his plays criticising the dominant white government in South Africa, which enforced separation of blacks and whites in the system known as apartheid. Fugard's play *Sizwe Bansi is Dead* was first performed in Cape Town in 1972, at the height of the apartheid era. The Cape Town theatre group, The Serpent Players, worked with Fugard to create a drama that reflected the harsh realities of black people's experience in the townships. The set was designed to be as simple as possible, so that the action was not interrupted by set changes. The play was initially condemned as a piece of propaganda designed to criticise the white South African government. However, its themes of oppression and self-realisation secured the play an international audience and a lasting legacy as an effective contemporary protest play.

Plot summary

The story of the play moves backwards in time to explain how the character of Sizwe Bansi, a migrant labourer from a South African township (a settlement allocated for black people), came to reinvent himself. Much of the action takes place in a photographic studio belonging to a man called Styles. In the studio, Styles takes family portraits as well as photographs for identification cards (a legal requirement for black South Africans). Styles is friends with Buntu, a local man who provides shelter for migrants looking for work, and who has taken in Sizwe Bansi.

Read the following extract from the play. In this scene, Buntu is helping Sizwe Bansi to understand what will happen if he remains illegally in the city of Port Elizabeth. He is reading out the letter that Sizwe Bansi has been sent by the authorities and which includes specific orders.

Text 1

BUNTU. Listen... [*reads*]. 'You are required to report to the Bantu Affairs Commissioner, King William's Town, within three days of the above-mentioned date for the...' You should have been home yesterday!... 'for the purpose of repatriation to home district.' Influx Control.
You're in trouble, Sizwe.

MAN   (Sizwe Bansi). I don't want to leave Port Elizabeth.

BUNTU. Maybe. But if that book says go, you go.

MAN. Can't I maybe burn this book and get a new one?

BANTU. Burn that book? Stop kidding yourself, Sizwe! Anyway, suppose you do. You must immediately go apply for a new one. Right? And until that new one comes, be careful the police don't stop you and ask for your book. Into the Courtroom, brother. Charge: Failing to produce Reference Book on Demand. Five **rand** or five days. Finally the new book comes. Down to the Labour Bureau for a stamp… it's got to be endorsed with permission to be in this area. White man at the Labour Bureau takes the book, looks at it – doesn't look at you! – goes to the big machine and feeds in your number…

[*Buntu goes through the motions of punching out a number on a computer… card jumps out, he reads*]

'Sizwe Bansi. Endorsed to King William's Town…' Takes your book, fetches that same stamp, and in it goes again. So you burn that book, or throw it away, and get another one. Same thing happens.

[*Buntu feeds the computer, the card jumps out.*]

'Sizwe Bansi. Endorsed to King William's Town…' Stamp goes in the third time… But this time it's also into a van and off to the Native Commissioner's Office; card around your neck with your number on it; escort on both sides and back to King William's Town. They make you pay for the train fare too!

From *Sizwe Bansi is Dead* by Athol Fugard

Vocabulary

rand: the currency used in South Africa

Activity 1

In pairs, improvise a short scene to act out what would happen between Sizwe Bansi and the official at the Labour Bureau. When staging the scene, think about:

- where you would position the audience
- how the man in the Labour Bureau could be represented using the actor's physicality
- how you could use the performing area to indicate power relations between characters.

With your group, evaluate the impact of the scene on your audience. How did you deal with the many bureaucratic characters who are described? How clear was Fugard's message in your staging?

Reflection point

Think of a recent campaign or protest – perhaps a climate change protest. How did people express their views? How could you portray scenes of similar protest in theatrical form? Create a short scripted scene that could be used in a devised piece and that reflects the key messages of the campaign.

Develop: Brecht's ideas for educating the audience

Practitioner Bertolt Brecht embraced a range of disciplines, including writing plays, poetry and political commentary.

Spotlight on practitioner:
Bertolt Brecht (1898–1956)

Born into a middle-class family in Munich, Brecht was greatly influenced by what he saw as the senseless slaughter of World War I. His first play, *Baal*, was performed in 1918 and was acclaimed for its poetic language. In 1925, when Brecht was working as dramaturg at director Max Reinhardt's celebrated Deutsches Theater in Berlin, he began to develop his 'epic theatre' – a form of theatre designed to communicate political messages to audiences. Epic theatre was characterised by:

- the presence of the **ensemble**: actors were visible to the audience at all times and often doubled as musicians
- the half-curtain: hung halfway down the vertical stage space, this made transitions between scenes visible to the audience
- *Verfremdungseffekt* (**alienation effect**): this was achieved by having actors play multiple roles
- stark lighting: Brecht's lighting was never used to create an illusion, but to illuminate the action – reminding the audience that it is watching a play
- comedy: this was either created through songs or characterisation intended to provide opportunities for direct address to the audience.

Collaboration with the composer Kurt Weill enabled Brecht to develop both a clear political narrative and a distinctive style. After Hitler came to power in 1933, Brecht's communist political leanings forced him into exile. However he continued to work in both northern Europe and the USA. He returned to Germany in 1947 and, two years later, established his theatre company the Berliner Ensemble.

Activity 2

Research one of the following plays by Brecht.

- *Mother Courage and Her Children*
- *The Caucasian Chalk Circle*
- *The Good Person of Szechwan*

How might he have intended the play to be staged to emphasise the political aspects? What might his political intention have been? Use a mind map, like the one below, to organise your ideas.

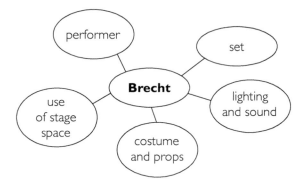

Key terms

ensemble: the group of performers who come together to make a production

alienation effect: distancing an audience from the action to ensure they do not forget that they are watching a play

In plays such as *Mother Courage and Her Children* and *The Good Person of Szechwan*, Brecht transports the audience to a different place and era from their own. By distancing the audience from the setting, Brecht believed that they would see his social and political messages more clearly. However, his characters are not the two-dimensional villains of the agit-prop tradition, and they often face the consequences of their actions.

To help the audience clearly see the choices that his characters made, Brecht developed a method known as 'Gestus' by which an actor physically demonstrates the social message. For example, in *Mother Courage and Her Children*, the audience observes Mother Courage changing sides in a long-running war in order to profit by selling her goods to members of the winning army. Ultimately, these decisions cost her the lives of her children. In a scene near the end of the play, Mother Courage is asked to pay for her daughter's burial. She counts out the coins one by one, before placing one back in her purse. This Gestus (the physical moment of keeping one coin) shows how, even in the midst of her grief, she is still thinking about money. Use of the technique stops the audience empathising with her.

The 1949 production of the play included Brecht's wife Helene Weigel in the lead role. This production was specifically intended to limit the audience's sympathy for Mother Courage and included Weigel's famous 'silent scream' Gestus, intended as a representation of the consequences of her actions. Some commentators regard *Mother Courage* as a successful example of his epic theatre in action, while others regard it as a great example of the tragic genre and have criticised the extent to which Brecht can be considered a political playwright.

Activity 3

Look back at Text 1 — the extract from *Sizwe Bansi is Dead*. How might the actor playing Bantu use Gestus to indicate his frustration with the bureaucratic system facing the people of the townships? Discuss this in small groups, then stage the scene to reflect the character's growing frustrations.

Apply: How might a director use Brecht's methods to communicate Fugard's message?

Read this extract from later in the play *Sizwe Bansi is Dead*. Here, Buntu is trying to explain to Sizwe the process through which he must apply for a job.

Text 2

MAN. I think I will try to look for some jobs in the garden.

BUNTU. You? Job as a garden-boy? Don't you read the newspapers?

MAN. I can't read.

BUNTU. I'll tell you what the little white ladies say: 'Domestic vacancies. I want a garden-boy with good manners and a wide knowledge of seasons and flowers. Book in order.' Yours in order? Anyway what the hell do you know about seasons and flowers? [*After a moment's thought.*] Do you know any white man who's prepared to give you a job?

MAN. No. I don't know any white man.

BUNTU. Pity. We might have been able to work something then. You talk to the white man, you see, and ask him to write a letter saying he's got a job for you. You take that letter from the white man and go back to King William's Town, where you show it to the Native Commissioner there. The Native Commissioner in King William's Town reads that letter from the white man in Port Elizabeth who is ready to give you the job. He then writes a letter back to the Native Commissioner in Port Elizabeth. So you come back here with the two letters. [...] and he says when he reads the letters: Ah yes, this man Sizwe Bansi can get a job. So the Native Commissioner in Port Elizabeth then writes a letter which you take with the letters from the Native Commissioner in King William's Town and the white man in Port Elizabeth, to the Senior Officer at the Labour Bureau, who reads all the letters. Then he will put the right stamp in your book and give you another letter from himself which together with the letters from the white man and the two Native Affairs Commissioners, you take to the Administration Office here in New Brighton and make an application for Residence Permit, so that you don't fall victim of raids again. Simple.

From *Sizwe Bansi is Dead* by Athol Fugard

Activity 4

In small groups, allocate the two roles and nominate a director. Stage the various scenarios Buntu describes by creating the different characters. Try to demonstrate the difference between characters and reveal the tragi-comic tone of Fugard's text. Discuss how you might use Brecht's methods to communicate the key political and social messages of the scene to an audience.

1.3 Genre case study: Symbolist drama

Big question

- What are the key features of symbolist theatre?

Starting point: The European symbolist tradition

Like political theatre, **symbolism** grew out of a broader cultural movement. The term 'symbolism' denotes the use of poetic images to replace concrete objects and was developed in reaction to the rise of **naturalism**. The symbolists were interested in spirituality, dreams and the imagination, and opposed matter-of-fact description. Symbolist painters such as Edvard Munch and Gustav Klimt used bold colours, often in a **montage** style, to represent people and places in dreamlike – and sometimes nightmarish – states. Symbolist playwrights were influenced by the work of these artists and writers. They regarded the theatre as an ideal visual platform for representing their ideas.

In Europe at the start of the 20th century, actor-managers started to bring the works of playwrights, such as Maurice Maeterlinck and Alfred Jarry to audiences. In Scandinavia, the later plays of August Strindberg and Henrik Ibsen mix naturalism with symbolism using dream sequences and an exploration of the complex psychological forces that motivated their characters. Strindberg's *A Dream Play* (first performed in 1907) is a good example of a symbolist play that grew out of this theatrical movement. In the play, the daughter of a goddess comes to earth to report on the problems facing humankind. Within the story, time and space do not exist and events are disconnected. The ending is typically pessimistic: the main character opens a door to discover the meaning of life, only to find that there is nothing there.

Activity 1

In pairs, undertake some research into Strindberg's plays. Look closely at their production history and identify the theatrical methods used to create the symbolist effects. Copy and complete the table below and add further rows as your research develops.

Theatrical method	Intended impact
Music – often dreamlike, including use of string instruments	To create a nightmarish or dreamlike atmosphere
Set – large painted stage flats expressing extreme emotions	To communicate the central emotions in the piece
Lighting	
Performance style	

Explore: Symbolism in *Blood Wedding*

Blood Wedding is one of Spanish playwright Federico García Lorca's most famous plays. First staged in Madrid in 1933, it is based on a true story about a young couple who met a tragic end. In the play, Lorca uses symbolist techniques to dramatise the sense of fate that pursues the couple.

Spotlight on practitioner:
Federico García Lorca (1898–1936)

The Spanish playwright Lorca opposed the fascist regime that developed in central Europe in the 1930s. He was inspired by the symbolist plays of Strindberg and sought to use theatre as a platform for communicating with others. Lorca worked with La Barraca, a travelling theatre company that set up a simple stage in town squares and performed classical plays in the Spanish tradition. The experience of minimalistic staging of classic texts informed Lorca's interest in the use of poetic language alongside visual images. The poverty and repression of the rural poor, and in particular the brutal experience of many women, recur as themes throughout his plays. He drew on the 'poetic memory' of the folklore of the villages of his childhood to inform his symbolic images.

Plot summary

In this scene, Leonardo has arrived to see the 'bride-to-be' – a local woman about to be married to another man. Although Leonardo himself has been recently married, the 'bride-to-be' is his true love and he has ridden his horse at top speed to declare that he still loves her.

Text 3

LEONARDO. I'm tied to you. You know that. You made the rope. With your own hands. They can kill me, those others, but they've no right to spit on me. All your silver gleams so bright. It spits on people sometimes.

BRIDE-TO-BE. Liar!

LEONARDO. I don't want to speak. I have my pride. I don't want these hills to hear my cries.

BRIDE-TO-BE. My cries would be louder.

MAID. These words must stop. You must not speak of the past. (*The* MAID *looks at the doors; anxiety has seized her.*)

BRIDE-TO-BE. She's right. I shouldn't even look at you. But it burns my soul to have you coming here and spying on my wedding and making insinuations about the orange blossom. Go and wait for your wife at the door.

LEONARDO. Can it really be that you and I cannot speak?

MAID. (*raging*). No. No, you cannot speak.

LEONARDO. After I got married I've thought night and day about whose fault it was and every time I think of this I think of another fault that eats the one before. But there's always someone. There's always someone to blame!

BRIDE-TO-BE. A man on his horse knows a lot and can do a lot to squeeze love out of a girl lost in a desert. But I've got my pride. That's why I am getting married. And I will lock myself away with my husband who I have to love more than everything.

LEONARDO. Your pride won't help you. (*He comes closer to her.*)

continued

BRIDE-TO-BE. Don't come near me!

LEONARDO. Do you know the worst thing? The worst thing we can do to ourselves? It's to keep silent. To keep silent and burn. What use was my pride to me and not looking at you and leaving you awake night after night? No use! All it did was fan the flames! And you think that time will cure everything and that walls will cover everything up, but it's not true. It's not true. When you get to the heart of things, you cannot make them disappear!

BRIDE-TO-BE. (*trembling*). I can't hear you. I can't bear to hear your voice. It's as if I had [...] fallen asleep in a bed of roses. And it pulls me, and I know I am drowning, but I go back. I go back. [...]

LEONARDO. There could be no peace for me unless I said these things. I got married. You get married now.

MAID. (*to* LEONARDO). And she is. She is getting married!

VOICES. (*singing closer now*). Little bride, little bride, open your eyes.

BRIDE-TO-BE. Open your eyes! (*She runs out to her room.*)

From *Blood Wedding* by Federico García Lorca, Act 2

Examples of symbolism in the play include:

- verbal: the 'bride-to-be' makes reference to the orange blossom, a symbol of new love
- performative: the personification of aspects of the world of the play, such as the hills being able to hear
- choral: the use of the voices to represent the inner thoughts of the 'bride-to-be'.

Activity 2

In pairs, answer the following questions:
What are the key symbolic images in the text? Note them down and comment on what they represent.

- Who are the 'voices' and what role do they play in creating mood and atmosphere?
- How does Lorca use the character of the Maid to develop tension and communicate a sense of the forbidden?
- How could a director visualise the key images in performance? Could they use design elements? Stage space? Characterisation?

Develop: How could you use Suzuki's theories of acting to stage a symbolist text?

Spotlight on practitioner:
Tadashi Suzuki (b. 1939)

Japanese theatre director and philosopher Tadashi Suzuki deals with, what he considers, the fundamental issues of our times. Over four decades, he has developed a form of physical symbolist theatre inspired by classical Japanese Noh theatre (see page 24). He believes that actors should use their whole body as a tool for expression. The Suzuki method of actor training is inspired by martial arts and requires immense energy and concentration. The breath creates both a rhythm for the actor's movement and a centre of energy in the body.

In his theatre, actors are usually:

- physically fit
- committed to working with the company for a lengthy period of time
- classically trained in Noh and Kabuki styles of theatre
- have a good understanding of classical Greek theatre
- have movement training and are interested in the role of the body in performance.

Suzuki has directed a number of Greek tragedies and Shakespearean plays, including *The Trojan Women*, *Oedipus Rex* and *King Lear*. His productions have been performed all over the world, usually by companies that include a broad range of nationalities. Like Lorca, Suzuki often focuses on the plight of women in the patriarchal society of Japan, and draws upon images from that country in both the past and present.

Case study:
The Trojan Women, Tadashi Suzuki (2014)

One famous example of Suzuki's performance style is his interpretation of the Greek tragedy *The Trojan Women*, first performed in 1974 and restaged in 2014. Originally set in the ruins of Troy after the end of the Trojan Wars, Suzuki instead stages his action in war-torn Japan at the end of World War II, costuming his dispossessed citizens in tattered kimonos, carrying their belongings in pieces of cloth. Suzuki uses Brechtian '**multi-roling**' to symbolise the fall of Queen Hecuba – the actor removes the rags of a beggar woman to reveal the queen's ruined robes. In the final moments, in a symbolic act of blasphemy and defiance, the queen's daughter Andromache throws a bunch of flowers at a human statue of the gods, which doubles over in agony. In the style of the symbolist paintings of Dalí and Klimt, the stage backdrop consisted of brightly coloured fishnets, suggestive of the psychological and political tangle that follows the end of a war.

Now read another extract from *Blood Wedding*. Here, a **chorus** of woodcutters discusses the hunt through the forest for Leonardo and the bride-to-be.

Key terms

multi-roling: when an actor performs two or more roles within one play, characterising each one by changes in physicality, voice, costume, etc., while making it plain to the audience that the same performer is playing different parts

chorus: a group of performers who speak, sing or move in unison; the chorus may also narrate the action

---

Text 4

A wood. It's night-time. Huge damp trees. A dark atmosphere. We hear two violins.
Three WOODCUTTERS *enter.*
WOODCUTTER 1 Have they found them?
WOODCUTTER 2. Not yet. But they are looking everywhere.
WOODCUTTER 3. They'll find them soon.
WOODCUTTER 2. Sssssshhh!
WOODCUTTER 3. What?
WOODCUTTER 2. They are getting closer.
WOODCUTTER 1. They'll see them when the moon rises.
WOODCUTTER 2. They should let them be.
WOODCUTTER 1. The world is wide. There's room for everyone to live in it.
WOODCUTTER 3. But they'll kill them.
WOODCUTTER 2. They were right to run away. You have to follow your heart's deep feeling.
WOODCUTTER 1. They were each deceiving the other, and in the end the blood was stronger.
WOODCUTTER 3. Blood.
WOODCUTTER 1. You have to follow the path of blood.
WOODCUTTER 2. But when blood sees the light of day, the earth swallows it.

continued

WOODCUTTER 1. So what? Better to bleed to death than live with it **putrid**.

WOODCUTTER 3. Be quiet.

WOODCUTTER 1. Why? Do you hear anything?

WOODCUTTER 3. I hear the crickets. I hear the toads. I hear the night watching.

WOODCUTTER 1. But there's no sign of the horse [...]

WOODCUTTER 3. They'll seek them out and they'll kill them.

WOODCUTTER 1. But by then they will have mingled their blood and they will be like two empty jars or two dried-up streams.

From *Blood Wedding* by Federico García Lorca, Act 3

Activity 3

You are now going to work in small groups to stage the scene, drawing on some of Suzuki's ideas for creating symbolic theatre.

- Identify the sounds of a forest at night. Begin with one member of the group creating the sound of splitting wood, then add small animals and birds, then other sounds. Build a **soundscape**.

- Develop a choral style of movement for the woodcutters, starting with the group's breathing. Focus on using rhythm to create movement.

- Identify key language in the woodcutters' dialogue and develop a style of choral delivery to build tension. Deliver the dialogue at different volumes and speeds.

Vocabulary

putrid: decaying

Key term

soundscape: a collage of sounds used to create or change the atmosphere in a drama

Apply: How might a director use design to draw out the themes in a symbolist text?

Now read another scene from *Blood Wedding*. Here, Lorca returns the focus to the fleeing couple.

Text 5

BRIDE. I'll sleep at your feet.
I'll be the dog that lies at your feet
And watches over everything you're dreaming. [...]
For when I look at you
When I look at you
Your beauty's a flame
A fierce flame that burns me.

LEONARDO. One flame burns another
And the same small spark
Can burn up two blades of grass
That stand together.
Let's go!

He pulls her after him.

BRIDE. Where are you taking me?

LEONARDO. Somewhere where those men who are pursuing us
Will never ever find us [...]

continued

BRIDE.	You run! It's only right that I should die here With a crown of thorns on my head And my feet in the river And then let the leaves mourn me […]
LEONARDO.	Quiet. They're coming.
BRIDE.	Go!
LEONARDO.	Hush. They'll hear us. You first. I said, Go!

The BRIDE *hesitates.*

BRIDE.	Both together!
LEONARDO.	(*embracing her*). As you wish! If they separate us, it'll be Because they've killed me.
BRIDE.	And because I'm dead.

They leave, embracing each other.

The MOON *enters very slowly. The stage is lit by a strong blue light. We hear two violins. Suddenly we hear two piercing screams. The violin music is cut off. On the second scream the* BEGGARWOMAN *appears and remains with her back to the audience. She opens her cloak and stays centre stage like a huge bird with outspread wings. The* MOON *stands absolutely still. The curtain goes down in total silence.*

From *Blood Wedding* by Federico García Lorca, Act 2

Activity 4

In small groups, copy and complete the following table to describe how you could stage the scene to draw out the themes, using symbolic elements such as the Beggarwoman (death) and the moon.

Staging form	Set	Lighting (including multimedia devices)	Sound – position and volume (including music)	Costume and props
Proscenium arch				
Thrust				
In the round				

Reflection point

How could you use the techniques of the symbolist theatre in your devised work? What kind of design ideas might you include to create symbols that communicate visually with the audience?

Key term

proscenium: an arch or frame separating the stage from the seating area in a theatre, often intended as a picture frame or 'fourth wall' through which the audience views the action

1.4 Genre case study: The theatre of Asia

Big question

- How has Asian theatre changed over time?

Starting point: Key features of classical theatre – Kabuki and Noh

Theatre in Asia stretches back thousands of years. In the ancient royal societies of China and Japan, theatre was developed as a form of entertainment for the ruling elite. In this unit, you will explore how modern theatre practitioners have developed a contemporary response to classical forms and sought to find new audiences.

Spotlight on theatre tradition:
Kabuki

Kabuki is roughly translated as 'sing, dance, skill'. The art form began in Japan in the 17th century, with a female ensemble performing a series of stylised scenes reflecting ordinary life. By the 18th century, male performers had replaced women in the drama, playing characters of both genders. Puppets were also introduced as part of the spectacle, which often went on all day. After Japan opened up to the West in the 19th century, the elaborate and stylised performance style became more widely known.

Spotlight on theatre tradition:
Noh

Like Kabuki, Noh is a total art form combining drama, music and dance – the word roughly translates as 'skill'. Predating Kabuki by 200 years, Noh began as a courtly form of entertainment for the military leaders of Japan, the Shogunate. A traditional Noh performance includes a series of plays performed by highly trained actors. Until the mid-20th century, it was dominated by male actors. There are four major categories of Noh characters: Shite, the main protagonist; Waki, the main antagonist; Kyogen, or supplementary players; and Hayshi, the musicians. Only the Shite characters wear masks, signifying age, gender and social ranking. Noh plays fall into three broad categories of plot and two performance styles: the Geki Noh, which advances the plot; and the Furu Noh, which entertains using dance and acrobatics.

Activity 1

In pairs, conduct some research into the similarities and differences between Kabuki and Noh. Copy and complete the table below to organise your notes. The first line has been completed for you.

Theatrical method	Kabuki	Noh
Staging form	Thrust-style *hanamichi* walkway into the audience	Wooden structure with the actors seated on the stage when not performing
Set		
Lighting		
Sound		
Costume and makeup		
Performer		

Explore: Contemporary Chinese theatre

Case study:
Chinese puppet theatre

Shadow puppetry is a key feature of classical Chinese theatre. The jointed puppets are generally made of cardboard, leather or metal, and cut out to resemble specific characters or objects. The puppet is held by a cane close to a screen, and then lit from behind. The hands and arms of the character are manipulated with a series of attached canes. The projected shadows enable the player to tell a simple story, sometimes with the accompaniment of music or narration. Shadow theatre troupes were extremely popular during the Ming dynasty (14th–17th centuries).

Spotlight on practitioner:
The Finger Players

Established in Singapore in 1996, The Finger Players company uses a wide range of puppetry methods, including exposed puppeteers and shadow play. Starting with a commitment to making quality puppet theatre for children, the company has developed a repertoire of works that it performs at venues around the world.

In 2004, the company performed *Furthest North, Deepest South* – its first show for adults, in which all members of the company used theatre, mime and puppetry to communicate with the audience. *Itsy – the Musical*, based on the nursery-rhyme character of Itsy Bitsy Spider, includes a broad range of design elements, including mask. More recently, the company has added multimedia techniques and continues to experiment with new ways of presenting live shadow puppetry.

The company sometimes covers themes of love and loss, using symbolic theatre methods to create moving and multidimensional images. In the 2007 show *I'm Just a Piano Teacher*, a 40-year-old piano teacher who hates music remains at home with his overprotective parents. Later in the play, he conspires to kill them. The parents were represented by life-size puppets hung from the necks of the actors so that the audience could simultaneously see the face of each actor and the inanimate body – emphasising their oppressive behaviour.

I'm Just a Piano Teacher, The Finger Players

Case study:
Contemporary political play-writing

Traditional Chinese theatre, known as Chinese opera, dates back to the Ming dynasty of the 14th century. Actors were highly trained to excel in music and dancing. Chinese opera is still performed in large cities across China. However, in the tradition of Brecht – and in stark contrast to the ancient traditions of Chinese theatre – a new generation of playwrights has emerged in communist China, producing plays that promote democracy and free speech. These playwrights reflect the modern realities of their changing societies, including the rise of new technologies and the growth in large urban areas.

Modern Chinese theatre faces many challenges, including the political oversight of local authorities and competition from organisations importing successful commercial productions. Since the Cultural Revolution of 1966–76, in which Western texts were banned, the concept of inter-cultural theatre, in which stories from other societies are retold in a local production, has become increasingly popular. This has allowed Chinese playwrights who live outside the country to present stories of China's past in Western theatres.

Spotlight on practitioner:
Frances Ya-Chu Cowhig

Born in America to a Chinese mother, Frances Ya-Chu Cowhig is a playwright whose works have been produced internationally. As a teenager growing up in Beijing, Cowhig was influenced by the tales she heard of life in rural China. In recognition of the difficulties facing writers seeking to tell their stories from inside China, Cowhig claims to have made a commitment to contributing stories about modern China to the world of theatre and to helping people understand the situation in the country after the Cultural Revolution. Cowhig speaks honestly about how she feels as an American with Chinese heritage. In response to reviews of her 2013 play *The World of Extreme Happiness,* Cowhig expressed concern that her play might be seen as 'propagandistic': 'What I'm really interested in is complicating every side of the story – telling a story that is very much about all the things we're seeing in the headlines, but telling it through the lens of trauma and recovery, through the efforts of multiple generations of people who are trying to construct meaningful lives.'

Develop: Staging Cowhig's text

Read the following extract from *The World of Extreme Happiness* by Frances Ya-Chu Cowhig. In this scene, we meet Sunny, who works as a cleaner in a factory. She is desperately seeking promotion. Together with her friend Ming-Ming, she attends a self-help class run by Mr Destiny.

Text 6

The crowd continues to chant as **Ming-Ming** *pushes Sunny towards* **Mr. Destiny**.

Mr. Destiny Tell us, Sunny, what brought you here tonight?

Ming-Ming You want a promotion.

Sunny   (*softly*) I want a promotion.

Ming-Ming They can't hear you.

Sunny   (*louder*) I want a promotion!

Mr. Destiny Do you want a promotion, or do you need a promotion?

Sunny   I need a promotion.

Thunderous applause.

Mr. Destiny And why do you need a promotion?

Sunny *turns to* **Ming-Ming** *for help.*

Ming-Ming You deserve it.

Sunny   Because I deserve it!

Mr. Destiny What else?

Sunny   I want… no, I need to – move up in the world. Higher and higher. And make more money and have more power.

Mr. Destiny What will you do with that money and power?

Sunny   Spend it! And get more power! And buy nice things and a good education for me and my brother.

Mr. Destiny Say more.

Sunny   Then I'll go back to the countryside and laugh at everyone who's still poor… and living in dirt. Then I'll move back to the city, buy an apartment, improve myself, memorize every story about the Monkey King and Get Even Stronger!

From *The World of Extreme Happiness* by Frances Ya-Chu Cowhig,
Act 1, Scene 6

Activity 2

In small groups, allocate the three roles and discuss how the stage space might be used to create the sense of a busy room crowded with people. What is each character's intention in the scene? How might these be communicated to an audience? Consider the nervous physicality of Sunny and Ming in contrast to the confident instructor. How might the performers use gesture, movement and physicality to create their roles?

Now read another extract from *The World of Extreme Happiness*. Sunny has risen in status in the factory and has been asked by the factory owner, James Artemis, to promote the benefits of the factory to the press. Newly politicised, she has taken the opportunity to expose the harsh realities of low wages and poor conditions.

Text 7

Sunny	My section manager jumped out of a factory window. There was a – petition by his body. Filled with hundreds of signatures. Every name was a protest. In the countryside there are always reasons to protest and people telling you not to protest.

Qing Shu Min *turns off* **Sunny***'s microphone* [...]

Sunny *steps away from the podium and speaks directly to the audience, over* **Artemis**. *Dozens of camera flashes go off.*

Sunny	I want to say – to all my fellow migrant workers who are watching me right now – that I protest – and I ask you to protest with me. Ask – demand that you... that you get the same rights as people born in the city. If they say no... go on strike. Stop working. Make these demands every day – for a month. And – and if they still say no... if they still say no – go home. Let city people – try to live – for a single day without us. Stop selling them food and digging out coal. Stop building their houses and sewing their clothes. Let the city people go hungry. Let them... walk – naked. On the street. Without shoes. And live in houses with – with broken windows and –

Lights shift. The podium, **Artemis** *and* **Qing Shu Min** *disappear.*

Sunny *is backstage, more grounded and sure of herself than ever.*

Sunny	*(dreamy)* Chop off my arms – I can still strike. Hack off my legs – I can still walk. Rip out my heart – I will mysteriously recover. I can bathe in boiling oil and come out cleaner than I went in.

Gao Chen *places a black hood over* **Sunny***'s head. She doesn't struggle. He escorts her off.*

From *The World of Extreme Happiness* by Frances Ya-Chu Cowhig, Act 2, Scene 6

Activity 3

Work in small groups to consider how you might create the sense of growing menace as Sunny speaks out against the empty promises of the new capitalist world of business and industry. Use the following questions to help you stage the scene:

- How would you use space to create a sense of the audience for the speech?
- How would you position Sunny during the various stages of the scene?
- How would you stage the response of Artemis and his assistants, and his subsequent exit from the stage?

Apply: How might a director use The Finger Players' shadow puppetry to draw out the themes in Cowhig's play?

The innovative ensemble work of The Finger Players provides a useful opportunity to highlight the themes of oppression and resistance in Cowhig's play. The character of Sunny is both naïvely idealistic and intensely principled. The action unfolds in a way that creates both shock and empathy for the character. The position of the audience is critical to the success of this scene, as the playwright suggests that the audience for Sunny's speech is also the audience for the play. This is a case of 'breaking the fourth wall' – that is, bringing the audience directly into the world of the play.

Activity 4

In small groups, create a design concept for the scene in Text 7 that uses The Finger Players' theatrical methods of puppetry, set, and live and recorded music. Use the following list of key features of the scene to help develop your ideas:

- The scene is set in a large public auditorium.

- The space is full of members of the press.

- Sunny is described earlier in the text as being dressed as an idealised peasant.

- Artemis and Qing Shu Min are publicly humiliated.

- Gao Shen is waiting for Sunny to finish her speech and go backstage.

- The use of a black hood is suggestive of Sunny's fate.

Create some design sketches and notes for the set and costume. Make specific notes for the use of puppets – discuss the range of options for the use of puppets to represent or exaggerate characters, create various moods and change the atmosphere. For example, could the press be represented by giant puppets looming over the heads of the crowd to suggest their role in reinforcing the company's propaganda? Include details about the materials that are to be used for the puppets and how they will be manipulated. Consider using shadow puppetry to create the sense of menace.

1.5 Genre case study: Physical theatre

Big question
- What are the origins of the modern physical theatre tradition?

Starting point: Introduction to physical theatre

Physical theatre emphasises the use of physical movement, including dance and mime, to communicate ideas to an audience. Physical theatre practitioners tend to use devising methods (see pages 89–93) to create the performance, and often challenge traditional forms of staging. Some theatre historians consider that the use of modern physical techniques has its roots in the exaggerated style of the Renaissance or Restoration theatre, where actors played self-consciously towards the audience. Others believe that the Italian tradition of commedia dell'arte (see pages 52–53) provides the stylistic roots of the genre.

One of the most influential mime artists is Jacques Lecoq, who encourages students to focus on body, movement and space. For Lecoq, mime is a way of embodying a character and by doing so, creating a better understanding of it. His actors are therefore required to demonstrate a degree of flexibility and control. Practitioners such as Steven Berkoff (see page 120) were trained in the Lecoq school. Others, such as Peter Brook (see page 125), have been influenced by physical theatre forms drawn from Asian traditions, including Kabuki, Noh and **Kathakali**. The visual techniques used in Balinese theatre strongly influenced the work of Antonin Artaud (see page 198).

Choreographers of **postmodern** dance have also influenced the development of physical theatre, including companies such as Frantic Assembly, Gecko, Au Ments Dansa-Teatre, Not Man Apart, Out of Balanz and Zen Zen Zo. Rudolf Laban's style of choreography offers actors a code that they can use to describe the qualities of movement. The Tanztheater of Pina Bausch creates improvised pieces that include verbal and non-verbal language, often surreal and designed to challenge the audience.

Activity 1

Choose one of the physical theatre practitioners listed above, or another whose work you have seen. Conduct some research into the key features of their style, looking closely at their **repertoire** as it developed. Identify three key pieces of work and spot any transitions in their style.

Key terms
Kathakali: a traditional Indian dance that is perfected during a long period of training
postmodern: a late 20th century approach in art, architecture, performing arts and literature that typically mixes styles, often in an ironic way
repertoire: a body of work attributed to one person

Explore: Features of Restoration comedy

The plays of the mid- to late 17th century in England were known as Restoration comedies, as they were written after King Charles II had been restored to the throne. The plays were composed in response to an 18-year period of strict religious dominance, when the theatres had been closed and such forms of entertainment forbidden. Audiences were attracted by the topicality of the dramas and plots, which resemble modern TV soap operas. They are full of witty dialogue and comic business and often feature aristocratic characters behaving badly, particularly the celebrated character of the 'rake' — a wealthy man of the town whose primary purpose was to seduce women.

Read the extract below from George Etherege's play *The Man of Mode*, which was first staged in 1676. In this extract, an aristocratic lady, Mrs Loveit, is discussing her frustration with the character Dorimant, a classic Restoration rake. Here the actors might play with the letter to generate the comedy.

Text 8

[MRS LOVEIT's]

Enter MRS LOVEIT *and* PERT. MRS LOVEIT *putting up a letter, then pulling out her pocket-glass and looking in it*

MRS LOVEIT: Pert.

PERT: Madam?

MRS LOVEIT: I hate myself, I look so ill today.

PERT: Hate the wicked cause **on't**, that base man, Mr Dorimant, who makes you torment and **vex yourself** continually.

MRS LOVEIT: He is to blame, indeed.

PERT To blame to be two days without sending, writing, or coming near you, contrary to his oath and covenant! 'Twas to much purpose to make him swear! I'll lay my life there's not an article but he has broken — talked to the **vizards i' the pit**, waited upon the ladies from the boxes to their coaches, gone behind the scenes and fawned upon those little insignificant creatures, the players. […]

MRS LOVEIT: I know he is a devil, but he has something of the angel yet **undefaced** in him, which makes him so charming and agreeable that I must love him, be he never so wicked.

PERT: I little thought, madam, to see your spirit tamed to this degree, who banished poor Mr Lackwit but for taking up another lady's fan in your presence.

MRS LOVEIT: My knowing of such **odious** fools contributes to the making of me love Dorimant the better.

PERT: Your knowing of Mr Dorimant, in my mind, should rather make you hate all mankind.

MRS LOVEIT: So it does, besides himself.

From *The Man of Mode* by George Etherege, Act 2, Scene 2

Vocabulary

on't: shortened version of 'of it', common to the linguistic style of the period

vex yourself: upset yourself

vizards i' the pit: fashionable masked ladies, in this case, sitting in the orchestra pit, or stalls of the theatre

undefaced: not marked

odious: horrible or ugly (can mean physical form or behaviour)

Case study:
The Man of Mode, Nicholas Hytner, National Theatre (2007)

The performance style of the Restoration was characterised by actions and gestures, and the frequent use of **asides** to bring the audience into the secrets of the play. In a modern interpretation of the play, directed by Nicholas Hytner at the National Theatre in 2007, Dorimant is a wealthy socialite trying to woo as many women as possible in the midst of London's nightlife. The modern set included two revolving cubes, which enabled Dorimant to skip between different centres of seduction. With the aid of modern music and lighting, movement sequences were used to suggest the scale of deception and competition between the sexes.

Key term

aside: a comment directed at the audience that is not supposed to be heard by the other characters

Activity 2

The scene in Text 8 would typically be staged in Mrs Loveit's parlour, with comedy generated by the interaction between the lady and her servant. Analyse the text for information on the possibilities for comic stage business in this scene.

- What sort of props might the actors use to create comedy for the audience? Working in pairs, try staging the scene with and without the aid of furniture.

- Explore the pace of the scene by playing it without the text and using only non-verbal communication. How might the actor playing Mrs Loveit exaggerate the depth of her feelings for Dorimant?

- Identify an action or gesture which each character could repeat and which could act as a Brechtian Gestus to communicate the character's intent to the audience.

- Play the scene again, with the text in place, and consider the importance of movement and gesture to the text.

Reflection point

How do the comedies of the Restoration differ from contemporary comedies? Think about a comedy which you enjoy, either on TV or in a film or a play you have seen. What sort of characters does it involve? Were any of them representative of society?

Develop: Understanding contemporary physical theatre

A number of contemporary theatre companies have embraced a physical way of working that communicates directly with audiences.

Spotlight on practitioner:

Kneehigh Theatre

Kneehigh Theatre was formed by Mike Shepherd and Emma Rice in Cornwall in 1980. The company uses devising methodologies to create theatre that is a blend of different theatrical elements, ensemble in style and intended as a community event. The company has developed an extensive repertoire drawn from myth, folklore and the Cornish storytelling tradition.

Early work was intended to respond to the wild natural landscape of Cornwall and included the use of traditional instruments like banjos and mouth organs, and choral storytelling. Very often, this led the company to create large-scale site-specific theatre using the natural elements, such as rocks and trees, and by using the sounds of the environment. As the work has evolved, the company has integrated acrobatics, multimedia and synthetic musical devices.

The touring nature of the company enables it to work flexibly and in response to ideas as they evolve. In recent years, the company have established a semi-permanent home in a large circus tent which they have called the 'Asylum'. This versatile space is intended to promote the sense of enquiry in theatre-making which the company believes is missing from much traditional contemporary theatre. Among its repertoire, Kneehigh has staged reinterpretations of classic novels, films and plays, including *Brief Encounter, Hansel and Gretel, The Bacchae* and *Tristan and Isolt*.

The key theatrical elements are:

- multi-sensory storytelling: a range of elements such as set, lighting and puppetry come together to create powerful images appealing to the audience on a number of levels
- clear narrative arc: usually moral or mythical in nature – for example, the enduring power of love or impact of loss
- multi-roling ensemble: performers usually play instruments, dance and sing
- multimedia and puppetry
- pre- and post-show interaction: the show is part of a much bigger event in which the actors play music, speak to the audience and continue interacting in role
- magic realism: a theatrical genre which uses symbolic props, puppets, fantastical hybrid characters and parallel worlds to create a magical version of reality.

Read the following extract from *The Man of Mode*. By this point in the play, Dorimant is keen to rid himself of Mrs Loveit's affections. As you read, think about how you could use elements of physical theatre to represent the shifting dynamic between the two characters.

Text 9

MRS LOVEIT: You take a pride of late in using of me ill, that the town may know the power you have over me, which now (as unreasonably as yourself) expects that I, do me all the injuries you can, must love you still.

DORIMANT: I am so far from expecting that you should, I begin to think you never did love me.

MRS LOVEIT: Would the memory of it were so wholly worn out in me that I did doubt it too. What made you come to disturb my growing quiet?

DORMANT: To give you joy of your growing infamy.

MRS LOVEIT: Insupportable! Insulting devil! This from you, the only author of my shame! This from another had been but justice, but from you, 'tis a hellish and inhuman outrage. What have I done?

DORIMANT: A thing that puts you below my scorn and makes my anger as ridiculous as you have made my love.

MRS LOVEIT: I walked last night with Sir Fopling.

DORIMANT: You did, madam; and you talked and laughed aloud, 'Ha, ha, ha'. Oh, that laugh! That laugh becomes the confidence of a woman of quality.

MRS LOVEIT: You, who have more pleasure in the ruin of a woman's reputation than in the endearments of her love, reproach me not with yourself – and I defy you to name the man can lay a blemish on my fame.

DORIMANT: To be seen publicly so transported with the vain follies of that notorious **fop**, to me is an infamy…

MRS LOVEIT: **Rail on!** I am satisfied in the justice of what I did: you had provoked me to it.

DORIMANT: What I did was the effect of a passion whose extravagancies you have been willing to forgive.

MRS LOVEIT: And what I did was the effect of a passion you may forgive if you think fit.

DORIMANT: Are you so indifferent grown?

MRS LOVEIT: I am.

DORIMANT: Nay, then 'tis time to part. I'll send you back your letters you have so often asked for. [*Looks in his pockets*] I have two or three of 'em about me.

From *The Man of Mode* by George Etherege, Act 5, Scene 1

Vocabulary

fop: a man who is excessively concerned with dress and his own appearance
Rail on: Continue to rage against

Activity 3

In pairs, play the scene with one character leading the other around the space. Reverse the dynamic and discuss which is a better fit and why. Then try adding music (this could be recorded or developed using percussion or sound effects). Experiment with the style and pace of movement.

Apply: How might a theatre company use Kneehigh's methods to bring a Restoration comedy to life for a modern audience?

Kneehigh is committed to creating irreverent and challenging theatre. It is therefore interesting to consider how its methods could be applied to *The Man of Mode*, perhaps by developing a chorus who comment on the unfolding of the comic action or through the use of symbolic props. A company might also use aerial work (trapeze or ropes) to present the idea of voyeurism which is at the heart of Restoration theatre, with some characters hoisted into the air to spy on others. This reconstructed approach to storytelling mirrors the episodic nature of Restoration text where lots of different stories are told in parallel to entertain the audience. It is rather like the experience of overhearing a series of gossipy conversations in a café or on a bus or train.

Activity 4

Review the two extracts (Texts 8 and 9) from the play. Follow the steps below to create a short devised sequence to describe the relationship between Dorimant and Mrs Loveit.

- Direct the text towards the audience, marking the moment when a key revelation or moment is enacted with an exaggerated or stylised gesture or movement.

- Add a chorus whose role is to repeat specific phrases used by the two characters.

- Develop a soundscape for the scene by exploring a possible sound for each of the character's underlying feelings: Loveit's frustration, Dorimant's scheming and Pert's mischief. Where possible, add instruments, body percussion (use of parts of the body to create sound) or sound effects.

- Use the chorus to improvise a non-verbal scene between Dorimant and Loveit that shows her being wooed by Sir Fopling while Dorimant observes with delight.

- Try adding a choral narrative that explains and comments on the events to the audience. What might the chorus be/represent?

- Discuss the use of design elements to modernise the two scenes. What kind of colours and fabrics might be used in the costumes? How might Loveit's house be furnished?

Reflection point

How could you use the physical theatre techniques in your devised work? What sort of non-verbal language could benefit your staging? Try experimenting with movement and consider introducing elements of music and puppetry in the style of Kneehigh.

Thinking more deeply

Now that you have begun to explore how different theatrical genres, traditions and practices have developed from specific socio-political and socio-historical contexts, you might want to explore one of them further by attempting to emulate the features of political theatre in your own piece. Imagine that you have been asked to write or devise a short play to educate a contemporary audience on the key elements of a particular social or political issue. Here are some examples:

- the impact of industrial pollution on global warming
- the role of women in modern society
- the increasing gap between wealthy and poor
- the impact of mass immigration on the developed world.

Follow these steps to develop a text for performance:

1. Choose a specific topic and undertake some research. Identify five key messages from your research that you would want an audience to consider.

2. Identify an appropriate setting for a discussion of the issues – it could be a specific location or a neutral space.

3. Identify the key players in the drama – for example, a politician, an activist, a park ranger.

4. Create a short, scripted scene in which ideas can be introduced to the audience. Aim for a maximum of 10 minutes in duration.

5. Decide which practitioner's methods you could use to communicate the key messages to the audience. Which is the best fit for your key messages? You could conduct some further research into contemporary agit-prop companies to help you.

6. Try to write down your key aims and objectives and for the piece in terms of the style and communication of key messages.

Chapter 2

Performing from a text

In this chapter, you will explore how directors work with actors to develop characters. You will also consider how a company of actors, directors and designers could apply ideas from practitioners to bring a text to life for an audience.

2.1 Staging a text: Understanding context, genre, style and form

Big question

- How do the context, genre and style of a play influence performance?

Starting point: Exploring the social, historical and cultural context of a text

In order to understand the world of a play, you need to understand the context in which it was written. This includes the social conventions and artistic movements that may have influenced the playwright, as well as events in the wider world. There are three key aspects of context to explore:

- **Social context:** This refers to what was happening in broader society at the time the play was written – for example, the relative decline of the aristocracy in the late 19th century and early 20th century in Europe and the rise of a new industrial class.

- **Historical context:** This refers to historical events taking place in the country or region where the play was written that might have influenced the playwright – for example, the way in which the mass casualties of World War I in the early 20th century might have led to writers questioning the authority of the ruling class.

- **Cultural context:** This refers to the artistic movements and developments in which the playwright was operating, and from which their works might have sprung. For example, Samuel Beckett's plays responded to the work of other European writers of the late 1950s, which has been grouped under the banner of the **Theatre of the Absurd**.

Activity 1

Divide into three research groups. Each group should take one of the three key aspects of context: social, historical or cultural. In your groups, discuss what events, social changes and influences from your own country and culture in the 21st century would fall into your chosen category. Undertake some additional research if you need to, to get some more ideas. Look at images as well as words. Record your ideas in a mind map like the one below.

people from different
nationalities mix freely

Social context

technology drives
communication

Key terms

Theatre of the Absurd: a term referring to plays written after 1945 by writers such as Samuel Beckett and Eugène Ionesco, which influenced later playwrights including Harold Pinter; in a time of anxiety caused by the threat of nuclear warfare, and following the horrors of World War II, the plays seem to question the nature of existence or to represent it as meaningless and absurd

Reflection point

If theatre is a response to the world around us, why do we perform older plays at all?

Consider the context in which William Shakespeare lived and worked as an example. Shakespeare was born in 1564 and died in 1616, at the age of 52. He witnessed the reign of Elizabeth I, and the accession of James I to the throne. Born the son of a glove-maker in the rural town of Stratford-upon-Avon, Shakespeare was educated at the local grammar school. He then moved to London, where he became a popular playwright and entertainer, leading a company of actors who performed for both monarchs. Some key features of Shakespeare's context are as follows:

- **Social context:** During Shakespeare's lifetime, the population of London grew substantially, although there were great differences in the lifestyles of the urban elite and the urban poor, who lived in cramped and squalid conditions. Society changed too and social mobility, like Shakespeare's own, was possible. The rise of a new mercantile class can be seen in plays like *The Merchant of Venice*.

- **Historical context:** During Elizabeth I's reign, England experienced a period of warfare with other European countries. Victory during the Anglo-Spanish War gave the Elizabethan regime a degree of symbolic power which lasted for many years. However, there were internal threats to the monarchy: both Elizabeth I and James I faced rebellion and revolt as a result of questions of legitimacy and religious conflict. These are explored and reflected in many of the history plays, such as *Richard III* and *Henry V*, and the tragedies, such as *King Lear* and *Macbeth*.

- **Cultural context:** Shakespeare's emergence as a playwright was made possible in part by the opening of the first permanent theatre, James Burbage's The Theatre, in Shoreditch in 1576, two years after Shakespeare's birth. Thinking about how the idea of a permanent theatre space influenced the form and style of Shakespeare's plays is important. Without this, Shakespeare's own experience of drama may have been limited to the masques which were often performed as part of the Queen's royal journeys throughout England, or to the local, seasonal festivities at Christmas or midsummer.

William Shakespeare.

Activity 2

The outcomes of research into context may inform your decisions about how to stage a performance. Divide into small research groups. Each group should take a specific focus from Shakespeare's context:

- life in Elizabeth's court

- life as a tradesperson, such as a weaver (who makes clothes), a joiner (who works with wood) or a blacksmith (who makes items out of metal).

- life in a rural village

- seasonal festivities or traditions. (Which were the important ones? Look at midsummer, for example. How did they celebrate?)

When you have completed your research, discuss how this information might help you as an actor or director. Think about how a performer might use this information to develop a character, for example.

Queen Elizabeth I

Explore: Examining genre, style and form

Taken from the French word meaning 'category', the **genre** to which a play belongs determines its use of specific theatrical and textual conventions to communicate the ideas in the play to an audience. For a director, therefore, the genre and the conventions associated with it provide a template to draw upon and sometimes to work against.

The genres of tragedy and comedy are usually considered to have their origins in the classical periods of Greek and Roman theatre. At this time, most people could not read or write, so it was important for the audience to understand, through the performance itself, what kind of play they were watching. An example of a theatrical convention of tragedy, therefore, might be the death of the hero as a result of a miscalculation or a tragic flaw. This allowed the audience to experience the catharsis that ancient writers such Aeschylus and Sophocles intended with their plays. Other theatrical conventions of Greek tragedy include:

- the presence of a main character (protagonist) in conflict with a second character (antagonist)
- a chorus that narrates and comments on the action
- action that is linear and moves towards a **climax**.

Key terms

genre: the type, or category, of drama that a play belongs to
climax: the moment of greatest intensity in a play – often the turning point in the drama

---

Spotlight on practitioner:
Aeschylus (524–456 BCE)

Often described as the 'father of tragedy', Aeschylus is credited with expanding the number of characters in a play from a single actor and chorus, in particular to develop the relationship between a protagonist and an antagonist. His trilogy of three connecting tragedies, *The Oresteia,* is set against a backdrop of war and tells the story of the various betrayals and acts of revenge that marked the lives of the Greek warrior, Agamemnon and his wife and children. Aeschylus's plays have a strong moral and religious tone and reflect on humankind's position in relation to the gods.

Activity 3

In small groups, undertake some research to discover the conventions of the genre of ancient Greek comedy. Copy and complete this table to help you set out your notes.

Characteristic	Examples
Key playwrights	Aristophanes
Conventions of the text	
Types of character	
Performance conventions	Fast-moving action, knockabout comedy sequences
Design conventions	
Features of audience response	

The **style** of a play refers to how it is performed and is closely connected to its genre. The style of a play is best defined with reference to the choice of methods – it is the 'how'. For example, the style of a play might be naturalistic, epic, **melodramatic**, comic, and so on. Shakespeare's *A Midsummer Night's Dream* can be said to conform to many aspects of the comic genre: absurd misunderstandings between lovers, unintentionally funny language, **slapstick** and, structurally, a 'happy ending'. In performing and interpreting the play, a director might emphasise these humorous elements in their chosen style, downplaying any hints of cruelty in the misunderstandings. But, equally, they might decide to foreground or touch on other styles – whether naturalistic, epic or something harsher in tone.

The play begins with a father demanding his daughter's death if she doesn't marry the man he wants her to; how these lines are performed and how others react can determine the style. If they are not taken seriously, the comic tone might be maintained. The sheer number of ways *A Midsummer Night's Dream* has been interpreted and performed might suggest that the play is very much open to what the director and actors bring to it. Yet the energy, interleaving plot elements and the inclusion of fantastical elements lend themselves to a particularly physical form of theatre.

The **form** of a play relates to how it is *constructed*, and shaped – how events, ideas and relationships are conveyed. For example, the conventional form of many plays involves speech in the form of direct address to the audience or dialogue between characters within set 'spaces of time' (scenes, acts). These might create a single, linear form with a small set of characters brought together in a unity of action, as in Henrik Ibsen's *A Doll's House*, in which everything is tied to the narrative of the main character, Nora. In *A Midsummer Night's Dream*, the movement between three disparate sets of characters might be said to create an episodic form, with parallel narratives being established and then brought together as the play moves towards its dénouement. Conversely, a writer may omit such divisions of scene, time or defined character, and propose a much looser set of 'instructions' to the director or actor, which creates the space for non-verbal and physical elements to tell the story – if there is one.

Activity 4

Choose a play text that you are familiar with and identify the play's features relating to its genre, style and form. Make notes and share your ideas with a partner. Think about the following questions:

- What clues can you find in the text to suggest what genre the play might belong to?
- How would you describe the style? Is there a set style – or could the play be open to several interpretations?
- What characteristics of the play's form can you identify?
- How might the style and genre of a text affect the preparation an actor undertakes for a particular role?

Plot summary

A Midsummer Night's Dream is set in two distinct worlds: the court of Theseus, the Duke of Athens, and the forest on the outskirts of the city. The play tells the story of a nobleman, Egeus, who insists his daughter Hermia should marry Demetrius, a man she professes not to love. Hermia elopes with her lover Lysander to the forest, a magical place in which the king and queen of the fairies (Oberon and Titania) are in conflict. At the same time, some local workers meet in the same forest to rehearse an epic play to celebrate the marriage of Theseus to Hippolyta. The three worlds collide when Oberon uses magic potions to punish Titania and to resolve the love problems of Hermia, her best friend Helena, Lysander and Demetrius. When the plan goes wrong, misunderstandings occur, but these are all resolved by the end of the play.

Key terms

style: the distinct way in which a play is performed, often influenced by the specific time and place in which the play is written

melodramatic: a term first used in the Victorian era to refer to plays interspersed with songs and accompanying orchestral music; melodrama relies heavily on sensationalism and sentimentality, and often takes a strict view of morality

slapstick: fast-paced comedy including disaster or clumsy mishap, often played out in physical sequences, sometimes with the use of comic violence

form: the way in which a play is constructed

Develop: Focus on genre, style and form through examining production history

One way of exploring the genre, style and form of a particular play is to look closely at past productions. Different directors make different theatrical choices in response to these aspects of a play. They choose to focus on specific themes and ideas in a performance style that is influenced by the text.

It is useful to understand the following about the play's genre, style and form:

- **Genre:** The genre of the play is clearly comedy, owing to the nature of the characters and plot. The social and political relationships in the play seem to reflect the structures of Elizabethan society, particularly the contrast between the aristocratic court and the working-class characters outside it, yet both are sources of fun for the audience. Other generic aspects of the play relate to the festive and fairy-tale elements, which perhaps reflect the masques and celebrations of seasonal events, such as midsummer.

- **Style:** The style of the play is highly theatrical and fast-moving, as the action moves between court, forest and fairy realm. Shakespeare uses lyrical language for much of the dialogue in the play, and there is the potential for the epic and poetic in the speeches of Oberon and Titania. There is also potential for the informal and naturalistic in the exchanges between the artisans. However, these apparently separate worlds can appear to break down when the working-class labourers put on the epic drama of 'Pyramus and Thisbe'.

- **Form:** As stated above, the play has an episodic form created by three interlinking plots. The narrative journeys of three distinct groups of characters are brought together in the central, transformative space of the forest in which reality is temporarily suspended, but it is in the court that the action both begins and ends. The play itself also contains another play – an epic tragedy rehearsed by the workers, which is then put on as part of the royal celebrations.

Below are three case studies, detailing past productions of the play and the different ways in which three directors engaged with its genre, style and form to present it to audiences of different eras.

Case study 1:
A Midsummer Night's Dream, Herbert Beerbohm Tree, Her Majesty's Theatre, London (1911)

Staged in the Edwardian period by a theatre owner and actor-manager, the production style was informed by the intention to bring the forest to life with as much realism as possible, using props and sets. The stage included mechanical birds tweeting in simulated trees, a real stream, fairies wearing costumes that lit up, and live rabbits that foraged for food. The director made Shakespeare's plays popular with his audiences by focusing on the theatrical conventions which created spectacle and magic. The production included music by the classical composer, Felix Mendelssohn.

Case study 2:
A Midsummer Night's Dream, Peter Brook, Royal Shakespeare Company (1970)

Brook's staging of the play for the Royal Shakespeare Company posed a particular challenge to the established theatre audience of the 1970s. The production drew on the physical style of the play, including the movement of the fairies and pursuits of the lovers through the forest, and was staged in a blank white box that included acrobatic apparatus such as a trapeze. A chorus of male fairies in modern dress brought the fairy world to life, and a huge red feather represented Titania's bower (a shady place under a tree). Brook also emphasised the idea that the fairy world is a mirror image of the human world by doubling the characters of Theseus/Oberon and Hippolyta/Titania. This deliberately abstract, symbolic and 'unnatural' approach drew attention to the theatrical nature of the play, according to Brook, but also pointed to a psychological interpretation in which the erotic and emotional transformations in the forest were the manifestations of subconscious fears and desires.

A Midsummer Night's Dream, Peter Brook, Royal Shakespeare Company (1970)

Case study 3:
A Midsummer Night's Dream, Robert Lepage, National Theatre (1993)

Well-known for his interest in design-led theatre-making, the French-Canadian director's interpretation of the play drew on Brook's minimalistic style to create a nightmarish forest world. Lepage's **mise en scène** included a series of black screens at the back of the stage, surrounding a stage covered in grey mud with a watery pool in the centre. Over the pool hung a single lightbulb, which was put out by a female Puck costumed in a red leather cat suit – an act intended to suggest the power of the fairies. Lepage's interest in the spectateur (someone who experiences Shakespeare's language as a foreign language) led him to focus on the power of the image – on the form rather than the genre. The production was highly visual and included the use of Javanese instruments to create a soundscape for the play.

Key term

mise en scène: the various elements that make up the staging of a play

43

Activity 5

Which aspects of the play's context, genre, form or style has each
director foregrounded and why? To what extent might each production
reflect – or challenge – the era in which the play was being staged?

A Midsummer Night's Dream, Robert Lepage, National Theatre (1993). Additional production
images are available online.

Activity 6

Divide into three groups. Each group should take one of the case studies
and research the production further, considering the following questions.

*   Case study 1: Which stylistic choices made by Beerbohm Tree would
    create the effect of magic most effectively, and why?
*   Case study 2: Why was it important to Brook to mirror the human
    and fairy world and how did he achieve it?
*   Case study 3: How did Lepage make his production reflect the
    influence of theatre forms from different parts of the world, and what
    might this say about his interpretation of the play?

Present your ideas to the other groups.

Reflection point

How influential do you think past productions of a text are on the
development of a director's ideas for staging the text? How much
does a director have to consider the values and attitudes of a
modern audience? Make some notes.

Apply: Staging a scene

Read the opening scene from *A Midsummer Night's Dream* set in the
palace of Theseus, Duke of Athens.

Plot summary

The Duke has been preparing for his wedding. Egeus, one of his courtiers, comes to complain that his daughter Hermia is refusing to marry Demetrius. Instead she has fallen in love with Lysander. Egeus asks the Duke to enforce his decision that his daughter should marry Demetrius.

Vocabulary

vexation: irritating act
filch'd: stolen
dispose: get rid of

Text 1

Athens. The palace of THESEUS.

Enter EGEUS, and his daughter HERMIA, LYSANDER, and DEMETRIUS

EGEUS: Happy be Theseus, our renowned duke!

THESEUS: Thanks, good Egeus: what's the news with thee?

EGEUS: Full of **vexation** come I, with complaint
Against my child, my daughter Hermia.
Stand forth, Demetrius. My noble lord,
This man hath my consent to marry her.
Stand forth, Lysander: and my gracious duke,
This man hath bewitch'd the bosom of my child;
[…]
With cunning hast thou **filch'd** my daughter's heart,
Turn'd her obedience, which is due to me,
To stubborn harshness. And, my gracious duke,
Be it so she will not here before your Grace
Consent to marry with Demetrius,
I beg the ancient privilege of Athens,
As she is mine, I may **dispose** of her:
Which shall be either to this gentleman
Or to her death, according to our law
Immediately provided in that case.

from *A Midsummer Night's Dream* by William Shakespeare, Act 1, Scene 1

Activity 7

In groups of four, work through these questions to explore how this scene might be performed.

Stage 1: What does this extract tell you about the context and genre of the scene?

- Find out about the royal court of Queen Elizabeth I during Shakespeare's time. What might the playwright have wanted to suggest about the rule of law in this scene?
- The play is generally regarded as a comedy. However, as mentioned earlier, this opening scene might hint at darker tones. How could the scene be played to draw out these darker tones?
- Alternatively, are there ways of making Egeus, or the situation comic, ironic or in some way lighter in tone to match the overall genre?

Stage 2: Identify the three key moments in this scene and create three frozen images that physically highlight the different moods. Focus on the use of space, especially levels, to help reflect the power relationships between the characters.

Stage 3: Create a short sequence that uses a physical style, including movement and language, to inform the audience about the formal relationships and style of the court. Consider what a modern equivalent of Queen Elizabeth I's court might be.

2.2 Staging a text: The role of the director

Big question

- How do directors create a concept for staging the text?

Starting point: The role of the director

Being a director involves different skills at different stages of the production process. A professional company usually works on a production for between four and six weeks. You will probably have longer than this for the scripted performance you create with your group.

The first step in the production process is for the director to meet with the design team and begin to describe his or her overarching vision for the text in performance. This central idea could be described as a 'concept' for the production. For example, you might describe a director's **production concept** for Shakespeare's play *Hamlet* as 'death'.

In the next stage, the director holds early read-throughs with the actors and the lead designers for each **production element**. During the read-through, the production team discuss their initial ideas for the look and feel of the production with the actors. The designers might refer to **mood boards**, **sketches**, **scale drawings** and **model boxes** to bring the world of the play to life for the actors.

During the rehearsal and development stage, the company of actors works closely with the design team. Rehearsals might include sessions with a movement director, voice coach, fight specialist or live musicians.

In the final stage of the process of moving 'from page to stage', the director oversees the technical and dress rehearsals. The cast makes final preparations to ensure that staging is refined for performance. The director's concept should now be visible on stage.

Activity 1

Read the description of the director's tasks on this page, then compile a table like the one below to organise these tasks into a timeline.

Week / Date	Task	Purpose
1	Meet with design team – set, costume, lighting and sound; explain concept for staging the text	Communicate vision to design team
2		

Reflection point

How can you apply your learning about the role of a professional director to your own work with your group. What might be the concept for your scripted piece? Try to identity the themes in your text and consider whether one of these might form the basis of the concept.

Explore: Developing characterisation skills

One of the director's main tasks is to help the actors bring dramatic characters to life. In some productions, the director will work alongside the playwright or a dramaturg to translate the text into a live performance.

Actors use a range of performance skills to create their characters. These skills can be broadly divided into two categories.

Physical skills	Vocal skills
Gesture, posture, facial expression	Inflection, intonation, tone, emphasis
Movement – quality, pace, tempo	Accent, dialect, speed, volume

To help actors to understand and develop the character's backstory, a director might use some of the techniques of the Russian naturalistic director Constantin Stanislavski.

Spotlight on practitioner:
Constantin Stanislavski (1863–1938)

Known as one of the leading theatre practitioners of the 20th century, Stanislavski began his career as a character actor, but turned to directing out of concern about the superficial performance style of the time. His reputation rests on the development of a system for actor training and rehearsal technique, commonly known as 'the system', which aims to encourage the 'art of experience' in contrast to the 'art of representation'

In his system, an actor might be asked to consider the character's **super-objective**. The actor might also be asked to map the character's **through-line** so they can identify key moments in the character's journey and analyse the motivations behind their actions. In 1896, Stanislavski co-founded the Moscow Art Theatre. Over the following years, the company produced a series of plays written by the leading naturalistic playwrights of the time, including Henrik Ibsen (1828–1906) and Anton Chekhov (1860–1904). Stanislavski's ideas have influenced many other practitioners and are still used by actors across the world.

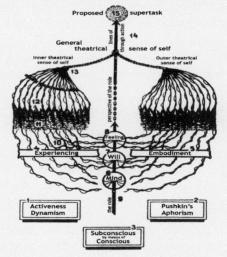

'Diagram of Stanislavski's system', based on his 'Plan of Experiencing' (1935)

Activity 2

In small groups, research one of Stanislavski's key productions. Identify how production elements such as sets, lighting, costume, props and sound were used to create the world of the play. Create a short presentation to share with the class.

Key terms

super-objective: the purpose which a character works towards during the play
through-line: the journey of a character from the start to the end of the play

Using the following extract, you are going to try out some of Stanislavski's techniques to develop the character of Puck from Shakespeare's *A Midsummer Night's Dream*.

Text 2
Enter PUCK
PUCK:
Through the forest have I gone.
But Athenian found I none,
On whose eyes I might approve
This flower's force in stirring love.
Night and silence.--Who is here?
Weeds of Athens he doth wear:
This is he, my master said,
Despised the Athenian maid;
And here the maiden, sleeping sound,
On the **dank** and dirty ground.
Pretty soul! she durst not lie
Near this lack-love, this kill-courtesy.
Churl, upon thy eyes I throw
All the power this charm doth owe.
When thou wakest, let love forbid
Sleep his seat on thy eyelid:
So awake when I am gone;
For I must now to Oberon.
Exit

From *A Midsummer's Night Dream* by William Shakespeare, Act 2, Scene 2

Plot summary

In the play, we are introduced to Puck, a fairy, and the jester and servant to Oberon, King of the Fairies. He is often mischievous, playing pranks on human characters.

In Text 2, Puck is searching for two young people from Athens who are wandering through the forest. He is seeking Helena and Demetrius, to carry out Oberon's orders that magic be used to bring the two characters together. Unfortunately, he comes across the wrong pair, Hermia and Lysander.

Vocabulary

Weeds of Athens: a reference to the clothes worn by people from Athens
despised: hated
dank: damp and cold
churl: a derogatory term for a young man, meaning ill-bred

As a director working with the performer playing Puck, you would need to plan a series of activities to develop the physical and vocal characteristics of the quick-witted and mischievous fairy.

Activity 3

Work in pairs, with one of you as director and one as the performer playing Puck (swap roles afterwards so you each get a turn as the actor). Explore the possibilities of the character's movement, with the director instructing the actor to begin in a neutral posture.

- Ask your actor to imagine they are filling their body from the feet upwards with the physical shape of the character.
- Pause in the centre of the body to explore the character's 'centre of gravity'.
- Move upwards into the arms and hands, prompting them to be aware of the range of possible gestures.
- Move finally to the shoulders, neck and head, and ask them to consider facial expression and posture.
- Now give them permission to experience the movement of their character. Guide them around the room, adjusting pace and tempo.

One of Stanislavski's key techniques for creating naturalism was to ask his actors to inhabit the wider world of the character, from before the beginning of the play into the world beyond it. To achieve this, Stanislavski developed a tool known as 'the magic if'. The actor asks themself the question 'what if?' before a specific action. For example, 'What if

Activity 4

Consider what might happen to Puck if he does not carry out Oberon's wishes. Create a short improvised scene. Remember to draw on the physical aspects of characterisation from Activity 3.

Puck decided not to obey Oberon?' By exploring the answer through **improvisation**, Stanislavski believed the actor could understand the emotions experienced and use them to enhance their performance.

Develop: Exploring the given circumstances of a scene

In order to understand the intentions of a character, actors might want to explore the '**given circumstances**' of a scene. This is a term developed by Stanislavski to describe the work undertaken by an actor to consider the events immediately preceding a scene as well as the specific circumstances of the scene including the time of day and location.

To help achieve this, the actors might ask each other a series of questions, working as researchers to develop their understanding of the context of the scene.

Activity 5

Consider the given circumstances of the extract from *A Midsummer Night's Dream* in Text 3 below.
- One student working as director should ask the actors to work in pairs. Give each pair a specific focus – for example, location in the forest.
- Each pair should then devise five questions that can be used to explore the given circumstances – for example, 'What do you hear/see/smell around you?'
- The company should then re-form into different pairs, where one actor poses the question and their partner provides the answer in role. Where appropriate, ask your actors to physically explore the space and begin to build an imaginative picture of the forest scene.

Text 3
LYSANDER:

[*Awaking*] And run through fire I will for thy sweet sake.
Transparent Helena! **Nature shows art**,
That through thy bosom makes me see thy heart.
Where is Demetrius? O, how fit a word
Is that vile name to perish on my sword!

HELENA:

Do not say so, Lysander; say not so
What though he love your Hermia? Lord, what though?
Yet Hermia still loves you: then be content.

LYSANDER:

Content with Hermia! No; I do repent
The tedious minutes I with her have spent.
Not Hermia but Helena I love:
Who will not **change a raven for a dove**?
The will of man is by his reason sway'd;
And reason says you are the worthier maid.
Things growing are not ripe until their season

Plot summary

In Text 3, Helena and Lysander, the incorrect target of Puck's magic, awaken in the forest. On waking, Lysander is overcome with feelings of love for Helena, vigorously exclaiming his new-found passion. Given how fiercely Lysander had previously declared his love for Hermia, another young woman, Helena is understandably shocked.

Vocabulary

Nature shows art: a reference to the Elizabethan idea that a person's emotions were visible in their heart
change a raven for a dove: replace a less attractive bird with one considered to be beautiful

continued

So I, being young, till now ripe not to reason;
And touching now the point of human skill,
Reason becomes the **marshal** to my will
And leads me to your eyes, where I o'erlook
Love's stories written in love's richest book.
HELENA:
Wherefore was I to this keen mockery born?
When at your hands did I deserve this scorn?
Is't not enough, is't not enough, young man,
That I did never, no, nor never can,
Deserve a sweet look from Demetrius' eye,
But you must **flout** my insufficiency?
Good troth, you do me wrong, good sooth, you do,
In such disdainful manner me to woo.
But fare you well: **perforce I must** confess
I thought you lord of more true gentleness.
O, that a lady, of one man refused.
Should of another therefore be abused!
Exit

From *A Midsummer's Night Dream*
by William Shakespeare, Act 2, Scene 2

Vocabulary

marshal: the leader of an army
(Lysander is saying that his desires are
now led by reason)
flout: make fun of
Good troth... good sooth:
Elizabethan exclamations related to the
importance of truth in relationships
perforce I must: it is necessary for
me to

Next the ensemble needs to develop a good understanding of the
physical and vocal demands of the production style. From an early point
in the rehearsal process, the director may bring the actors together for
ensemble work, including movement work.

Spotlight on practitioner: **Théâtre de Complicité**

Complicité is an international theatre company based in
London. Founded in 1983 by Annabel Arden, Fiona Garden,
Marcello Magni and Simon McBurney, the company began
as a theatre collective. Over three decades, it has developed
a unique approach to devising theatre that now has a global
following. Each piece of work is created after a period of
extensive research and as a result of collaboration with
a range of artists, including visual artists, film-makers and
dancers. The performances often feature dazzling use of
lighting, projection and video, integrated with intricate
ensemble choreography and powerful acting.

Activity 6

Using Text 3, divide your company into two groups. One group should
develop a physical language for the fairy characters and the other should
work on the physicality of the young Athenians.

Use the **shoaling** (from shoal of fish) technique used by Complicité
to develop a shape and rhythm for your group. The group should move
closely together and form a triangular shape, with a leader identified at

Key term

shoaling: moving together as a group

the top of the triangle. The leader moves the group swiftly around the space, taking care to maintain its physical shape. The leader brings the group to a halt and then the group changes direction so that a new leader emerges and moves the group on. You can use music to create and alter the pace, and deliver a series of commands (for example, 'softly') to alter the quality of the movement. Use physical **levels** to explore the qualities of movement when closer to the floor.

Once the physical shape of the group has been established, the ensemble can begin to develop **choral movements** to establish a group identity.

Apply: Focusing on a specific theatrical moment

When shaping the production concept, a director will identify key moments in the drama as being critical for the process of communicating the interpretation. These key moments might focus on the journey of one character or might mark a transition point in the **group narrative**. In *A Midsummer Night's Dream*, for example, you might identify the moment where Puck applies the fairy juice to the eyes of the wrong Athenian pair as being key to the journey towards the play's **dénouement**. The play's key themes and ideas need to be clear in the way the moment is staged. In this scene, the young couple might be observed by the invisible fairies who could form a chorus around them.

Key terms

levels: divisions of the vertical space to create visual interest for an audience
choral movements: simultaneous group movement of the actors
group narrative: the story created by the group of performers for the audience
dénouement: the final moments in the drama, usually involving an element of either resolution or dramatic climax
stage flats: large pieces of scenery designed to frame the stage picture
gobos: a stencil placed inside a lantern to cast a pattern or shape of light on stage

Activity 7

Consider how you could communicate the key themes in *A Midsummer's Night's Dream* in Act 2, Scene 2. Copy and complete the following table to indicate how you might communicate these themes through your production methods. The examples make reference to the themes of light and dark in the forest, but you can replace these with your own ideas.

Production methods	How will you communicate the key themes?
Set	Use of large jagged **stage flats** to indicate the darkness of the forest. Or use scenery to suggest the forest canopy that protects the young Athenians.
Lighting	Use forest **gobos** to create the imagery of the green forest
Sound	Sound of flies swarming above a site of decay. Alternatively, the sound of the birds moving in the trees.
Performers	Fairy chorus move in a stylised sequence to create an atmosphere of wakefulness and suggest a nightmarish world; likely to include elements of aerial work where the Athenian characters might be lifted from the floor and moved around by the fairies
Use of space	
Multi-media	

Reflection point

Work together as a group of performers to identify five lines from *A Midsummer Night's Dream* which could be used to create a physical sequence that would bring the fairy kingdom to life.

Evaluate the success of this piece by asking the following questions:
- How clearly did you communicate the key themes?
- What kind of atmosphere did you create?
- Did the mood shift at all?

As director, how will you encourage your ensemble to provide feedback to one another?

2.3 Approaching the text as a performer

Big question

- How do performers communicate a character for an audience?

Starting point: The importance of genre for an actor

Actors respond to the genre of a text, as well as its style and form, in order to develop appropriate physical and vocal skills. Commedia dell'arte is a genre of theatre which emerged at the same time as Shakespeare was developing his career as a dramatist in 16th-century London.

Key term

lazzi: stock jokes of commedia dell'arte, involving comic improvisation

Spotlight on theatre tradition: **Commedia dell'arte**

Commedia dell'arte means 'comedy of the profession'. It was an early form of professional theatre, originating in Italy, which was popular in Europe between the 16th and 18th centuries. Plays in this genre are usually built on the interconnected stories of stock, or archetypal, characters. The characters represent social archetypes from all levels of society, including higher-status characters, such as The Doctor and The Captain and working-class characters such as the servant. 'Inamorati' characters were lovers – often the main subject of the play's narrative.

Commedia dell'arte performances were a mixture of script and improvisation, and always included **lazzi** – jokes or foolish routines, well-known to audiences and performers of the time. Commedia troupes toured Europe and often performed as part of local festivals. Actors often changed troupes and usually played the same character, including some that were masked, like Arlecchino (Harlequin) and some that were unmasked, such as the Innamorati. Commedia had a significant influence on the development of theatrical forms, such as melodrama and pantomime.

Activity 1

Research the character types of commedia dell'arte. Copy and complete the table below to help you organise your ideas. Add rows to the table as you explore the full range of characters.

Character	Masked or unmasked	Social role and status	Characteristics – costume, physical and vocal skills
Arlecchino (Harlequin)	Masked	Servant	Tight-fitting, colourful suit (checked?); fast-moving; often speaks directly to the audience
Il Dottore (The Doctor)			
Il Capitano (The Captain)			

Explore: Developing physical characterisation in the style of a specific genre

As a performer approaching a text in a particular genre, it is important to understand the range of physical skills required for performing in that genre. The following example, which explores one of the most significant commedia texts, Carlo Goldoni's *A Servant to Two Masters*, shows how genre might inform performance.

Spotlight on practitioner: **Carlo Goldoni (1707–93)**

Goldoni was a playwright from the Venetian Republic. Educated as a lawyer, he later started managing a theatre and began writing plays. During his career, he wrote a number of plays in Italian and French, as well as operatic librettos. Goldoni wanted to move beyond the comedy of masks and mystery popular at the time, and to represent real life through plot and character. Many experts believe he laid the groundwork for the naturalistic theatre that arose in the 19th century. However, it is his commedia-like comedies for which he is best known, and for his translation of the elements of commedia into a formal written format. In *The Servant of Two Masters*, the unravelling of the confusions of the plot towards a happy ending may reflect Goldoni's desire that theatre should provide a respite from the challenges of life. The play is about an enterprising servant attempting to make money by taking on two jobs at the same time – perhaps reflecting Goldoni's entrepreneurial approach to his own career as he reinvented himself within a range of different professions.

Commedia **troupes** crossed borders of nationality and language, so they relied on a highly visual physical language in performance. The lazzi in this play would have delighted the audiences of the time. The **zanni**, or comic actors, would develop **set pieces**, which often dealt with bodily functions, such as eating or toileting.

Key terms

libretto: the words to an opera
troupe: a group of touring actors who perform in different places
zanni: the name given to the stock comic characters in commedia dell'arte
set piece: a scene that audiences would recognise as typical of plays in the genre

Harlequin, a commedia dell'arte stock character

Il Dottore or the Doctor, a traditional commedia dell'arte character

Chapter 2 Performing from a text

Read the extract below, from the opening of the play. A servant,
Truffaldino, introduces himself to Pantaloon (a gentleman whose daughter
has just got engaged), Pantaloon's servant Smeraldina and his neighbour
The Doctor. Although she does not speak in this scene, Clarice is referred
to. She is the daughter of Pantaloon. As you read, choose one character
and consider the physical challenges the actor might face, such as
managing the fast-paced dialogue and movement. How might the physical
style influence your use of movement and gesture?

Text 4

Pantaloon.   Who are you, my good friend? and what is your business?

Truffaldino.   [to Pantaloon., pointing to Clarice.] Who is this fair gentlewoman?

Pantaloon.   That is my daughter.

Truffaldino.   Delighted to hear it.

Smeraldina.   [to Truffalindo.] What's more, she is going to be married.

Truffaldino.   I'm sorry to hear it. And who are you?

Smeraldina.   I am her maid, sir.

Truffaldino.   I congratulate her.

Pantaloon.   Come, sir, have done with ceremony. What do you want with
me? who are you? who sends you hither?

Truffaldino.   Patience, patience, my good sir, take it easy. Three questions at
once is too much for a poor man.

Pantaloon.   [aside to Doctor.] I think the man's a fool.

Doctor.   [aside to Pantaloon.] I think he's playing the fool […]

Pantaloon.   Will you tell me who you are, or will you go about your business?

Truffaldino.   If you only want to know who I am, I'll tell you in two words. I
am the servant of my master. [Turns to Smeralinda.] To go back to
what I was saying—

Pantaloon.   But who is your master?

Truffaldino.   [to Pantaloon.]. He is a gentleman who desires the honour of
paying his respects to you.

from *The Servant of Two Masters* by Carlo Goldoni, Act 1, Scene 1

Activity 2

- In groups of four, choose one character each from the extract.
  Choose a physical stance for the actor which represents their status.
- Start to move the character around the space (without any contact
  with other characters). Begin to observe the pace and rhythm
  of movement.
- Now allow your character to interact with others, using a simple
  non-verbal greeting. Note whether your character gravitates towards
  some characters more than others.

Make some notes about the physical style that you are beginning
to develop. How does it affect movement, gesture, posture and
facial expression?

Commedia actors were highly skilled at performing in the exaggerated physical style that characterised the genre. Now focus on the scheming servant Truffaldino, a typical zanni character of the genre. In this scene from later in Act 1, Truffaldino is trying to secure the service of the second of two masters.

Text 5

Truffaldino.	I'm sick of waiting; I can hold out no longer. With this master of mine there's not enough to eat, and the less there is the more I want it. The town clock struck twelve half an hour ago, and my belly struck two hours ago at least. If I only knew where we were going to lodge! [...]

Enter Florindo in travelling dress with a Porter carrying a trunk on his shoulder.

Porter.	I tell you, sir, I can go no farther; the weight's enough to kill me.
Florindo.	Here is the sign of an inn. Can't you carry it these few steps?
Porter.	Help! the trunk is falling.
Florindo.	I told you you could not carry it; you're too weak; you have no strength at all. [*Flor. re-arranges the trunk on the Porte's shoulder.*]
Truffaldino.	Here's a chance for sixpence. [*To Florindo.*] Sir, can I do anything for you?
Florindo.	My good man, be so good as to carry this trunk into the inn there.
Truffaldino.	Yes, sir, let me take it, sir. See how I do it. [*To the Porter.*] You be off! [*Truffalindo. puts his shoulder under the trunk and takes it by himself, knocking the Porter. down at the same time.*]
Florindo.	Well done!
Truffaldino.	It weighs nothing. A mere trifle. [*Goes into the inn with the trunk.*]
Florindo.	[*To Porter.*] There! You see how it's done.

From *The Servant of Two Masters* by Carlo Goldoni, Act 1, Scene 2

Activity 3

In small groups, allocate one aspect of Truffaldino's character to each actor: greed, intelligence, deception, charm.

Move into the playing area, focusing on making your characteristic clear for the audience.

- Start at level 1 (very minor) and develop a clear sequence of gestures you can use to demonstrate the characteristic – for example, using lots of arm movements to confuse Florindo.

- After a minute or so, raise the level of exaggeration towards 10. At the highest level, you should become a **caricature** of Truffaldino.

- Explain to the rest of the group the impact of exaggeration on posture, gesture and the pace and quality of movement.

Key term

caricature: an imitation of a person in which certain striking images are exaggerated for comic effect

Develop: Exploring vocal skills

Alongside the physical aspects of character, it is important to consider the vocal aspects. There is a range of vocal techniques, which can be used to create different effects in performance.

Vocal technique	Definition and effects
Volume	The amount of sound created can be varied to create mood or atmosphere.
Pitch	The particular level (high or low) of a voice can be varied to suggest different tones or emotions.
Pace	Controlling the speed of the vocal delivery of a text can help to convey character or the style or mood of the scene.
Pause	A short period of silence or stillness in a performance can be used to create dramatic interest or tension.
Inflection	Changing the way the voice rises and falls. Can be used to communicate meaning and intention in dialogue.
Intonation	Changing tone can indicate attitude or emotion.
Accent	The way words are pronounced can be used to indicate nationality, ethnicity or where a character is from.
Emphasis	Stress on a particular word or sound to enhance its significance.

Due to the visual nature of the genre, commedia actors sometimes used a nonsense language now known as Grammelot to communicate relationships between characters and enhance the comedy. Grammelot is a sort of improvised babble and can consist of nonsense words, as well as noises and grunts. It can be a useful rehearsal tool for developing understanding of the shifting tensions in a scene.

Activity 4

Reread Text 5, then work with a partner to annotate a copy of the text to indicate where there are opportunities for the actor to use any of the techniques listed in the table above. When you have finished, stage the exchange between the characters using Grammelot rather than the text. Focus on the use of space and the physical language between the two actors. Finally, perform it again with the real words, but using the emphases, tone and pace generated by the use of Grammelot to provide dramatic interest.

Apply: Drawing out the farce

Commedia is closely linked to the theatrical genre known as **farce**. Understanding of the style of commedia will allow you to identify the elements of farce in *The Servant of Two Masters* and explore how an actor might apply their physical and vocal skills to the genre. It is precisely this combination of performance skills that is required to create the fast pace demanded by a farce.

Reflection point

How might you use the physical characteristics of a commedia character to inform your development of a character from another comic text?

Key term

farce: a genre of comedy often characterised by a series of unlikely coincidences, a fast pace and careful comic timing; from the French 'farcir', meaning 'to stuff'

Spotlight on theatre tradition: **Farce**

In farcical plays, the audience is entertained by absurd situations, crude characterisation and physical sequences. In modern farce plays, actors may be seen coming into and out of doors narrowly missing each other, dropping heavy objects from a significant height and narrowly missing the head of the person standing underneath, or confusing one person for another.

Activity 5

Conduct some research into modern playwrights who are considered to have embraced the farce genre, such as Alan Ayckbourn or Alan Bennett. Make some notes on the characteristics of the plays and try to find some reviews of performances. Use the following questions to help you.

- What is the subject of the farce?
- How is the comedy created?
- How have playwrights adapted the commedia genre to make it appeal to a modern audience?

Read the extract below from Act 2 of *The Servant of Two Masters*. By this point in the play, Truffaldino is running from one master to another, trying to keep up his various deceptions. In this scene, two waiters serve dinner to the two different masters, Beatrice and Florindo, in two different rooms. The greedy servant follows the waiters and takes food off every plate, all for himself!

Text 6

Truffaldino.	[*to Beatrice*]. Dinner is ready for you in that room, sir.
Beatrice.	Go and put the soup on the table.
Truffaldino.	[*makes a bow*]. After you, sir.
Pantaloon.	A queer fellow, that servant of yours. [*Goes in.*]
Beatrice.	[*to Truff.*]. I want less wit and more attention. [*Goes in.*]
Truffaldino.	Call that a dinner! one dish at a time! They have money to spend, but they get nothing good for it. I wonder if this soup is worth eating; I'll try it. [*Takes a spoon out of his pocket and tastes the soup.*] I always carry my weapons about. Not bad; it might be worse. [*Goes into room with soup.*]

Enter First Waiter with a dish.

1st Waiter.	When is that man coming to take the dishes?
Truffaldino.	[*re-entering*]. Here I am, friend. What have you got for me?
1st Waiter.	Here's the boiled meat. There's another dish to follow.

[Exit 1st Wait.]

Truffaldino.	Mutton? or veal? Mutton, I think. Let's taste it. [*Tastes.*] No, 'tis neither mutton nor veal; 'tis lamb, and very good too. [*Goes towards Beat.'s room.*]

Enter Florindo.

continued

Florrindo.   Where are you going?

Truffaldino.   Oh dear, oh dear! [*Aside.*] [...]

[*Florindo goes into the other room—as soon as he is in Truffaldino quickly takes the dish in to Beatrice.*

Enter 1st Waiter with another dish. Florindo calls from his room.]

Florrindo.   Truffaldino! Truffaldino! am I always to be kept waiting?

Truffaldino   [*coming out of Beatrice's room*]. Coming, sir. [*To 1st Waiter.*] Quick, go and lay the table in that other room, the other gentleman has arrived; bring the soup at once.

1st Waiter.   Directly.

[*Exit 1st Waiter.*]

Truffaldino.   What may this dish be? This must be the 'fricandeau.' [*Tastes it.*] That's good, upon my word.

[*Takes it in to Beatrice.*]

Abridged from *The Servant of Two Masters* by Carlo Goldoni, Act 2, Scene 2

Here the actor playing Truffaldino needs to balance plates while eating, drinking and moving rapidly around the stage. The actors playing the waiters also contribute to the pace and visual comedy. One way of managing the physical demands of the form is to use Stanislavski's technique of units and objectives (see Unit 2.2). The technique can be applied to the demands of the farce.

Activity 6

Read Text 6. On a copy of the extract, draw a line every time an action finishes. Each one of these is a 'unit of action'. Number each unit, then for each one, assign each character an objective . Record your findings in a copy of the table below. An example has been given.

Unit of action	Character's objective
1. First waiter brings plate of food for Florindo	1st waiter: deliver food Truffaldino: eat some food and deliver remainder to Florindo

Next you need to develop the physical and vocal language of the farce. Start with the stage directions – for example, '*Takes a spoon out of his pocket and tastes the soup*'. The actor would need to consider the status given to them as the master comic actor and the focus of the action. The actor therefore needs to make decisions about all the physical skills. For example, they might decide to hold the tray high in the air and spin around a couple of times, taking something from the tray each time they turn away from the waiters, to hide the fact that they are taking food and eating it.

Activity 7

In groups of three or four, allocate each person a role from this scene.

*   Mark up the stage space using small items of furniture or masking tape, indicating the location of each of the four doorways – one each into the two rooms where Florindo and Beatrice (the masters) are, and two into and out of the kitchen.
*   Perform the sequence at top speed several times, without the text, until the style of movement and the use of specific gestures have been established.
*   Drop the speed to a conversational level, paying attention to the rhythms that you have established between the actors.

In Lee Hall's 1999 production of the play, actor Jason Watkins, playing Truffaldino, brought this scene to life using several physical techniques.

Case study:
A Servant to Two Masters, adapted by Lee Hall, Royal Shakespeare Company (2000)

In this production, the actors performed on a **thrust stage**. In this scene, therefore, the actor playing Truffaldino was able to share his manic greed and comic deceit with the audience seated on three sides of the auditorium. The four doors were arranged at the back of the stage, and entrances and exits of the two masters were timed to perfection, with Watkins moving with the plates at a frantic pace to ensure that he was always in view of Florindo and Beatrice when he was called. His body was elongated as he aimed to catch a plate with one hand and open a door with another. His facial expressions were a combination of delight and exhaustion as the scene wore on. His delivery of the text was fast-paced and used a range of intonation and accent to bring the comedy to life. The combination of physical and vocal skills helped to drive the pace and energy of the scene. (Production photos are available online.)

Key term
thrust stage: a stage that extends into the audience area, with seats on three sides of a 'T'-shaped acting space

An example of a thrust stage.

Reflection point

How could you use your understanding of the genres of commedia and farce to inform the development of a character you are portraying in your own performance? Annotate a copy of the text with ideas for physical and vocal work.

2.4 Staging a group text performance for a modern audience

Big question

- How can you stage a text for a modern audience?

Starting point: Adapting a text to modernise the style

When approaching a text written centuries ago, the world of the play may seem unfamiliar and the characters unrecognisable. Even the language may seem remote and inaccessible. However, one of the reasons that such plays are still popular today is because the playwrights wrote about 'universal' human experiences – the problems and joys that people at all times and in all places have experienced. Many modern playwrights have adapted classical or **canonical texts** to appeal to contemporary audiences. Lee Hall's adaptation of Goldoni's play is a good example of this.

Let's start with the process of adapting the text. Here Lee Hall describes his approach to adapting Goldoni's text in his introduction to the play in 1999:

> My project has been to reinstate the actual Goldoni play rather than to create my own riff on it [...] it seemed more appropriate to reinstate Goldoni than reiterate my own preoccupations.

One way of understanding the process of adaptation is to use a flowchart. The diagram below describes the range of considerations for a modern theatre company seeking to adapt a classical text.

Location: What sort of place would the characters now live and work in?

↓

Status relationship: Is there a modern equivalent to the job or social roles that characters might perform?

↓

Situations: What would be the modern equivalent to the situations that the characters find themselves in?

↓

Personal props: Are there modern equivalents to the personal objects or props that a character might use?

↓

Clothing and appearance: What is the modern equivalent to any clothing item?

Key term

canonical text: a text considered to be of significant cultural value as a work of art

Activity 1

Review the extracts from *The Servant of Two Masters*. Use the flowchart above to make notes on the possible options for a 21st-century production of the play. For example, could the scheming servant Truffaldino become a personal assistant serving the needs of two masters who both reside in gleaming modern apartments?

Explore: Using contemporary design elements to modernise the text

You could design Goldoni's play to create a contrast with the original 18th-century aristocratic setting or, as adaptor playwright Lee Hall indicated, to sympathetically recreate the comedic farce in a period style. The action moves rapidly between Pantaloon's house, Brighella's inn and the streets outside. Traditionally, commedia was performed by touring troupes, so staging had to be simple. Companies used just a few key props and items of costume to differentiate between characters. Today, companies have access to sophisticated technology to enhance the action – for example, a sense of a bustling urban street could be created using projected images. You might also want to draw upon popular youth culture and insert modern props, such as mobile phones. An original commedia production would probably have been performed in an 'end-on' form, with the audience facing the stage. In a modern production, you might place the audience in thrust or **in the round**.

Key term

in the round: a staging form in which the audience surrounds the stage on all sides

Activity 2

Collect some images of 18th-century Venice to develop your understanding of the colours and shapes of the period, such as the rich brocades and velvets of the Venetian court. Copy and complete the table below to record your ideas for designing the text for a modern audience.

Design element	18th-century Venice	21st-century design
Staging (for example, thrust, proscenium arch)		
Set		
Lighting (including multimedia)		
Sound		
Costume		

In the first production of Hall's adaptation, the audience was transported to 18th-century Venice, but easily understood the narrative because the language had been modernised and contemporary references brought the jokes to life. The set consisted of a few key items of furniture and props. To indicate the aristocratic houses, a chandelier and baroque chair were 'flown' on to the stage during set changes. The colour scheme was also highly symbolic. Gold and red fabric was used to indicate wealth, and browns and creams to indicate lower-status dwellings and situations.

Develop: Establishing the theatrical style and pace of a scene

Read this extract from *The Servant of Two Masters*. Here Truffaldino is confronted by his two masters following a chaotic dinner service. Truffaldino continues to lie to them. Thinking that they have been tricked by two deceitful servants, Florindo enlists the innkeeper Brighella to help unravel their identities.

Text 7

Enter Truffaldino brought in by force by Brighella and the 1st Waiter.

Florindo.	Come here, come here, don't be frightened.
Beatrice.	We shall do you no harm.
Truffaldino.	[aside]. H'm, I still remember the thrashing.
Brighella.	We have found this one; if we can find the other, we will bring him.
Florindo.	Yes, we must have them both here together.
Brighella.	[aside to Wait.]. Do you know the other?
1st Wait.	[to Brig.]. Not I.
Brighella.	We'll ask in the kitchen. Someone there will know him.
1st Wait.	If he had been there, I should have known him too.

[Exeunt 1st Wait. and Brighella].

Florindo.	[to Truff.]. Come now, tell us what happened about that changing of the portrait and the book, and why you and that other rascal conspired to drive us distracted.
Truffaldino.	[*signs to both with his finger to keep silence*]. Hush! **[To Flor.]** Pray, sir, a word with you in private. [*To Beat., just as he turns to speak to Flor.*] I will tell you everything directly. [*To Flor.*] You must know, sir, I am not to blame for any thing that has happened; it's all Pasqual's fault, the servant of that lady there [*cautiously pointing at Beat.*]. It was he mixed up the things, and put into one trunk what belonged to the other, without my knowledge. The poor man begged and prayed me to take the blame, for fear his master should send him away, and as I am a kind-hearted fellow [...] I made up all these stories to see if I could help him [...] Now I have told you the whole truth, sir, as an honest man and a faithful servant.

From *The Servant of Two Masters* by Carlo Goldoni, Act 3, Scene 3

In this extract, there are a number of entrances and exits, as well as an aside between Truffaldino and Florindo. The tone and style of the scene is therefore comic confusion with rapid-fire delivery of the text, including use of a range of areas of the stage space.

Activity 3

Divide into small groups and allocate roles to each of the actors. Each group will also need a director, who can provide a beat, either by clapping or using a small percussive instrument, such as a drum.

- Pace out the scene by reading the dialogue and working out how the stage space might be used to create the comedy for the modern audience. Notice the natural rhythm of the scene.
- Introduce a faster rhythm, using your instrument of choice – try changing the use of space as the scene progresses.
- Introduce a piece of fast music and play the scene without speaking the words.
- Consider how the change of pace changes the actor's gesture and movement. Discuss with your group.

Apply: Choosing scenes for a scripted performance for an audience

The genre, form and structure of the play may determine whether there is one clearly identifiable moment of dramatic climax. Where the structure of the play is **cyclical** or **episodic**, there may be a number of moments of theatrical tension or interest.

Imagine that, as a group, you have been working on *A Midsummer Night's Dream* and are beginning to plan a theatrical interpretation. To help you understand the themes and ideas in Shakespeare's comedies, you have all agreed to research other examples, such as *As You Like It*. For example, you may have decided to highlight the theme of power in your performance of *A Midsummer Night's Dream* – specifically the abuse of power. In order to present approximately 30 minutes of performance, you have chosen to focus on the two powerful male characters of Theseus and Oberon, respectively lord of the court and king of the forest of Athens. To create depth and contrast in the presentation, you have decided to include a lighter scene, including the fairy characters, alongside two of the darker scenes, which show the two characters in conflict. The performance will be staged in a thrust style, using a range of multimedia devices, such as projections and live film feed. The play will be updated and set in a modern landscape.

Text 8 is one of the key scenes you have chosen. As you read the extract, start to think about the options for performing and designing the scene. At this point in the play, Oberon confronts his fairy queen Titania, accusing her of having feelings for Theseus.

Key terms

cyclical: describing a circular structure where the actions at the beginning of the play are revisited at the end

episodic: a series of complete scenes, each of which contains a unified story or set of actions

Vocabulary

rash wanton: a reference to Titania's suspected infidelity

buskin'd: a thick-soled boot worn by warriors, a reference to Hippolyta's status as Queen of the Amazons

---

Text 8

Enter, from one side, OBERON, with his train; from the other, TITANIA, with hers

OBERON:	Ill met by moonlight, proud Titania.
TITANIA:	What, jealous Oberon! Fairies, skip hence: I have forsworn his bed and company.
OBERON:	Tarry, **rash wanton**: am not I thy lord?
TITANIA:	Then I must be thy lady: but I know […] the bouncing Amazon, Your **buskin'd** mistress and your warrior love, To Theseus must be wedded, and you come To give their bed joy and prosperity.

continued

OBERON:	How canst thou thus for shame, Titania,
	Glance at my credit with Hippolyta,
	Knowing I know thy love to Theseus? [...]
TITANIA:	These are the forgeries of jealousy:
	And never, since the middle summer's spring,
	Met we on hill, in dale, forest or mead,
	[...] But with thy brawls thou hast disturb'd our sport.
	Therefore the winds, piping to us in vain,
	As in revenge, have suck'd up from the sea
	Contagious fogs; [...]
OBERON:	[...] Why should Titania cross her Oberon?
	I do but beg a little changeling boy,
	To be my henchman.
TITANIA:	Set your heart at rest:
	The fairy land buys not the child of me.
	His mother was a votaress of my order:
	And, in the spiced Indian air, by night,
	Full often hath she gossip'd by my side,
	And sat with me on Neptune's yellow sands,
	[...] But she, being mortal, of that boy did die;
	[...] And for her sake I will not part with him.
OBERON:	How long within this wood intend you stay?
TITANIA:	Perchance till after Theseus' wedding-day.
	If you will patiently dance in our round
	And see our moonlight revels, go with us;
	If not, shun me, and I will spare your haunts.
OBERON:	Give me that boy, and I will go with thee.
TITANIA:	Not for thy fairy kingdom. Fairies, away!
	We shall chide downright, if I longer stay.

Exit TITANIA with her train

From *A Midsummer Night's Dream* by William Shakespeare, Act 2, Scene 1

Activity 4

Annotate a copy of Text 8 to show how the performers might use the space at different moments. Now try staging the scene, focusing on Oberon's desire to demonstrate his power over Titania.

- How might the performers use their physicality to indicate the tension between them?

- How might the production concept – for example, the use and abuse of power – influence the use of **proxemics**?

- How might the performers use costume and props to support their performance?

Key term

proxemics: the physical distance between actors on stage, often used to signify the relationships between characters

2.5 Preparing an individual performance for an audience

Big question

- How can you create an integrated, individual scripted performance?

Starting point: Making text choices

When artists decide to create a 'one-man' or 'one-woman' show, they think carefully about their choice of performance material. In the same way as a company of actors makes choices about the presentation of a whole text, individual actors may choose to highlight a particular theme or message for an audience. Solo performances often draw on the same production elements as group performance – including lighting and sound, puppetry, masks, props and costume – but in the individual performance you must put together for your course the core focus will be on your individual vocal and movement skills.

A solo performer can draw on, and explore dramatically, any number of texts. These might include:

- individual monologues or speeches from established playscripts
- **transcripts** of real-life conversations or events (for example, trials or official inquiries)
- news reports or articles
- poems or extracts from prose fiction or non-fiction
- song lyrics
- essays or speeches
- or any other written texts which could be adapted or utilised in performance.

Key term

transcript: an accurate written account of a conversation, which might include speech utterances such as 'Um' or 'Err', as well as pauses and hesitations

---

Activity 1

A student selects the following 'texts', with the intention of using at least three of them to explore a theme in performance:

- Shakespeare: a speech by Puck, a mischievous fairy, on his/her powers to trick humans (Act 2 Scene 1 of *A Midsummer Night's Dream*)
- extract from 'Goblin Market', a poem by Christina Rossetti
- a children's story about Loki, the **trickster** character from **Norse** mythology
- an oral transcript in which an old man remembers the pranks played by his friends on '**All Fool's Day**'.

Vocabulary

trickster: an archetype in traditional stories, such as the zanni in commedia dell'arte, a figure who is cunning and fools other people

Norse: relating to Scandinavia and Iceland

All Fool's Day: the first day of April, when traditionally people play tricks on one another

Activity 2

On your own, think about what unifying theme, idea or question could link the texts. You could use one of the possibilities below, or come up with your own. Share your ideas with a partner or small group.

- clowns, jesters and fools
- the trickster
- 'What fools these mortals be!' (a line from *A Midsummer Night's Dream*)
- the hoax
- fake news.

Explore: Presenting an individual performance

Activity 3

Below are three of the texts from the initial list. Read them carefully and begin to think about how you could use any two of them as part of a structured sequence with one other text.

Text 9

PUCK: I am that merry wanderer of the night.
I jest to Oberon and make him smile
When I a fat and bean-fed horse **beguile**,
Neighing in likeness of a **filly** foal;
And sometime lurk I in a gossip's bowl,
In very likeness of a roasted **crab**,
And when she drinks, against her lips I bob,
And on her wither'd **dewlap** pour the ale.
The wisest aunt, telling the saddest tale,
Sometime for three-foot stool mistaketh me;
Then slip I from her bum, down topples she,
And 'tailor' cries, and falls into a cough;
And then the whole **quire** hold their hips and laugh,
And **waxen in their mirth** and **neeze** and swear
A merrier hour was never wasted there.
But, room, fairy! here comes Oberon.

From *A Midsummer Night's Dream* by William Shakespeare, Act 2, Scene 1

Vocabulary

beguile: to charm

filly: young female horse

crab: a roasted wild apple (commonly put in bowls of drink)

dewlap: lower neck or jaw

quire: choir

waxen in their mirth: laugh very hard

neeze: sneeze

Text 10

Old Man: um [.] so me and jim [.] my best mate from school, like [.] so we played knock-down ginger, which was when you rapped on some adults' door then ran away [.] but thing was, [laughs] the challenge was to see who could leave it longest [.] like, you knocked then waited as long as you dared, before running away [.] well, jim, he was always braver than me [.] I was a right chicken [.]

Text 11

'Lie close,' Laura said,
Pricking up her golden head:
'We must not look at goblin men,
We must not buy their fruits:
Who knows upon what soil they fed
Their hungry thirsty roots?'
'Come buy,' call the goblins
Hobbling down the glen.
'Oh,' cried Lizzie, 'Laura, Laura,
You should not peep at goblin men.'
Lizzie cover'd up her eyes,
Cover'd close lest they should look;
Laura rear'd her glossy head,
And whisper'd like the restless brook:
'Look, Lizzie, look, Lizzie,
Down the glen tramp little men.
One hauls a basket,
One bears a plate,
One lugs a golden dish
Of many pounds weight.
How fair the vine must grow
Whose grapes are so luscious;
How warm the wind must blow
Through those fruit bushes.'

From 'Goblin Market' by Christina Rossetti

Activity 4

In the scene in Text 9, Puck is describing how he changes shape to trick people. In Rossetti's poem (Text 11), Goblin men try to tempt two sisters enjoying a summer's walk to try their wares. Look at the grid below setting out some of the key vocal and physical 'tools' at your disposal as a performer.

Vocal	Physical
• pitch, projection, volume, articulation • pace, pause, breathing, cueing • tone, inflection, accent, repetition, emphasis	• body: posture, gesture, facial expression, eye contact • movement: timing, direction, energy, pathways, repetition • use of space: levels, personal/general space, proximity

With a partner, work through both columns to check your understanding of each term. Now decide how you might use these skills to portray the character of Puck in Text 9 and the two sisters in Text 11.

For example:

Puck: [1] I [2] am that merry wanderer of the night

[1] proximity: close to audience, as if taking them into his confidence

[2] emphasis: strong – to focus on himself

Activity 5

How would a performance of these texts differ in style from a performance of Text 10, the real-life transcript? How could you mimic the patterns of everyday speech? Think about the pauses and hesitations (indicated by the [.]) and how and where this might have been spoken. Perhaps it was a radio interview – so the speaker might be very static in terms of delivery and movement. Write down one way in which you could use this speech as a contrasting element to the dynamics of a performance using Puck's speech.

Activity 6

You are now going to work on the characters more closely. Assuming the actor's neutral stance (feet shoulder width apart, hands by your side, knees relaxed), imagine you are adopting the character of Puck working from the tip of your feet to the crown of your head. Move around the space and notice the centre of gravity, or central point of energy in the character. Experiment by shifting the energy around the body. Now add some gestures and start to explore the space, focusing on developing your fairy movement style. Return to the text and explore what happens to the delivery of Shakespeare's language as you move. Do you emphasise certain words or sounds?

Next consider how you might use Text 11 to create a character who resembles one of the goblin men. Start by developing a rhythmic walk which creates the sense of temptation and menace in the poem. Now develop a physical vocabulary for the character which includes representation of the act of carrying the goblin wares. Finally consider how you could move between the characters of Puck and goblin and what 'shape-shifting' might look like in performance as you move from between lightness of a spirit and the heaviness of a goblin.

Develop: Links and transitions

It is important that you make effective links between the individual sections of your individual performance. For example, you could use:

- one of the texts as a central narrative to which you return several times (interspersing parts of Puck's speech with other trickster pieces)
- the same music or song as a recurring motif in your pieces
- an object or prop which appears in, or is used in, each fragment or piece
- a particular movement, such as dance
- lighting or sound themes or changes
- multimedia devices including projection or short films as a backdrop
- a real-life documentary piece (like the transcript on page 66) as a counterpoint to the drama.

You could also add verbal links – giving your own explanations, which make your theme or idea clear.

Remember, too, that you can edit and adapt the text or texts you have chosen to create an effective dramatic sequence. For example, you could select just some of Puck's lines. This will be informed by the style you want for your performance. Previously you explored how style can be shaped by aspects of the text. In Peter Brook's 1970 'empty space' production of *A Midsummer Night's Dream* (see page 125), the physical style of the performance was developed with the use of acrobatics and aerial techniques. In this production, symbolic props were used to suggest the power and influence of Oberon and Theseus. You can find more information about the design of this production in Chapter 4.

Now read the following extract, which follows on immediately from Puck's earlier monologue.

Text 12

OBERON: My gentle Puck, come hither. [...]

Fetch me that flow'r; the herb I showed thee once:
The juice of it on sleeping eyelids laid
Will make or man or woman madly **dote**
Upon the next live creature that it sees.
Fetch me this herb, and be thou here again
Ere the **leviathan** can swim a league.

PUCK: I'll put a **girdle** round about the earth
In forty minutes.

Exit Puck

OBERON: Having once this juice,
I'll watch Titania when she is asleep,
And drop the liquor of it in her eyes;
The next thing then she waking looks upon,
Be it on lion, bear, or wolf, or bull,
On meddling monkey, or on busy ape,
She shall pursue it with the soul of love.
And ere I take this charm from off her sight,
As I can take it with another herb,
I'll make her **render up** her page to me.

Abridged from *A Midsummer Night's Dream* by William Shakespeare,
Act 1, Scene 2

Vocabulary

dote: to be fond of someone

leviathan: huge whale

girdle: a belt

render up: to give something to someone

Activity 7

Reread Text 12, paying particular attention to the instructions Oberon gives Puck. Then work in small groups to follow the steps below to explore a possible style for the fairy characters who could be on stage throughout this scene, observing the action. Remember that the physical and vocal style of the fairy characters needs to match the overall style of the production concept.

- Firstly, divide into groups of five, with one person nominated to act as director.
- Start with an actor's neutral stance. Use a piece of music or create a percussion beat to move the fairies around the space.
- Start to use non-verbal sounds to create a soundscape for the movement of the fairies – focus on the quality of sound: hard or soft, sharp or lyrical.
- Now move back to the text and work on your own. Consider how a fairy might respond to Oberon's words and movements.
- Now focus on developing the individual physical and vocal characteristics of the character of Puck – how might you convince the audience of the fantastical nature of the character?
- Now that you have a company full of individual Pucks, ask one individual to introduce themselves non-verbally to the rest of the actors.
- Notice the similarities and differences between your own interpretation and that of others.

The character of Puck lends itself to a range of different interpretations. Conduct some research into previous interpretations of the role.

Apply: Key design questions to consider when creating an individual performance

Audiences and critics who saw Peter Brook's 1970 production of the play commented on the highly visual style and minimalistic approach to a classical text. However, some critics felt that the white box in which the play was staged detracted from the musicality of the original verse by making the interpretation too modern. Others were impressed by the playful nature of the performance. Since it was first performed, most have agreed that this innovative interpretation was a landmark in theatre history.

As you prepare your individual performance, try to draw your ideas together, using a series of key questions:

- As an individual performer, how would you highlight the key themes in the texts chosen?
- How could you use design elements to bring the text to life?
- How could you ensure that the style of the performance is consistent throughout?

Activity 8

Use these questions to identify an appropriate sequence of scenes and texts.

- Look more closely at the overall plot line of your chosen playscript and try to select three or four key scenes that might form the basis of an individual performance. (You can narrow or edit these down later.) Make some notes on the reasons for your choice. Try to identify a specific theme or idea which you can focus on.
- Undertake some research on the theme or key idea and identify material which might be useful as part of a performance – this might include poems, extracts from letters or the first page of a novel.
- Create some design sketches which illustrate your ideas for staging.
- Decide on some link devices which you can use to create effective transitions between scenes and make a coherent performance for the audience.

Chapter 3

Devising

Devising is a key skill in the theatre. There are no set methods for devising, and companies and practitioners approach the process in many different ways. However, there are some important elements to be taken into account when you are creating your own devised piece. In this chapter, you will learn about these key elements and explore ways in which to approach the devising process.

3.1 Introduction to devising

Big question

- What are the key elements of devising a creative piece?

Starting point: What is devising?

Devising is the theatrical process of creating original performance work. It is often undertaken by a group, but it can also be an individual process. A devised piece often originates with a **stimulus**, tradition, style or the work of a particular practitioner. Devising can be a lengthy but exciting process. It requires deep exploration of an initial stimulus, and the work shifts and reshapes frequently throughout the process. The final production may be very different from your initial ideas – the work is intended to be the product of a full creative process.

Imagine that you are going island-hopping in the Greek islands. If you go straight from the first island to the last without visiting any in between, you will only gain a superficial view of the area. It is only by exploring other islands that you will understand the area as a whole. Once you have visited them all, you might decide that you have a favourite island or two and head back there for a longer period of time to explore further. You will still reach your destination, but your journey will be more varied, your experience richer, and your knowledge at the end, much broader.

The early stages of devising are similar. Your ultimate destination is the final idea that you and your company decide to take further, but many 'islands' should be explored before picking your favourite and settling on that destination.

Key term

stimulus: the starting point for a new piece of developed performance work; the finished piece can either be directly related to or inspired by the stimulus, or it can provoke a new direction of ideas

Activity 1

Many individual practitioners are known for their creation of devised pieces. Find the names of three individuals or theatre companies who were or are famous for their collaborative approach to creating original drama. For each practitioner, find a quotation or write a single-sentence summary of their approach to the devising process or their feelings about it.

Explore: What is the first stage of devising?

During your course, you will be asked to undertake two devising tasks. In one, you will need to work as a group to devise a play from a stimulus. The stimulus can be literary, artistic, from current events or from historical events. In the other task, you will work as a group to devise a play inspired by a given theatre practitioner, tradition or style. The crucial first step in the development of a devised piece is a thorough exploration of your stimulus or research on the practitioner, tradition or style on which you intend to base the finished piece. Think of this in terms of studying a map of the islands and deciding where to go first. This research will give you the depth of information you need to start making decisions about what it is you want to achieve. It may also allow you to dig deeper and find a more interesting angle that you had not originally considered.

Below is an example of a short research journey. Your own may be much more complex. Do not be afraid to explore different paths and loop back to another 'island' if it is not working.

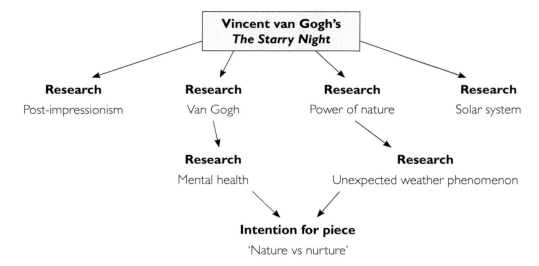

Once you have settled on your overall intention, it is important to keep it in mind throughout the rest of the process. In a directed piece of theatre, this intention is referred to as the 'directorial concept'. It is essentially what you hope to communicate to your audience, and it should inform all the dramatic elements you choose:

- design
- structure
- acting style
- script
- practitioner/tradition/style.

Everything that you decide or develop from that point on needs to be created with this concept in mind. Keep asking yourself, 'Does this decision help communicate our overall intention/concept?'

Activity 2

Think back to a devised piece that you have worked on in the past, either for an exam or in class. Draw a diagram like the one on the previous page to outline the journey you took to reach the final intention for the piece. Notice how you made links and discoveries.

Develop: Enhancing communication and spontaneous ideas

Communication within a group is vital to the success of a devised piece. As the drama develops, it is important that everyone is aware of and participates in the decisions. Have regular meetings and, if possible, set up a group chat or email circular so that you can keep in touch about ideas, even when you are not in the rehearsal room. This will also allow you to share visual ideas as well as verbal ones – for example, you may see a poster, an article in a magazine or even notice the shape of a building that you feel fits in to your ideas and research. If you can photograph these images for inspiration and share them instantly with the group, you will automatically be creating a bank of ideas.

Activity 3

Collaboration and the ability to develop ideas together are important skills to keep your group working well. Begin your first devising session together by playing a game of word association. One member of the group begins by saying a random word, then the rest of the group take it in turns to follow each word with another that they associate with the previous one. For example:

egg ➜ breakfast ➜ morning ➜ sun ➜ sky ➜ space ➜ empty ➜ hungry

Start with simple objects and work up to rounds of the game that are deliberately more abstract. For example, you may wish to start a round with an emotion and see where it takes you. Starters might be:

- objects: backpack, clothes hanger, candelabra, music speaker, kiwi fruit
- emotions: disappointment, cheer, anger, love, embarrassment.

Next see if you can work together to bring the chain back to the original word once more. Using the egg example above, 'hungry' could loop back around to 'egg'.

As you continue to devise, remember this activity. Not only can it promote a strong working relationship within your group, but it will remind you to look for unexpected connections and to explore tangents as you discuss your stimulus. By making sure that you have fully explored different possibilities, you will find that your work becomes richer and the intentions behind your ideas will also become clearer to you. Establishing a strong working relationship as a group will make sure your work is cohesive and based on full collaboration.

Respect the different personalities and preferred approaches of your group members, and give everyone an equal opportunity to express ideas. You may, for example, have someone in your group who has excellent ideas but who is not always as confident at expressing them as other group members. Make sure everyone has a chance to be heard. You must be able to demonstrate that you can work as a well-formed ensemble on stage, so practising this in all aspects of the devising process will lead naturally to a seamless group dynamic in performance.

Apply: Staying on target

You will learn how to break down the devising process throughout this chapter, but here is a checklist of potential tasks in the process for you to keep in mind.

1. Use a large sketch book, notebook or digital tool to record the group's ideas.

2. Write a schedule that includes targets for each week and tasks for each lesson.

3. Collaborate on all aspects of the devised piece, including the writing of the script.

4. Include movement sections using the ensemble.

5. Create smooth transitions, possibly using music and **tableaux**.

6. Use peer and teacher feedback throughout the process.

7. Film your work, if possible, and watch it so you can improve it.

8. Take photos of each rehearsal, if possible, and create a photo journal with captions for each photo.

9. Create a version of the script with sound and lighting cues for the technician.

10. Once the piece is finished, write programme notes including photos of the cast and a brief summary of each scene. Highlight the themes and message you want to convey to the audience.

11. Run a **technical rehearsal** for sound and lighting.

12. Run a full **dress rehearsal**.

13. Walk through the piece at double time to make sure you remember the staging and the transitions. Check that props and costumes needed for changes are in position.

14. Make sure the piece is the correct duration by timing it.

15. Before the final performance, warm up physically and vocally.

Key terms

tableau: a still moment in which actors position themselves to suggest relationships between characters, highlight an emotion or increase tension

technical rehearsal: a rehearsal that takes place before the dress rehearsal, in which all technical elements (lighting, sound, set, costume, etc.) are brought together and run through to check for any errors or issues

dress rehearsal: a full performance, with all costumes, set, lighting, sound, etc., as if it was being performed to an audience

Reflection point

Make a list of the areas that you feel you might find the most challenging. As you journey through the devising process, refer back to this list and make note of any moments when you overcome your fears. Discuss any initial concerns with your group so that you can look out for each other.

3.2 Devising from a stimulus

Big question

- How do performers use a stimulus to create a piece of theatre?

Starting point: What is devising from a stimulus?

A theatre company often creates performance material based on a stimulus. They might choose their own stimulus or be commissioned to devise a piece of work based on a stimulus given to them by someone else. For example, an art gallery might commission a piece based on an artist, to be performed at the opening of an exhibition. In this example, the theatre company might take a biographical approach, showing key moments in the artist's life, or devise in response to a series of paintings.

When devising, companies tend to work together democratically, with each performer contributing to the creation of the piece. Actors might take turns in directing scenes. Mime, movement and music can be used as well as drama, and actors might take on different roles, such as choreographer, musician, singer, set or costume designer, in order to create a successful, holistic piece of theatre.

The stimulus that begins the process can be taken from a range of forms, and may be visual, aural or linguistic material. Some examples are shown in the table below.

Literary	Artistic	Current event	Historical event
• **Poem:** 'To The Moon' by Percy Bysshe Shelley • **Short story:** 'The Yellow Wallpaper' by Charlotte Perkins Gilman • **Speech from a play:** Hamlet: 'I will tell you why…', *Hamlet* Act 2, Scene 2, by William Shakespeare • **Opening paragraph from a novel:** *The Night Circus* by Erin Morgenstern	• **Painting/ photograph/ sculpture:** *The Lady of Shalott* by John William Waterhouse • **Piece of music:** 'Numb' by Portishead • **Photograph:** an ice sculpture (see page 77)	• **News story:** 'Great Pacific Garbage Patch' • **News clip:** Footage of the London riots, 2011	• **Documented event:** Fall of the Berlin Wall • **Key moment:** Rosa Parks sitting at the front of a segregated bus • **Biography:** Frida Kahlo • **Historical photograph:** *The Falling Man* – by Richard Drew

Choose a stimulus that you feel will give you the opportunity to explore several different paths at first. If the stimulus doesn't offer enough dramatic possibilities, you are limiting the options for your overall intention, as well as the dramatic potential of the final piece.

Activity 1

In groups of four, take a column each from the table above and choose one type of stimulus from it (for example, poem). Individually, research one of the examples of that stimulus type that you think would make a starting point for a devised piece. Come back together as a group and discuss your ideas. Which do you think will work best? Why?

Explore: Moving from ideas to exploration

When choosing and developing a stimulus, it is helpful at first to ask yourself if it has performance potential. Does it inspire a piece of drama? You can ask questions about the stimulus to create initial ideas, or identify emotions and moods that it provokes. These could be recorded in a diagram like the one below before further discussion, to see if they generate a strong idea for a piece.

Activity 2

Imagine you have been given the photograph below as a stimulus for a piece of devised theatre. It shows an ice sculpture of a carriage (an 'artistic' stimulus).

In groups, discuss the image and construct a mind map of your initial ideas. Think about the following questions:

- What mood does the image evoke?
- What are the qualities of the ice – its texture, temperature and ability to last?
- How might you use the idea of something being transparent?
- The carriage cannot function as a vehicle so what is the purpose of making it?
- Is the construction strong or fragile?
- What type of movement does the image inspire?
- What might a wheel represent? Circularity? The wheel of fortune?

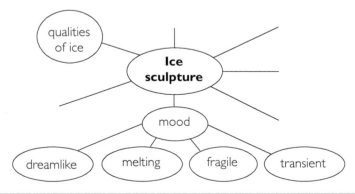

Once you have some initial ideas in a diagram, you can decide which areas you are most interested in. You can then research and explore these areas in greater detail. For example, based on the ice sculpture, you might choose to explore the idea that nothing lasts forever. This could open up new avenues in which you discuss love, age, consumerism, and so on.

Activity 3

Look at the start of the thought development process below:

wheel ➜ cycle ➜ life ➜ fortune ➜ fate ➜ societal expectations vs freedom to choose?

How might this be developed for another three steps?

Using the trigger words below, write down possible areas of exploration to move your diagram from observational to more conceptual or thematic ideas, focusing on finding a deeper meaning that you can begin to really work with:

- sun
- fragile
- fairy tale.

As you follow this process, you may find that additional ideas start to link or overlap. You will begin to see patterns that interest you that you can explore to give your research, and the finished piece, greater depth. For example, the final idea for 'wheel' above might link well with your final idea for fragility: 'life is fragile – repercussions of our decisions'.

Make sure that you know when your devised piece is to be performed so that you can plan of how long to spend on each preparation stage.

Stages of devising: the 7 Es

i) Early: discussion, decision-making and research into initial ideas

ii) Exploration: improvisation, experimenting with style, developing early scenes

iii) Emerging: development of plot, character, script

iv) Evolving: adapting and shaping throughout the rehearsal of your piece

v) Embellishing: final rehearsals, including technical and dress rehearsals, adding the finishing touches to your piece

vi) Enactment: performance of the piece

vii) Evaluation: you should continually evaluate your work as you produce it, but you will also be required to give a 3-minute spoken evaluation of your piece.

Activities 2 and 3 above would be part of the 'Early' stage. When you have responded to your stimulus and undertaken research, the next stage, 'Exploration', often begins with improvising around your findings. If you are using an existing story for your work, you could try improvising a scene based around a pivotal moment, or you could experiment with the story's setting or context, perhaps making links to contemporary society. If your group is using a more abstract initial idea, avoid the temptation to solidify plot ideas just yet, as you can bring this together in the 'Emerging' stage; rather, this part of the process would be to discover different ways of expressing your thoughts and ideas. It will help to crystallise the style that you feel works well for your piece. For example, if you follow the thought process above, you might want to capture a mood of feeling trapped by social expectations by creating movement sequences or tableaux that represent the feeling of entrapment in an abstract way. The techniques of physical theatre might also be used to develop an improvisation focused, for example, on the effort involved in carrying the blocks of ice. Consider the weight, texture and size of the blocks and mime the creation of the sculpture. You might consider using a drumbeat to underscore the action and create tension.

Or, you might begin with a more naturalistic approach, perhaps by improvising an interview scene. For example, you could create a scenario in which a character has tried to protest about a situation in which they feel trapped, and has been arrested. You could therefore improvise a scene set in a police station, or perhaps a witness or expert being interviewed for a news item. Here, you can embellish your improvisations with facts and stories from your research.

At this stage, you are just trying out ideas and there are different ways of doing this. For example, still using the wheel example above, you could try several further exercises:

- **Conceptual tableaux:** Pick out four or five emotions or moods that your idea provokes. For each of these, create a tableau that represents this. Avoid creating a 'story' with these images; instead use your body as a personification of the emotion or mood. Think of yourself as an expressionist painting in a gallery with a caption printed under it: 'You are the emotion!' For the wheel, try 'Freedom', 'Trapped', 'Peer pressure', 'Consequence'.

- **Scene:** Improvise a scene in which a young person is trying to tell their strict parents that they want to study at university rather than take over the family business as had always been assumed.

- **Movement sequence:** Choose a piece of music that you feel harnesses the mood of your current idea. For 'the wheel', for example, you could try creating a hectic rush-hour sequence accompanied by fast-paced music, to highlight the society that your potential characters might inhabit. From here, the start of another idea might emerge – that your characters might want to rebel against this society.

Activity 4

Look back at your final ideas from Activity 3 and choose one to explore through improvisation. You could divide the ideas between the members of your group so everyone can improvise a specific scene based on one of them. Use the example exercises above, or come up with your own ideas for improvisation.

Throughout your exploration, do not be afraid to throw out ideas that do not work or fit. Having enough preparation time is crucial, and you will be able to work more efficiently on a piece that flows and excites you, than on a complicated puzzle that does not fit together. Considering and discarding ideas is the essence of devising and does not mean that you are 'failing'. Instead, you will develop a stronger piece by being bold, adaptable and creative in your thinking.

As you develop short scenes or sequences through your improvisations, you can begin to link pieces together. You may establish clear character roles through this exploration, or you may decide that your piece is leaning towards a more chorus-based approach. Once you have some of these details in place, you can begin to think about structuring the piece as a whole and working on more specific details. However, you should still remain flexible in your approach through the next stages, which are discussed in the rest of the chapter.

Develop: The structure of a devised piece

As you develop more ideas, you will soon recognise whether you are leaning towards a stylised piece – perhaps with elements of physical theatre – or a more realistic piece with naturalistic acting (or a mixture of the two). This will determine the way in which you communicate to your audience and how you choose to structure your piece.

Think about plays that you have seen or studied in the past. The way that they are structured and presented has a huge impact on the way that an audience views the play and its characters. Shakespeare, for example, always wrote his plays in five acts, with the fifth providing a resolution or denouement. This structure goes all the way back to Aristotle's theory for the structure of a Greek tragedy. The following diagram is often used to represent the plot structure of a tragedy:

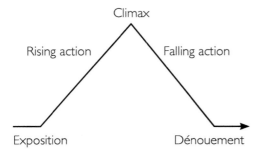

Not all plays follow a strict five-act structure, of course, but many do still follow a clear linear structure: they have a beginning, middle and end that move chronologically from the start of the plot to its conclusion. However, particularly over the last century or so, playwrights have become increasingly experimental with their structures. For example, In the play *Betrayal* by Harold Pinter, the action is written backwards – the first scene of the play is chronologically the last. The play opens with a couple reminiscing about the affair that they had in the past. The rest of the play shows, in reverse order, how that affair had started, developed and fizzled out.

Devices such as flashbacks and flash-forwards, and the inclusion of movement sequences or multimedia elements can often enhance tension or delay a 'reveal'. It is important to develop a clear idea of your piece's flow and structure so that it feels purposeful.

Activity 5

Think of some plays that you have seen or studied, films you have seen or books you have read that have interesting plot structures. Copy a table like the one below, adding more rows as needed to record the effect the structure had on you, the audience or reader.

Play/film/novel	Structure	Effect on audience/reader
For example, *Betrayal* by Harold Pinter (play)	Storyline moves from 'present' to past with each scene.	Audience knows the outcome from the start and understands more and more with each scene why the relationship did not last.
For example, *The Seven Deaths of Evelyn Hardcastle* by Stuart Turton (novel)	Each chapter starts the same day over again from a different character's perspective.	The reader slowly builds up a clearer overall view of the 'day' and starts to make links and theories of their own.

The table below outlines some possible structures.

Structure	Explanation	Effect	Example
Linear	Plot develops chronologically	Shows a clear chronological passing of time (although the starting point might shift). This gives the audience a clear, easy-to-follow sense of the plot.	We see the student tell their parents at the beginning of the play and see the consequence unravel. *or* We see the scenes that lead up to them telling their parents, so that the piece builds to a climax.
Non-linear	Use of flashback and flash-forward	Offers different versions of the story to make the audience consider which outcome is better.	We see the student tell their parents their desire to study. The action then splits into two paths – show one outcome and then flashback to the first scene again and show the opposite one.
Circular	Returning the action to the beginning again	The audience gets to decide which path was taken or (unlike the example above) can muse as to whether there might have ever been a third option.	Perhaps as above, but the first scene repeats once more at the end.
Binary	Split into two distinct sections	This might present two perspectives on the same narrative told from the point of view of two different characters. It can limit the scope for development.	We see the story told from the student's and the parents' perspectives.
Palindromic	The first half is mirrored by the second (ABCDEDCBA)	Allows the middle scene to be the climax; the scenes before build up to, for example, the revelation of a secret, and subsequent scenes show the aftermath, with each scene 'reflecting' the earlier one in some way through a character or situation.	We are shown the lead up to and the aftermath of the student telling their parents – the central climax scene is the only one in which the parents are present. The scenes either side are mirrored in location and other characters are involved.
Rondo	The first scene is repeated as each alternate scene	Useful if you want to have a recurring motif to highlight an issue or a theme. The repeated scene can be very short, like a chorus for a song or a refrain.	The first scene is the student opening their excellent exam results. This scene is repeated throughout but each time a chorus member joins to comment upon the action. The student's actions, however, remain the same in each of these repeated scenes.

Next, think about the more detailed structural devices:

- **Opening:** How will you start your piece? With a **prologue**?

- **Transitions:** The way in which you move between scenes is as important as the scenes themselves. Transitions should be smooth and uphold your chosen style.

- **Movement sequences:** Some elements of your piece (for example, intense emotional moments) may be easier to express through movement.

- **Repetition:** Repeat scenes or movement to make the audience notice connections and patterns.

- **Reversals:** You could include a 'turning-point' moment – perhaps a shift in the main character's circumstances, or a moment when the audience's perceptions are overturned.

- **Ending:** How will you close your piece? By freezing the action and fading the lights? With an **epilogue**?

Key terms

prologue: originating in classical Greek drama (the term means 'before word') and traditionally took the place of a first act, filling in everything that needed to be known before the play proper began

epilogue: a short scene or speech at the end of a play, reflecting on what has happened

Activity 6

Decide which overall structure will work best for your piece. Which structural devices from the list above will you use? Are there any that lend themselves to your chosen structure particularly well? Why?

Within the scenes themselves, there are many dramatic techniques that can enhance your structure. Some examples are outlined below.

Technique	Explanation	Possible use
Tableaux	Still moments, in which actors position themselves to suggest relationships between characters, highlight an emotion or increase tension.	Could be used to 'mark the moment' (dramatic devices to emphasise or draw attention to a key aspect of the drama).
Split scene	Using different areas of the stage simultaneously. Often (but not always), the action in one area continues, while the other freezes.	Can create different locations on stage or create a deliberate contrast between characters' lives.
Mime	Purely physical – acting with no speech or noises from the actor, often without physical props.	Could be used to create a dream sequence or to represent a character's inner thoughts.
Slow motion	Intense slowing down of movements, requiring careful choreography and strength of physicality.	Can be used to create tension and suspense, or to mark a moment.
Narration	A performer commenting upon the action of the play, possibly offering the audience extra details and information.	Can be used to link scenes together or to offer 'truths' and commentary not made clear by the action.

Apply: Shaping the piece through direction and roles

Once you have decided on the structure, you can begin directing the scenes. Often in a devised piece, the whole ensemble takes on a directorial role, as well as designing the performance collaboratively. Whether taken on by an individual or the whole group, the role of a director is important in ensuring that the overall message and intention continues to be communicated effectively in each scene as the piece develops. The intention will, of course, also influence your design decisions.

Spotlight on practitioner:
Katie Mitchell (b. 1964)

Katie Mitchell is a British director who has worked with the Royal Shakespeare Company, the Royal National Theatre, the Royal Court, the Young Vic and the Donmar Warehouse. She is influenced by the later work of Constantin Stanislavski (see Unit 2.2) and believes that meticulous preparation before entering the rehearsal phase is key to a successful production. In her book, *The Director's Craft: A Handbook for The Theatre*, she sets out clear guidelines to her systematic approach to directing a play. A great deal of her work takes a feminist approach, ensuring that female voices are heard in the theatre.

Mitchell's intense preparation and rehearsal periods have resulted in a style that has become known as 'extreme' naturalism. Whereas Stanislavski wanted his audience to believe in and connect emotionally with the characters on stage, Mitchell also seeks to provoke and challenge. She does not allow her naturalistic influences to prevent her from deconstructing or fragmenting plays, and more recently she has started to use multimedia in some of her productions. In *Waves*, for example, a production inspired by Virginia Woolf's novel of the same name, Mitchell uses live video feeds to provide often extreme close-ups of the actors' faces, to show a character's perspective. The actors also created abstract 'pictures' using props and feeds filmed at interesting angles as they performed were live-projected onto the large screen upstage. In this way, the characters were often able to express inner **monologues** and the audience were given more of an overall sensory experience rather than a linear naturalistic narrative.

The techniques used by contemporary practitioner Katie Mitchell demonstrate that, even with a naturalistic style of acting, you are not tied to a chronological or even coherent narrative, and that it is possible to produce experimental or abstract work. The beauty of theatre is that you can express your intentions in many different forms and styles.

Key term

monologue: a sustained speech made by a character; can be directed at another character or the audience

Waves, Katie Mitchell, Cottesloe Theatre / National Theatre (2006)

Activity 7

In a similar way to Stanislavski, Katie Mitchell encourages detailed preparation before a rehearsal begins. She creates lists of factors and circumstances that will affect the scene and the characters within it, in order to give the actors a clear view of the world of the play. Continue to explore your scene inspired by the ice sculpture stimulus in Activity 2. Use some of Mitchell's preparation techniques to see how you can develop character. Copy and complete the following table.

Place	Where is this scene taking place?	
Character biographies	What events have shaped this character in the past?	
Immediate circumstances	What has taken place in the hours leading up to this scene?	
Time	When does this scene take place – time, season, year? Where does it sit in relation to previous or forthcoming scenes?	
Events	What happens in the scene to affect the behaviour of the characters?	
Intentions	What drives the characters?	
Relationships	How do the characters view each other, and how does this affect their behaviour?	

Reflection point

Use the table below to write an evaluation of what you have achieved so far in this unit.

How did the group use the stimulus to create ideas for a piece of devised theatre?	Write a paragraph to summarise the discussion about the stimulus, using the mind map as a guide.
Was physical theatre used to create an environment?	Choose a scene and explain how physical theatre was used in place of a set to create an environment. Include photographs.
Was music used to underscore the action? What effect did this have on the mood of the scene?	Explain how the music was created and which instruments were used (remember that the voice is an instrument).
Which skills have you used so far?	Comment on how the following were used and to what effect: physicality, timing, vocals, unison, canon (repetition where one part overlaps with the next), focus, spatial awareness, strength, balance.
Which scenes will you work on in the next rehearsal?	Reflect on the other scene ideas you have and decide which one could be worked on next. Should the whole group work on this? Explain your decision.

3.3 Script and design

Big question

- How can you develop your practical ideas into a workable production?

Starting point: Creating your script

Actors, directors and the ensemble work in different ways to achieve a stylised devised work. The process is a collaborative one and each company has its own distinct approach to such work. Most – but not all – companies capture their final performance in a final scripted format. If you have been researching and improvising as a group, you will probably find that the script has already started to evolve. Improvising around your ideas will mean that you are already developing the language of your piece.

Spotlight on practitioner:
Sally Cookson (b. 1960)

Sally Cookson is a director known for creating theatrical versions of novels and stories from *Jane Eyre* to children's classics such as *Treasure Island*, *Peter Pan* and *We're Going on a Bear Hunt*. Her approach is to discuss, workshop, improvise and devise with her actors directly from the book, rather than creating a script or adaptation in advance. Consequently, she considers her work as 'evolving' and often redrafts right up to the first night. Cookson seeks to create worlds from simple props, inventiveness with physicality and ensemble precision.

Cookson was asked to adapt and direct Patrick Ness's children's novel *A Monster Calls*, the story of 13-year-old Conor whose mother is terminally ill. One night, Conor is woken by something at his window: a monster in the form of a talking tree. It announces it will tell the teenager three tales, after which Conor must tell a fourth story.

Cookson worked directly from the novel rather than writing a script, and collaborated with dramaturg Adam Peck, who used the themes and dialogue from Ness's novel to help create a working document for the company to use in rehearsal. The designers all took part in the devising process. The set was designed so that the actors had space to perform physical theatre and the tree could 'grow' on stage. Ropes were used to represent the tree monster and were tied around the actor playing the monster so he could climb and run with them. They could be moved to different parts of the stage depending on the scene, and were not always visible. Props were used sparingly to allow for movement in the space and for the audience to use its imagination. Costumes were designed to be appropriate for the physical work required on stage. (Production photos can be found online.)

Activity 1

New writing often takes place in a workshop environment, where actors improvise and a playwright or director will write down 'golden lines' that develop naturally. Divide your group into actors and a playwright/director.

- **Actors:** Improvise around a very simple and short scenario related to your piece.
- **Playwright/director:** Note down any lines that are particularly clever, well structured or entertaining, that you think could become part of the script. Also note down any story development that worked well (or didn't).

Highlight the lines and story arc that you want to keep. Then try the scene again, this time with the director shaping and **blocking** the scene. Repeat the process as often as necessary to get a smooth version that you are happy with as a group.

Explore: Staging your piece

Fairly early in your process, you will have an idea of what **stage configuration** will best suit your piece and communicate your intentions – that is, the layout of the stage and the position of the audience. The configuration you choose depends upon how you want your audience to feel or react during your piece. For example, if you want the audience to feel trapped and claustrophobic, you may wish to set your piece in the round.

Key terms

blocking: the path of an actor's movement on stage, including entrances and exits

stage configuration: the layout of the stage in relation to the audience

Activity 2

Consider each of the following stage configurations. Research any configurations that you are not familiar with, then copy and complete the table to note down possible advantages and disadvantages of each one.

Configuration	Advantage	Disadvantage
In the round	Immersive atmosphere. Could make the audience feel uneasy – they can see each other so could enhance a piece about society as they have to examine themselves, etc.	Blocking is a challenge – could not use if a piece needed split scene
End-on		
Thrust		
Traverse		
Promenade		
Immersive		

Develop: Adding further design elements

All the different elements of design need to work together to promote your overall concept. Set, lighting, sound, costume and props must all be carefully chosen and designed to promote your message and reflect the style that you have chosen for your piece. For example, you may design a realist set and focus your action in a realistic environment. Alternatively, you may adopt a symbolist style (see pages 20–23) and use levels and lighting to suggest mood and location.

When choosing your design, always be aware of its potential to reveal information to your audience. For example, if you decide to costume a cast all in white, but one actor also has a red scarf, this will instantly let the audience know that this character is special somehow.

Activity 3

Copy the mind maps below and add any more functions you can think of to each of them. For each of the five diagrams, note the messages you want to convey through them and consider how you might do that.

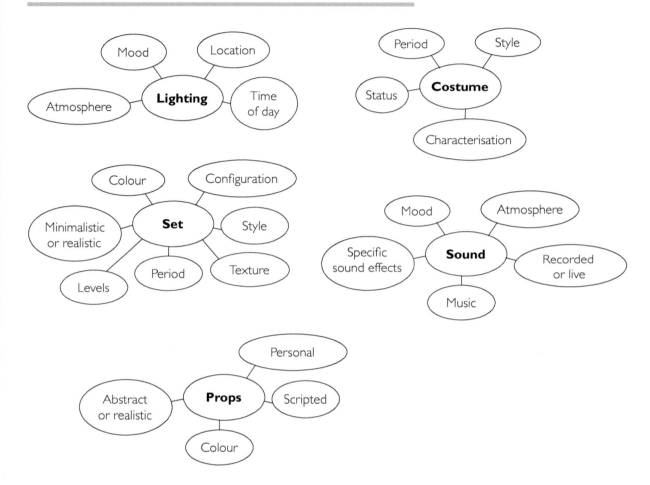

Apply: Taking inspiration from other practitioners' work

You are now going to continue to hone a scene from your piece. Think about the meaning and visual messages that you want to represent through your blocking and design. The 'world' that you create on stage will impact the audience from the moment they enter the space, and will continue to do so throughout the performance, so it is vital to get the effect you want. Remember that you can create a theatrical 'world' with whatever is available to you – set and costume do not need to be elaborate to make an impact. For example, imagine a piece of theatre in which chairs for the audience are arranged in a circle in a studio, with low lighting. The piece is in the round and all the actors are in white leggings and white tops. The piece would feel immersive for the audience and the actors would instantly read as an ensemble in which none of them yet have their own identity. This example is simple and yet demonstrates a conscious decision about design.

Spotlight on practitioner:
Robert Wilson (b. 1941)

Texas-born Robert Wilson's theatre is often referred to as either 'theatre of visuals' or 'theatre of images'. He wants every moment of his productions to create a careful 'stage picture', telling a story or communicating an idea visually. He considers all design aspects, down to the fabric of costumes and the materials and proportion of furniture, to be of equal importance to dialogue and music. Wilson explores time and space on stage and enjoys playing around with narrative, often preferring a non-linear approach. In 1992, he founded The Watermill Center in Long Island – a research, study and inspiration centre in which projects and workshops are held, exploring fusions of genre, art forms and cross-cultural approaches. This melding of style and genre is typical of Wilson's work and to achieve this he collaborates with a range of artists, performers and musicians. This image is from Robert Wilson's famous production of Woyzeck in which he collaborated with musician Tom Waits. Notice the precision of the design and the actors' physicality.

Woyzeck, Robert Wilson, Betty Nansen Theater, Copenhagen, Denmark (2000)

Activity 4

Have a look at the image above, from Wilson's Woyzeck. Discuss with your group what the 'stage picture' represents for you. What mood does it provoke? What do you see happening? Now use this method to enhance your own work: choose a scene from your piece and rehearse it, taking pictures throughout. At the end of your rehearsal, look back at your pictures and discuss whether the images communicate what you intend them to. Do they make sense if taken out of context? Now play around with blocking and proxemics to see if you can create clear 'stage pictures' that still work with the flow of your piece. Think about depth, levels, clarity of physicality and facial expressions. Run the scene again. Has it changed?

Key context

Woyzeck is a play by Georg Büchner written in 1836. It was found 'unfinished' in fragments after his death and no one knows the original intended order of the scenes. The play centres on a poor soldier who is working several jobs to provide money for his common-law wife, Marie, and their child. Due to his struggle to provide for his family, he is rarely able to spend time with them. One of Woyzeck's jobs involves being experimented upon by a doctor who has put him on a diet solely of peas. His mental state deteriorates throughout the play and, when he finds out that Marie is having an affair, he kills her, and then himself. The play was disliked at the time of its finding, as it sought to expose the plight of poverty and mental illness, but was finally performed in 1913 and has since become famous for its fascinating combination of **German Naturalism** traits and **expressionist** style.

Key terms

German Naturalism: not to be confused with a naturalistic acting style, Naturalism was a genre and movement from around 1880 to 1900 which tackled difficult or taboo subject matter, centring around working-class protagonists. The characters are seen as victims of their socio-economic background, 'controlled' by external forces.

expressionist: Expressionism was an artistic movement which emerged in the early 1900s, which aimed to provoke an emotional response in the audience through more abstract forms. In theatre, scenes could be nightmarish and often episodic.

3.4 Devising in response to a practitioner, tradition or style

Big question

- How do actors, directors and designers use the hallmarks of a practitioner or style when devising?

Starting point: Investigating context

When researching your devised piece in response to a practitioner, style or tradition, one of the most important considerations is context. This will include biographical information, historical or cultural background and political views. For example, a practitioner's childhood experiences might have influenced the style of their performance work in later life. To begin your investigation:

- find or create a timeline of political and historical events that took place throughout their lifetime to analyse what might have influenced their thinking

- find out whether they had any drama training and who might have influenced them in their acting, writing and directing career

- consider the various disciplines they studied and how this may have influenced their devised material.

You may find this information in biographical and autobiographical writings, as well as in magazine and newspaper articles and books. Some play texts have informative introductions that include information about the practitioner or style. Some practitioners also write about the methods they use to create work. If they have also written plays, you could study at least one of their plays in detail and rehearse sections for performance in order to develop an understanding of the required style.

Theatre traditions from around the world may have many different origins – for example, through ritual or having been specifically designed for a certain audience demographic. In order to understand the style or tradition you wish to respond to in your devised work, you should thoroughly investigate its origins and development.

Activity 1

In groups, choose a practitioner to research. Divide the questions below among group members and then share your findings.

- Who were the main influences on their work?

- With whom did they collaborate?

- What theatre companies did they establish or work with?

- What was their approach to devising work? List the key features of their style.

This activity could be used to explore many practitioners before you decide which to exclusively focus upon as a case study.

Explore: Frantic Assembly's physical theatre style

What follows in this unit is a detailed example of the process of using a practitioner as the inspiration for a devised piece. You can adapt this process for other practitioners, theatrical traditions or styles.

Spotlight on practitioner:
Frantic Assembly

Frantic Assembly is a UK theatre company formed by Scott Graham and Steven Hoggett in 1994. They have developed a recognisable style of striking physical sequences alongside often very naturalistic text. A large amount of their work is formed and devised in collaboration with different writers and they have developed a reputation for their knowledge and expertise in approaches to devising. However, Frantic Assembly have also used their unique style to interpret established classical texts, notably Shakespeare's *Othello*. Their approach to physical theatre has enabled them to name and develop techniques and exercises which they discuss in their book, *The Frantic Assembly Book of Devising Theatre*.

The company uses a variety of physical exercises to warm up, before embarking on contact improvisation activities designed to translate textual themes into a visual format. A series of trust exercises are performed in order to develop a close bond between the actors before they move on to undertake more physically challenging tasks. Once trust has been built, one actor can lift another, or several actors might lift one actor above their heads and help the elevated person perform actions, such as walking along a wall with their body parallel to the ground.

Emotion is a huge driving force for Frantic Assembly's physical sequences. Think about the last time you were so overcome with emotion that it was difficult for you to put how you felt into words. Perhaps you were so happy that you felt like you could fly, or so enraged that you felt that you might burst. It is in these hard-to-express moments that Frantic Assembly's techniques can help with on stage. Their productions often centre on domestic circumstances – family life, spousal relationships or friendships, which are situations their audiences will recognise. Love, in its different forms, is often a key theme within their productions and, as such, many of their techniques centre upon demonstrating relationships between characters through movement.

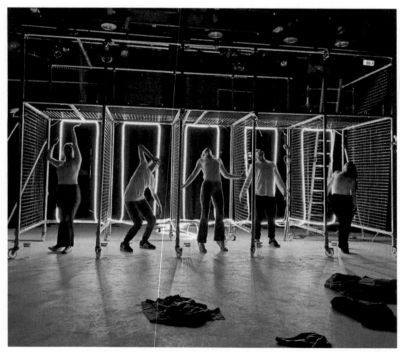

An example of an A Level devised piece using Frantic Assembly as the chosen practitioner

One of Frantic Assembly's most famous **contact improvisation** techniques is called 'chair duets'. This is a process in which two performers can represent a clear idea of their relationship using a simple repertoire of physical movements. Often, chair duets are set to music to further enhance the mood of the duet. For example, a chair duet could be created to demonstrate a romantic sequence, or it might represent two friends having an argument. Sequences such as these can represent and express emotional moments that are difficult to put into words.

Activity 2

1. As a group, research chair duets. There are some good examples online given by Frantic Assembly themselves. Notice how the actors create a sequence of deliberate movements that connect to each other.

2. Discuss what 'story' you feel that the performers are trying to express. The movements may be tender and loving or they may feel like a rejection or conflict.

3. Next, research some more of Frantic Assembly's techniques, such as 'round-by-through' and 'hymn hands'. Do you think that any of these techniques might be useful to explore in creating scenes for your piece?

4. Write a list of music that you would like to try using with these techniques, giving reasons for your choices.

Key term

contact improvisation: a system in which movement is initiated by physical contact between two bodies; they may roll, fall, turn, jump while giving support to each other, giving and taking weight

Develop: Researching a practitioner

The 'chair duet' is just one of many techniques that Frantic Assembly use – there are many others. When investigating practitioners, traditions and styles, explore as many of their techniques, methods and characteristics as possible. Having a comprehensive understanding of these elements will ensure that your finished piece fully reflects the characteristics of your chosen starting point.

During the course of your research, you might also consider the following:

- the social, cultural, historical, political and geographical context of the development of the style or when the practitioner was working

- the purpose of the drama

- the artistic or political intentions of the practitioner or tradition

- a practitioner's working methods and any related theatre companies

- whether it is associated with a specific type of venue or stage configuration

- how production roles should work to reflect the practitioner, style or tradition (actor, director, ensemble, etc.).

As you carry out this further research, you may come across many different accounts of professional productions that clearly bear the traits and methods of your chosen practitioner, tradition or style. You can choose one of these to focus on as a case study, which will essentially become a stimulus for your group. Remember that while you can deviate from the themes and plot of this case study production, the stylistic essence must be evident in your own devised piece. Look at the production as a source of inspiration and a starting point for ideas.

Activity 3

Make a list of all the productions you can find that are related to, or renowned for being heavily influenced by, your chosen practitioner, tradition or style. In your group, select a production or two each to investigate. Bring your findings together and discuss which of these productions you, at first glance, find the most interesting, or that you agree have the most potential. You can then research two or three in greater detail before deciding upon the production that you will use.

Consider:

- The style of the piece – is it very true to your chosen practitioner/ style/tradition?

- Are the themes and content giving you any ideas? Remember that you do not have to use the same themes and content – it may be more rewarding if you don't. However, the content of the production may act as a stimulus in itself.

- Does the production excite and interest you? Are you inspired to create a piece in a similar style?

- Do you think that the production offers you enough inspiration 'offshoots' to work with? Choose the production that gives you the widest range of mini stimuli ideas and the most possibilities to explore.

A group of students has followed the process in Activity 3 and is now trying to decide between Frantic Assembly's version of Shakespeare's *Othello*, and a play written by Abi Morgan called *Lovesong*, as their focus.

Othello is a Shakespearean tragedy about jealousy. Iago is jealous of Othello's military success and that he has managed to marry their senator's beautiful daughter. He plots to make Othello believe that his wife, Desdemona is having an affair, when in fact she is innocent. Othello lets his jealousy overcome him and eventually kills Desdemona in a rage.

Lovesong follows the story of a married couple, which cuts from scenes from the early days of their marriage to the last part of their relationship in the 'present' (when they are in their seventies) using flashbacks, transitioned through beautiful Frantic movement pieces. The play is performed by four actors: two play the younger couple and two play the older version of the same couple. All four actors are often on stage at the same time, as present-day and flashback scenes cross over each other. The set is a simple domestic scene of kitchen table and fridge stage right, and bed and wardrobe stage left. The bed and wardrobe have hidden entrances to help keep crossovers smooth.

Two pairs of actors representing one couple in a dress rehearsal of *Lovesong*, Abi Morgan, Franctic Assembly, Lyric Hammersmith (2011)

The students have condensed their comparisons of both productions in the table below:

Othello (2008, reworked in 2014)	Lovesong (2011)
Abridged and adapted from Shakespeare	New writing
Contemporised	Non-linear plot – fluid transitions between present-day and flashbacks
Use of movement sequences to show relationship	Use of movement to enhance emotional moments and characterisation
Exploration of status and trust	Exploration of the reality of love and marriage over time

After weighing up the pros and cons of each production, the group of students have decided to use *Lovesong* because:

> We felt that *Lovesong* offered more opportunities to try out ideas that interested us. We liked the fact that the piece is non-linear as we would also like to experiment with fluid time. *Lovesong* has very widely relatable content and we want to make sure that whatever we choose to develop as our content, that it also has that familiar feel to it. We also realised that the ideas we discussed for *Othello* all sounded too similar to the original production and we wanted to write something completely new.

Apply: Exploring a particular production

Once you have decided on the production you want to study in depth, you need to work as a group to investigate the features of that production which might inspire your own devised piece.

Activity 4

You have chosen to focus on *Lovesong* as a production that interests you, as you believe that it provides more 'islands' for you to explore. Find out even more about it. What aspects of the production inspire or interest you personally? Write down what has intrigued you about this piece so far. It could be the way that time is presented or the domestic themes within the play.

The diagram below shows some notes that the students made in response to Activity 4.

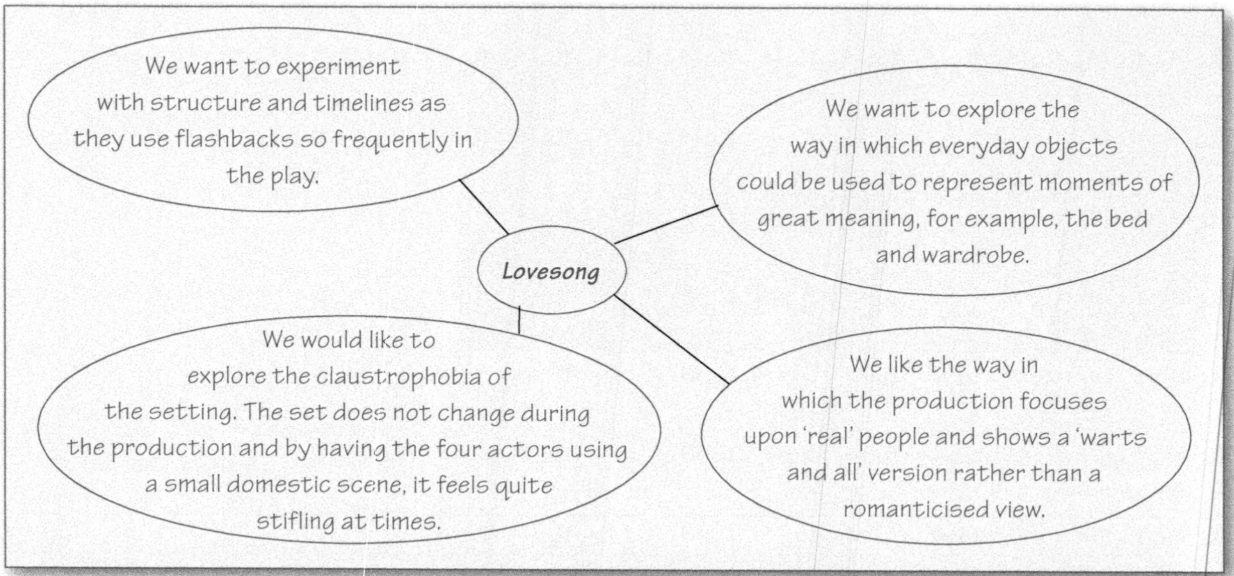

We want to experiment with structure and timelines as they use flashbacks so frequently in the play.

We want to explore the way in which everyday objects could be used to represent moments of great meaning, for example, the bed and wardrobe.

Lovesong

We would like to explore the claustrophobia of the setting. The set does not change during the production and by having the four actors using a small domestic scene, it feels quite stifling at times.

We like the way in which the production focuses upon 'real' people and shows a 'warts and all' version rather than a romanticised view.

Notice that the aspects that these students have picked out are all directly related to the investigation of the production itself. These initial observations then become a stimulus-style starting point:

Activity 5

In your group, expand the observations from the *Lovesong* diagram above, adding ideas and discussion points. Start with the 'everyday objects' observation. How might you use a kitchen table, for example? Consider how it could be carried, lifted and positioned to accompany movement. If the table itself is moved, each movement and placement of the table should have a reason behind it and not be executed just for visual effect. Or would you keep the table as a constant and make your ensemble move around it? The table might become a bed or a place of refuge, somewhere to hide behind. What would it represent for your piece and, consequently, what sort of subject matter or narrative might be explored?

Read the example below, which shows how one group has moved their work from theory into practice.

We have decided to explore using a kitchen table as a constant representation of 'home' in a piece about a child growing up. We were inspired by the use of the simple furniture in *Lovesong*, which remains constant throughout the play, both in the 'present' scenes and the flashbacks. We also noticed the way in which many Frantic Assembly productions focus on family situations and relationships, and felt that following a child growing in a family home would maintain a feel of the practitioner.

Activity 6

Look at the structure for a devised piece outlined in the table below. In groups, discuss how effective this structure might be. Copy and complete the table with notes about how you might approach improvising each scene. When might you use Frantic Assembly's style of movement and when would you keep the scenes naturalistic?

Possibilities of scenes	Improvisation ideas
Flowers and 'It's a girl' balloon on the table	
As a baby – parents up all night	
As a toddler – cooking/feeding	
As a 5-year-old – birthday party	
As a 10-year-old – doing homework	
As a teenager – misses curfew – parents up late at night again	
As a young adult – comforted after a break up	
As an adult – having wedding hair done	
Flowers and 'It's a girl' balloon on the table	

Reflection point

Evaluate the success of your performance at each stage of the process, using the table below.

Are the characters distinguishable from each other and are their relationships believable?	Give a list of *dramatis personae* (the characters and the names of the actors playing them). Ask for peer feedback on relationships to check whether they are clear.
When and where is the piece set?	Give a detailed description of how this is achieved through set, lighting, music, costume and dialogue.
How much can your chosen practitioner's style or tradition's approach to making theatre be detected in the performance?	Look back at your research and see how you have used approach and techniques in your piece.
What changes were made between the technical rehearsal and the dress rehearsal?	The technical rehearsal was mainly focused on lighting and sound, but you may have discovered some problems that needed solving before the dress rehearsal. Outline these and give some detailed examples of what was changed and how.
What purpose did the chorus serve?	Explain what the chorus did in each scene. Give detailed examples.

3.5 Apply your skills

Big question

- How can you devise from a range of starting points including a given stimulus and a practitioner, style or tradition?

Starting point: Investigating a stimulus

Read the following poem, which could be used as a stimulus for your first devised piece.

Text I

The Road not Taken

Two roads diverged in a yellow wood,
And sorry I could not travel both
And be one traveler, long I stood
And looked down one as far as I could
To where it bent in the undergrowth;

Then took the other, as just as fair,
And having perhaps the better claim,
Because it was grassy and wanted wear;
Though as for that the passing there
Had worn them really about the same,

And both that morning equally lay
In leaves no step had trodden black.
Oh, I kept the first for another day!
Yet knowing how way leads on to way,
I doubted if I should ever come back.

I shall be telling this with a sigh
Somewhere ages and ages hence:
Two roads diverged in a wood, and I –
I took the one less traveled by,
And that has made all the difference.

Robert Frost

Explore: Exploring different ideas

The ideas below are designed to help you explore in a practical way. Remember – the most effective approach to a devising process, after initial discussion, is the practical exploration route. By trying out ideas practically, you will discover new angles and possibilities, and be able to enhance your ideas to achieve a more sophisticated outcome.

Exploration I

Write down your own individual instant reactions to the poem.

1. How does it make you feel?

2. What do you think it is about?

3. Are there any lines or images which particularly stand out for you?

4. Does the poem resonate with your life, or make you relate it to currents events?

As a group, discuss your initial thoughts. Did any of you have the same first reactions? Did any of your group members' thoughts about the poem surprise you? These discussions will enable you to develop an initial mood and atmosphere to work with, which you can later remember when you come to design your pieces. Notice small details such as 'yellow wood'. This could imply a certain species of tree, or that the time of year is autumn. Do these details change anything?

Exploration 2

In order to begin practically exploring your ideas from the Exploration 1, try identifying key words or phrases that have potential visual or movement vocabulary. For example, for the line 'Two roads diverged in a yellow wood', you could:

1. Use your bodies to represent travelling down two paths. Begin by moving in unison and then gradually split off into different, contrasting movements.

2. Allow your physicality to 'grow', from small subtle movements of your fingers, into your arms, shoulders, torso and legs. Experiment with the 'size' of your movement. What are you making each path represent?

3. As an ensemble, explore the visual impact of the poem by creating 'conceptual tableaux' as explained in Unit 3.2. If possible, film sections or take photographs to document your work, remembering to invent captions for each. This might be the line from the poem with a short explanation of what the group has created. This practice will create evidence of your working practice and will help you write an evaluation of your process.

Exploration 3

Some lines might inspire musical or vocal ideas – for example, 'I shall be telling this with a sigh'. Experiment with tempo, pitch, tone and volume. Try different ways of exploring the word 'sigh' vocally, and combine with movement.

Exploration 4

Create a series of scenarios as a basis for improvisation.

1. The road is literal: explore improvising the poem at face value – a group of hikers deciding which route to take. This would give you a naturalistic feel.

2. The road is metaphorical: create a scenario in which someone has to make a difficult decision. This could give you a non-linear or fragmented approach.

3. The road is spiritual: the split represents moral, emotional or spiritual choices. This could open up more abstract avenues.

Exploration 5

A chorus can be used to comment on the actions and emotions of the characters. You could use an ensemble for this purpose. Try a simple exploration at first, adding a chorus of 'yellow' trees or represent the 'grassy' path. Then take the chorus further by experimenting with the idea of them as the two paths, commenting upon the pros and cons of the characters' decisions.

Develop: Bringing cohesion to exploration

By undertaking detailed and varied exploration as above, you will emerge with a range of ideas and routes to try. The next step is finding links and piecing bits together, like a puzzle, deciding which to explore further and which to discard. This allows you to move the work away from a direct response to the poem, down more creative paths. After this, you can take the process forward using the structuring and design stages in this chapter.

Activity 1

Give each of the Exploration activities above a title. Write these and a summary of the content on separate pieces of paper to create a large mood board. Work as a group to rearrange and add to your ideas – perhaps include photographs to add inspiration for your intended aesthetic. You could use string to link certain parts or create a flow chart, or 'to-do' sections. This visual prompt will add to your digital bank of ideas and will help you to physically see and keep on top of your progress.

Reflection point: Evaluating your devised work

Once you have performed your devised piece from a stimulus, you need to reflect on the process of creating and rehearsing, as well as the final performance. Copy and complete the table below to record ideas to support your three-minute spoken evaluation. Give specific and detailed examples of each point in the table and evaluate how successful you were.

Title of piece	
In response to the stimulus, briefly describe the journey from stimulus to devising.	
Basic plot or structure developed with dramatic intention	
Character(s) played	
Physicality used: stance, gait, eye focus, facial expressions, movement, gesture, reaction	
Dialogue and vocal delivery – pitch, diction, accent, pace, tone, fluency, intonation, rhythm, stress, pause, silence	
Key words – monologue, duologue, choral speech	
Design: set, costume, lighting, sound, props – give a description of the purpose/ function/ mood/ atmosphere, etc. What does it communicate to the audience?	
Intention, themes and message. How clear is the message? Did the audience understand what you were trying to communicate?	

For all of the above, check that you have considered any changes that were made and why. If the final piece could have been improved, how would you seek to do this?

Apply: Responding to a theatrical style or tradition

Theatre of the Absurd and Noh theatre

Read the section on the Theatre of the Absurd (see pages 174–179) – a style that you might choose for a devised piece. Then look back at the section on Noh theatre (see page 24). This is an example of a tradition. You can adapt many of the techniques covered in this chapter to apply to traditions and styles. The diagrams below highlight a few characteristics of both Theatre of the Absurd and Noh theatre. Notice how these instantly transform into a first-stage stimulus-style exploration.

Activity 2

For this activity, choose to focus upon either Theatre of the Absurd or Noh theatre. Research and make a list of famous Absurdist- or Noh-inspired productions, with key content and themes of the production, in a table like the one below.

Theatre of the Absurd	Content/themes	Noh theatre	Content/themes
Rosencrantz and Guildenstern are Dead by Tom Stoppard (1966)	Shakespeare's play *Hamlet* from the point of view of the two *seemingly* most insignificant characters. Identity, fate, existentialism, language.	For example, *Takasago* by Zeami Motokiyo	A priest unknowingly meets the spirits of the 'Twinned Pines' in the form of an old married couple. Symbolic of marital harmony and long-lasting love.

The combination of your knowledge of the characteristics of your chosen style or tradition and of the production that you have selected, becomes a kind of new stimulus starting point. You can then approach the devising process in a largely similar way to a stimulus-inspired piece, going through the stages outlined earlier in this chapter.

- Make regular checks to ensure that your piece upholds the style, tradition or practitioner methods that you have chosen

- Use a past professionally performed production as an investigation case study. Remember that your piece does not need to have the same content or themes as your case study, but it must be clear that you have used the production as your inspiration.

Chapter 3 Devising

Revenge tragedy

Revenge tragedies are originally attributed to the Roman philosopher and dramatist Seneca. However, there was a revival of the tradition in the Elizabethan and Jacobean eras, and most well-known revenge tragedies performed today are from this period. A revenge tragedy follows a protagonist whose purpose in the play is to seek revenge for an antagonist's wrongdoing.

There are several 'ingredients' that a revenge tragedy usually contains:

- ghosts or supernatural elements
- scenes of madness
- murder or very gory scenes, often with multiple corpses
- play within a play
- disguises
- usually one avenger, who usually dies.

William Shakespeare's *Hamlet* contains many elements of a revenge tragedy. Hamlet is the Prince of Denmark who is told by his late father's ghost that he was murdered by Hamlet's uncle. Thus, Hamlet is incited to seek revenge on his uncle. It follows the pattern because:

- the ghost of Hamlet's father tells him of the wrongdoing
- Hamlet pretends to be mad to cover up his distress at this news
- there are many murders in the play – the final scene sees almost all the cast killed off on stage
- Hamlet asks some visiting players to put on a show with a story that restages the way in which his uncle murdered his father. Hamlet wants proof of his uncle's guilt from the way he reacts to the play
- Hamlet is sent away and returns, initially in disguise
- Hamlet is the avenger, and he dies at the end.

If you were to choose to work with revenge tragedy for your devised piece, you would need to research other revenge tragedies and find a past production to use as your case study. You and your group would then have to discuss and explore a way of creating a piece in this style or tradition.

For example, you could research a specific production of *Hamlet*, looking at the way in which each of the revenge-tragedy ingredients was handled on stage. The ghost in the Elizabethan and Jacobean periods would have just been a costumed actor. A contemporary production, however, might also choose to add effects: lighting, multimedia, stage smoke or a gauze. All these factors could be researched to give you ideas for how to devise your own play.

Activity 3

Imagine that your group has decided to use the 2017 Almeida Theatre production of *Hamlet* as a case study. This production, directed by Robert Icke, was highly contemporised, and Hamlet was played by Andrew Scott. (There are many resources online about the show, including clips from the production.) Consider the following approaches that you might undertake as a way in to the '7 Es' stages of devising:

1. Look at the ways in which this production handles certain scenes and relates them to contemporary society. Technology was prevalent in the production: for example, the ghost was caught on CCTV footage shown on large screens upstage, in a set that resembled a security surveillance room. Throughout the show, live-feed cameras were used as if submitting footage to a newsroom. How might you make use of technology and surveillance in your own devised piece? Could this help you with the 'play within a play' convention?

2. Andrew Scott played the title role with a heavy focus on the grief of his character. His interpretation leans more towards the idea of Hamlet's mental health being genuinely fragile, rather than the idea of him 'putting on' the madness. Write down other ideas of how you could link a revenge piece to the theme of mental health. Could you also bring in elements of disguise here?

3. The royal family in the play were filmed for news footage. Research some news stories of people seeking revenge. You could also look at the way in which celebrities and royal families are pursued by the press. How could you mould these stories into a revenge tragedy?

4. There is no reason why you cannot devise around the play itself. Choose a pivotal scene and improvise different outcomes, or improvise the 'missing scenes' (scenes that we know must happen within the story, but are not seen on stage). Do these improvisations spark any further ideas?

5. Research revenge tragedies intensively and consider why the genre became so popular in the Elizabethan and Jacobean eras. Are we still fascinated by the genre? Think about popular television programmes or films. Do any of them follow a revenge-tragedy pattern?

6. Discuss in your group what people tend to want revenge for. What would push you to want to seek revenge on someone? You could also discuss philosophical questions, such as: 'Does everyone have a limit? If you push someone far enough, will they "snap"?'

These are just a few examples of how you could find your way in the 'Early stage' of a devised process. You will see that it involves a lot of initial questions, just as your work on a stimulus did. Check back to the later 'E' stages on page 78 and revisit the previous examples of devising processes to see how you could then move this work forward.'

Thinking more deeply

Producing a written analysis and evaluation

It is important to be able to evaluate, not only the process and production, but also your own personal contribution throughout your piece's creation and completion. You will learn a great deal about yourself and your ability to create and collaborate throughout this process. You may fall out temporarily with group members as it becomes a personal expression of your ideas. If this happens, take time to 'breathe' as a group by reminding yourself of your initial and overall intentions. The audience is the most important factor to consider when creating a piece.

In the 800-word written analysis and evaluation of the play you devise and perform in response to a practitioner, tradition or style, you will need to reflect honestly upon your artistic intentions and your own personal contribution to the success of achieving these in your piece. The following questions cover the areas that you will be expected to write about.

Intention:

- Which practitioner, style or tradition did we choose and why? Which specific elements of the methods or theory were applied?
- What did we decide was important to convey to the audience?

Process:

- Where did we start? How useful were our original ideas and how did they develop to the final piece?
- What style and structure did we use? Why?
- How and why did our piece change along the way?

Me:

- What was my role in the process?
- How did my role communicate my intention in the performance?

Overall:

- Was the piece successful in what we set out to achieve? If not, how would we adapt it were we to do it again?

Try writing a short paragraph for each of the above areas. Below are a few trigger lines and an example of an evaluative paragraph. You must ensure that your thoughts are personal reflections and that you offer alternatives for any elements that you feel did not work.

- Our original thought process led us to…
- We discovered…
- During our exploration…
- We realised that this was not communicating our intention effectively, so we…
- Having spoken to members of the audience…
- I personally wanted to convey…
- I felt that we were successful/unsuccessful because…

> Having spoken to some audience members, we realised that they found Scenes 4 and 7 quite confusing, as we touched upon new plot aspects that were not then fully expanded upon. I feel that we could have structured the piece more effectively; instead of eight scenes for a 20-minute performance, I would streamline and condense to six scenes, removing unnecessary 'padding'. This would maintain the pace of the piece and, consequently, the final scene would have a greater impact on the audience.

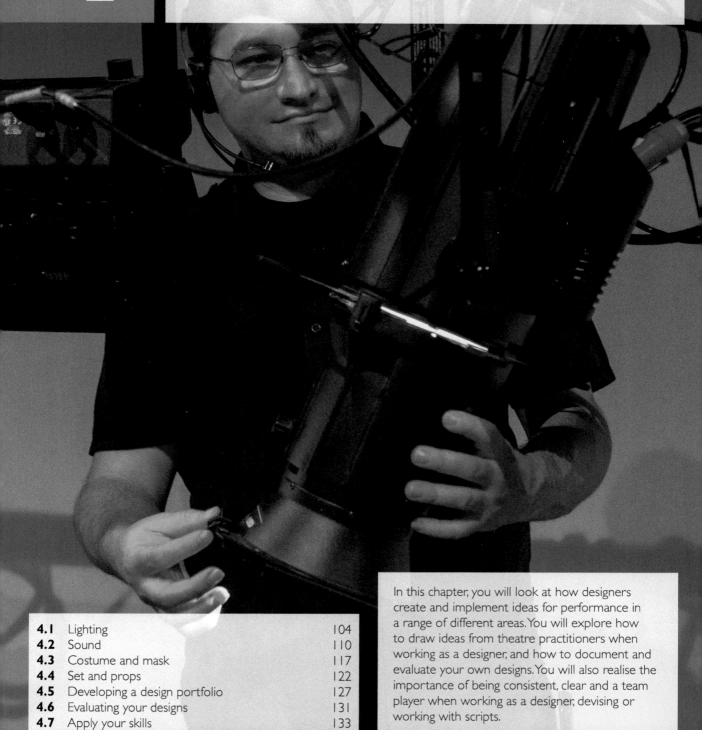

In this chapter, you will look at how designers create and implement ideas for performance in a range of different areas. You will explore how to draw ideas from theatre practitioners when working as a designer, and how to document and evaluate your own designs. You will also realise the importance of being consistent, clear and a team player when working as a designer, devising or working with scripts.

4.1 Lighting

Big question

- How do lighting designers create a design for performance?

Starting point: The purpose and history of lighting design

A lighting designer works with the director and the wider creative team to create the lighting design for performance. The design has to create atmosphere, respond to pointers in the script such as time of day and interior or exterior conditions, and consider both visibility and safety on stage. All this has to be done within a specific budget created by the producer or set by the company itself.

Activity 1

Research the following phrases related to theatre lighting. What do they refer to in modern theatre?

- 'in the **limelight**'
- a birdie being 'one under par'
- a top hat to protect your eyes

Key terms

limelight: a cylinder of lime that was heated to produce an intense bright white light; used in theatres before the invention of the lightbulb

footlights: lights used at floor level at the edge of the stage to provide general up-lighting of actors

downstage: the section of the stage closest to the audience

carbon arc lamp: the first form of electric light; the light is created by a spark or electric arc with two carbon rods with a gap between for air to pass between.

gel: a transparent coloured material placed in a gel frame at the front of a lantern to project colour onto the stage

---

Greeks (500 BCE): Earliest known form of stage lighting – theatres were built with the direction of the sun in mind and plays were performed in the afternoon, using sunlight to light the actors.

1600s: Chandeliers over both stage and audience; **footlights** began to be used on the **downstage** edge of the stage.

1870s: Limelight in general use in modern theatres (until the 1890s, when it was replaced with the **carbon arc lamp**).

1881: The Savoy Theatre in London installs the world's first electric lighting system, followed by Boston's Bijou's Theatre and the Metropolitan Opera House in New York City.

1580–1618: Candles introduced for theatre lighting, initially in Italy in both the academic and court theatres.

1780s: Oil lamps began to replace candles as the primary light source.

1816: The world's first gas stage lighting system was installed in Chestnut Street Theatre in Philadelphia, USA.

1877: **Gel** introduced to the theatre world.

Explore: The process of lighting design

A lighting designer will initially work alone, but they must liaise with others involved in a production. In professional theatre, a lighting department consists of a designer, a **production electrician** and a lighting operator. **Follow spot** operators may also be needed, depending on the scale of the production and the design created.

Below are the key stages of planning and carrying out a lighting design:

- Read the script and discuss ideas with the director and set designer.
- Watch rehearsals/run-throughs.
- Produce a **cue list**.
- Draw the **lighting plan**.
- Put the lights in the **lighting rig**.
- Focus the lights to make sure they are pointing at the correct part of the stage.
- Plot the lights – that is, program the lighting desk (usually done by the operator, under instruction from the lighting designer).
- Carry out a technical rehearsal.

Key terms

production electrician: the person responsible for the electrical design of all practical lighting elements

follow spot (spotlight): a powerful, moveable lighting instrument which projects a bright beam of light on to the stage/actors

cue list: a list of lighting states with a brief description

lighting plan: a drawing of the lighting design, showing the positions of the lights, lighting bars and further details, such as colours

lighting rig: the structure in which the lanterns (lights) are all placed

Activity 2

The images below and on the next page show the following key documents that a lighting designer might typically use. In pairs, decide which document you think is which. Discuss and make notes on why you think each of the following is important for lighting design:

- cue list
- focus sheet
- lighting plan/plot
- cue/plot sheet
- gel cutting sheet ('colour call').

Cue No.	Action/State	Page
LX0.5	Preset house lights and dim state on stage	1
LX1	On clearance, house lights out and crossfade to light through window	1
LX2	As Mr Jones enters, build state	2
LX3	End of Scene 1, check down to doorway as they exit	4
LX4	Change scene state	4
LX5	When set, general state for Scene 2 – dawn	5
LX6	Build state as sun rises	5
LX7	Snap blackout	8
LX8	Scene changes state	8
LX9	Scene 3 state	9

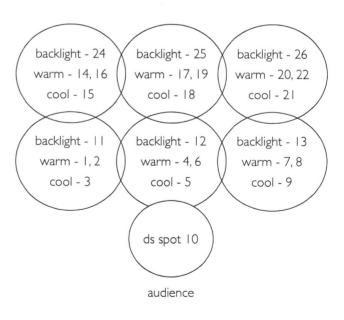

Cue no.	Memory	Up/down/time	Action	State notes
Preset	0.5	5	with 'half hour call'	houselights and preset on stage (dim windowgobo and blue wash
I	I	15/7	on clearance	houselights out & build state on stage (scene 1)
2	2	4	as Butler exits	check DSR – focus on sofa area
2A	2.5	3	as curtains are closed	check whole state – evening approaches
VIS3	3	0	VISUAL: light switch USR	switch practicals on & lift state

	1K Fresnel	CCT Fresnel	Source 4 Profile	Minuette Profile	Parcan	PC	Floodlight
343	6						
110					2		
024					2		
183					2		

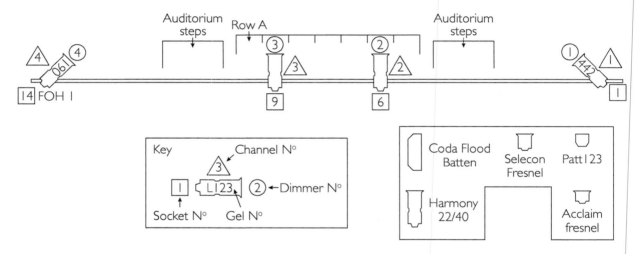

To effectively create light, you need to complete the following sequence:

Lantern + Colour + Position + Focus (gobos) + **Flow** = Lighting

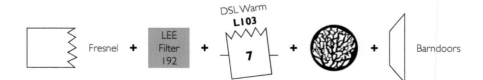

Different types of lantern create different effects. The table below gives some examples of lanterns you can use and why you might choose them for a design.

Lantern	Symbol used on a lighting plan	Purpose	Additional features
Flood		Simple lantern that will 'flood' the stage with light. Good for lighting the back wall or a **cyc** on stage. It has a wide beam, which can produce an unwanted spill of light, so should only be used for a specific effect or for lighting scenery.	Can come in a batten (four floods in a row). Can add gels.
Fresnel		A soft-edged spotlight. The size of the beam can be adjusted.	Can control the beam angle. Can add **barndoors**. Can add gels.
Profile		Profiles produce clearly defined 'spots' of light. They can be hard- or soft-edged. They are the most versatile and focusable lantern because the beam size can be adjusted. A followspot is a special type of profile lantern with a much stronger light.	Has shutters, which means a shape can be formed with the beam of light. Can use gobos to create shapes or patterns.
Parcan		The cheapest lantern available, as this is simply a 'can'. The light produced can be very intense. Not to be used for **general wash** as the beam can't be blended very well.	Can add gels. Suitable for strong colours or for special effect.

Activity 3

Select an extract from a play you are studying. In groups, use the information in the table above to decide which lanterns you would use to create the following effects:

- establishing a particular kind of atmosphere
- indicating the time of day
- highlighting key actors or scenery
- defining key areas of the stage through lighting.

Develop: Varying technology to develop designs

As lighting technology advanced, **scrollers** were introduced to easily create colour changes during performance, and **moving lights** were used to allow for repositioning/refocusing remotely mid-performance.

Lanterns are controlled by dimmers and the console (desk). In the past, operators only had the option of 'manual' (faders were pushed up and down), so cues could only be prepared two at a time (A/B deck). Today, desks are programmable, allowing operators to program cues into the computer memory. Operators now hit 'Go' to change the lighting states. However, manual desks can still be used for simple shows.

Key terms

cyclorama (cyc): a large curtain or wall (often concave) positioned upstage in a theatre

barndoors: a metal structure placed on the front of a lantern which enables a designer to shape the light, such as narrowing the beam to create the effect of a 'crack' of light

general wash: a general fill of light/colour evenly spread across the stage

scroller: a mechanical accessory that goes on the front of a parcan and which 'scrolls' through several colours

moving lights: automated/mechanical lights that can be refocused/repositioned mid-performance (unlike other fixed lanterns)

Activity 4

In pairs, look at the scenarios below. Decide whether a manual or programmed desk should be used and give your reasons.

- The opening of a performance that has several lighting cues in quick succession.
- During a scene, two lanterns need to be controlled separately to create the effect of time passing.
- A follow spot needs to be operated at the same time as a long-fade cue. There is only one operator.

Read the extract below, from the 1622 Jacobean revenge tragedy *The Changeling*, and then complete Activity 5.

Text 1

Enter Alibius and Lollio

ALIBIUS: Lollio, I must trust thee with a secret,
But thou must keep it.

LOLLIO: I was ever close to a secret, sir.

ALIBIUS: The diligence that I have found in thee,
The care and industry already past
Assures me of thy good continuance.
Lollio, I have a wife.

LOLLIO: Fie sir, 'tis too late to keep her secret: she's known to be
married all the town and country over.

From *The Changeling* by Thomas Middleton and William Rowley,
Act 1, Scene 2

Plot summary

The play illustrates the secrecy and corruption at the heart of an aristocratic court in a European country. This scene is set in a mad house involving Alibius, a jealous doctor, and his servant Lollio. In this extract, Alibius and Lollio are talking about Isabella (Alibius's wife).

Activity 5

Copy and complete this table, explaining how you would light this extract if you had decided to have Isabella on stage while the other characters are discussing her.

Character/place/theme	Location	Lantern	Colour	Why
Isabella (Alibius's wife)	Lit upstage centre			To reveal to the audience who they are talking about
Verse and prose		Profiles	Two different colours: 1) 2)	To indicate the high- and low-status characters
Entrance of Alibius and Lollio		Fresnel		
Alibius's jealousy		Profile	Green	

Apply: Using lighting in the style of a practitioner

Spotlight on practitioner:
Edward Gordon Craig (1872–1966)

Rather than simply lighting the actors and scenery, British theatre designer and director Edward Gordon Craig instead focused on lighting to show space and performance area. He felt that light was essential in evoking different moods, establishing the environment and creating the world of the story. In one notable performance of Henry Purcell's *Dido and Aeneas* in the early 1900s, he had an overhead bridge constructed for the lighting, from where he used colours (blue, amber and green) to transform the stage. Craig used lighting only to show movement in time, location and anything else that 'transitions' in performance. He believed that lighting design:

- should be kept simple and essential
- should use straight lines and play with scale, contrast and shadows
- should play a vital part in communicating the story.

His ideas marked the start of a shift away from the use of conventional footlights towards lighting from above and from the sides of the stage.

You are now going to think about Craig's approach to lighting in relation to the play *Mother Courage and Her Children* by Bertolt Brecht (see pages 15–16). Scene 1 of the play is set in Dalarna, Sweden, in spring 1624. A sergeant and recruiting officer are recruiting soldiers for the Swedish campaign in Poland. They stand shivering on a highway. The officer complains of the difficulty in recruiting soldiers from the untrustworthy townspeople. The sergeant declares that the people need war, as without war, there is no organisation.

Activity 6

Look at the image below, showing this scene from the play. There are four white arrows pointing to elements of the modern-day lighting design that follow Craig's key principles. In pairs, identify the focus of the lighting design on the stage.

If you were creating a lighting design for this scene, what three things would you change to make the location and environment of Swedish springtime clearer?

Reflection point

Make some notes for a lighting plot for a piece of devised work you have recently created. Think about:

- lanterns you might use
- colours and gobos you could add
- the shadows you create
- whether you use shutters or barndoors
- whether you would use a manual or a programmed desk.

4.2 Sound

Big question

- How do sound designers create a design for performance?

Starting point: Background to sound

A sound designer works with the director to decide what themes and emotions to explore in a production. It is important to remember that music and sound are used to create an experience. The design must create emotion, reflect the mood and underscore the actions. Sounds should evoke a reaction that indicates the feelings within a scene and prepare the audience for the action that will follow.

Sound is one of the youngest fields of stagecraft. People have always created 'noise' to enhance emotion, but it has come a long way from its earliest use in religious practices for healing or recreational purposes.

Activity 1

Research the following mechanical devices. How is each one used in modern theatre? In pairs, focus on one of these and present your research to the rest of your class:

- wind machine (aeoliphone)
- thunder sheet
- rain box
- rumble cart
- thunder run.

Romans (240 BCE): Machinery was used to create sound effects. The Romans invented a thunder machine using brass balls and a wind machine – a rotating wheel with fabric draped over it.

Medieval theatre (500–1500): Sound effects were needed to represent hell and the appearance of God in morality plays. Sound was heard through songs and instruments and used for transitions and ambience.

Victorian theatre (1837–1901): First use of recorded sound (1890) – an early record player played a recording of a baby's cry.

Greeks (532 BCE): Tragedies and comedies needed storms, earthquakes and thunder in performance. The Greeks created the stepped audience (amphitheatre) because they understood how sound travelled to an audience. It was the famous philosopher, Aristotle, who first noticed that the chorus sounded better when standing on a hard surface. This marked the beginning of understanding sound absorption.

Elizabethan theatre (1562–1603): Sound effects and music started being written into scripts. Theatre started to move indoors and sound was used to reproduce effects, as well as being used more symbolically.

17th–19th centuries: The development of mechanical devices for theatre became so highly developed, it led to **cues** in theatre.

Key term

cue: the trigger for an action to be carried out at a specific time

Explore: What does a sound designer have to consider?

The key features of a sound design are:

- **amplification** of voice and instruments
- live sound effects (**Foley**)
- pre-recorded sound effects and/or music
- modification of pre-recorded music or effects
- **voiceover**
- pre-show and post-show announcements
- composition of music
- creation of soundscapes
- scene-change sound effects
- placement of speakers.

Key terms

amplification: the process of increasing the volume of sound

Foley: the reproduction of everyday sounds, normally used in post-production film editing; in theatre, it is used off stage with a microphone to create live sounds as they happen in real time on stage

voiceover: speech played through the sound system, sometimes without a physical performer

Activity 2

Select an extract from a play you are studying. Using the features listed above, copy and complete the sound design ideas table below. The first line has been completed for you.

Act/scene	Page reference	Feature of sound	Idea
Act 1, Scene 2	12	Voiceover (pre-recorded)	To make the scene more Brechtian [see page 15], I would have the opening stage directions to the scene played to the audience as a voiceover recording.

To effectively create sound, you need a source. This source goes through a mixing desk, where any modifications to the sound are made, and from the **mixing desk** to the amplifier. The amplifier sends the sound to the speaker and the spectator hears the sound.

Key term

mixing desk: a console where sound signals are mixed and then output

You can remember this process using the mnemonic 'SMASH':

Source → **Mixing desk** → **Amplifiers** → **Speaker** → **Hear sound**

The table below gives some examples of equipment you can use to produce an effective sound chain.

Source	Mixing desk	Amplifiers	Speakers
Voice	Soundcraft Vi2000 Digital mixer	Yamaha PCN Power Amplifiers	Subwoofer speaker
Compact disc (CD)	Soundcraft Signature 10	4 Channel Amplifier	Floor monitor speaker
Piano	Behringer X32 Digital Mixer	Anthem M1 Monaural Class D amp	On-stage wedge speaker
Striking match (Foley sound)	Soundcraft Europa analogue mixing desk	Audio Control Savoy G3 Amplifier	FOH (front of house) speaker

Activity 3

Draw your own sound chain showing the different types of sources, desks, amps and speakers you might use in a devised performance you are working on.

Microphones are used to amplify voice, objects or instruments on stage. In larger performance spaces, they are crucial to ensure information is not lost when communicating with an audience. In the sound chain process, they form part of the source.

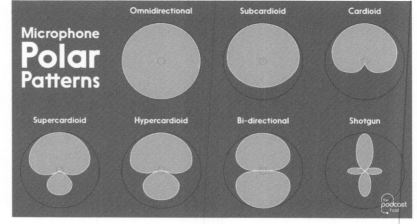

There are several microphone **pick-up** patterns that a sound designer needs to consider:

- omnidirectional: picks up from all around; best used for several instruments.
- cardioid: picks up from the front only; best used for solo singing or speaking.
- subcardioid: wider pick-up than cardioid, useful for duologues or duets.
- super/hypercardioid: narrower pick-up than cardioid; useful for loud sound sources and noisy stage environments.
- bi-directional (figure of 8): picks up from front and back with no side pick-up; useful for stereo recording or two or more instruments.
- shotgun: picks up from overhead; useful for choral or large group singing.

Key term

pick-up: the area around the microphone where sound signals will be in range

Activity 4

Working in small groups, look at the following stage situations. For each one, discuss which of the microphones listed above you would use. Make notes, giving reasons for your choices.

- A large choral ensemble talking in unison
- One single actor on stage talking with a stage whisper
- Groups of actors on stage, and duologues are spoken from the centre of the groups
- An actor with a drum that is beaten every time they say a certain word

Develop: The process of sound designing

A sound designer often works alone, but like a lighting designer, they must liaise with other members of the production company. In professional theatre, the technical specification of the design will be delivered and operated by a technician.

The different stages of sound designing are explained below.

1. Text analysis: Read through the script and highlight key themes, selecting anything that you need to question further.

2. Discussion with the director/actors and set designer.

3. Formulate a brief: From the director/designer discussion, write out your sound brief and give this back to the director to approve.

4. Research: Look at the themes, characters, time period and location, and start to gather ideas.

5. Sketch phase: You won't have specific timings for the final production yet, so you have to 'sketch' ideas. Get all audio ideas onto a computer, listen to them frequently, **layer** them and share them with other members of the creative team.

6. Plan a design that meets the parameters of your specified budget: This means that additional software for creating sounds would need to be budgeted for; the use of other sound artists or the hire of a recording studio would all need to be considered.

7. Get copyright or clearances: Look into the costs and rules around any soundtrack or effect you wish to use that is owned by someone else. When you are wanting to use someone else's music in something you are creating, you need to have permission from the copyright holder and you may need to apply for a PRS (Performing Right Society) licence to ensure the original composer/musician receives **royalties** for their work.

8. Production meeting: Bring together others within your team who are designing for a production – for example, costume or lighting.

9. Attend rehearsals throughout the process and make rehearsal notes.

10. Formulate and develop a cue list (see page 102 for an example cue list).

11. Create a sound schematic (see page 111 for an example).

12. Put cues 'in the book': This means the script that will be used during the performance to cue all of the technical elements.

13. Plot: Program the cues into the sound desk, if digital.

14. Technical and dress rehearsals: The dress rehearsal is the last rehearsal before the first performance where all costume and technical elements run. The technical rehearsal is for the designers and technical crew more than the actors, and this happens before the dress rehearsal, to make sure all the cues are going to work.

Key terms

layer: to stack two or more sounds together to achieve a sound effect/music track; this is usually done using a computer software package, where the tracks can be seen 'stacked' on top of one another

royalties: a sum paid to a composer or writer for each public performance of their work or each copy of it sold

Activity 5

Work backwards from the end point (when your devised performance is) and create a schedule timeline using the stages above. For example:

- Exam performance: 01.03.2022
- Dress rehearsal: 28.02.2022
- Technical rehearsal: 27.02.2022

Read Text 2 – another extract from *The Changeling*. The main plot action is set in Vermandero's Castle, in the port of Alicante. This opening scene is beside the castle gate. Jasperino and Alsemero are friends.

Text 2

Enter Servants

JASPERINO:	Backwards, I think, sir. Look, your servants.
1 SERVANT:	The seamen call: shall we board your trunks?
ALSEMERO:	No, not today.
JASPERINO:	'Tis the critical day it seems, and the sign in **Aquarius**.
2 SERVANT	[*Aside*] We must not to sea today, this **smoke will bring forth fire.**
ALSEMERO	Keep all on shore. I do not know the end – Which needs I must do – of an affair in hand Ere I can go to sea.
1 SERVANT	Well, your pleasure.
2 SERVANT	[*Aside*] Let him e'en take his leisure too: we are safer on land.

From *The Changeling* by Thomas Middleton and William Rowley, Act 1, Scene 1

Vocabulary

Aquarius: the astrological sign of water, supposedly favourable for sea travel

smoke will bring forth fire: a phrase more commonly known as 'there is no smoke without fire', which means if something seems to be bad, there is probably a good reason for it

Activity 6

Copy and complete the table below to analyse the scene's sound design. What themes are emerging? What information is in the stage directions for you to consider?

Sound idea	Reasoning	Source	Volume	Direction	Timing
Town bells	Sets the time/ location of the scene.	Recorded effect mixed through the mixing desk.	Quiet (– 20dB) underneath dialogue.	Upstage, on stage speakers. The sound is heard by actors and audience.	3 × chime (indicates middle of the day) (approx. 10 secs)

Activity 7

Text 2 lasts for approximately 35 seconds. Look at the bar chart below showing the layers and timing of the soundscape. Create your own soundscape bar chart and consider the following:

- From the options below, which three sounds would you layer to create a soundscape that runs for the whole extract?
- Would you use pre-recorded sounds, instruments, Foley sounds or a combination?

Consider the historical context (see page 38) and select sounds that would be appropriate:

- seamen calling
- rigging creaking
- waves crashing against the port
- ships' chains dropping
- ships' foghorn
- the loading and unloading of goods at the port.

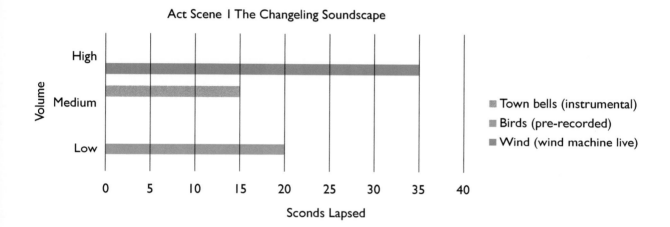

Apply: Using sound in the style of Brecht

You read about the German theatre practitioner Bertolt Brecht in Chapter 1 (see pages 15–16). Brecht used music and song with the intention of it commenting or conflicting with the action on stage. Often the style of music and the lyrics would be in **juxtaposition** with each other, which would help distance the audience (the alienation effect). Brecht used music to interrupt the flow of the story and to ensure the audience did not become emotionally invested. He would often have the source of the music visible to the audience. Musicians would not be placed in an **orchestra pit**.

Read Text 3 from *Mother Courage and Her Children*, which Brecht wrote in 1939. The markings + and / are outlined and used in Activity 8.

Key terms

juxtaposition: placing two elements close together or side by side to show similarities or differences

orchestra pit: an area of the theatre where musicians perform, usually located in a lowered area in front of the stage

Plot summary

It is 1631, and Mother Courage's wagon is outside a war-torn village. The Chaplain (a religious minister) enters, needing linen to bandage some peasants whose farmhouse has been destroyed. Kattrin wants to give him some shirts, but Mother Courage refuses, stating that the peasants have no money for her goods. Kattrin threatens her mother and the Chaplain takes the shirts anyway.

Text 3

Mother Courage's cart has stopped in a badly shot-up village.

Thin military music in the distance. Two soldiers at the bar being served by Kattrin and Mother Courage. One of them has a lady's fur coat over his shoulders.

MOTHER COURAGE: Can't pay, that it? […] They give us victory parades, but catch them giving men their pay.

SOLDIER: …I missed the looting. The double-crossing general only allowed an hour's looting in the town. + He ain't an inhuman…, he said. Town must of paid him.

THE CHAPLAIN *stumbles in*: There are people still lying in that yard. The peasant's family. Somebody give me a hand. / I need linen.

The second soldier goes off with him. Kattrin becomes very excited and tries to make her mother produce linen.

MOTHER COURAGE: I got none. All my bandages was sold to the regiment. \ I ain't tearing up my officers' shirts for that lot.

From *Mother Courage and Her Children* by Bertolt Brecht, Scene 5

Activity 8

What song/music do you think could be played to contrast to the words in the scene? Think about the key themes. For example, the use of Sam Smith's song 'Money on My Mind' could provide a source of aural juxtaposition because the lyrics describe that he doesn't have money on his mind and that he is doing something for the love of doing so. This would juxtapose the scene, as Mother Courage is doing this purely for her own gain – for her, everything revolves around money.

When would you start, break and end the sound cues? Remember that Brecht used music to break the emotional involvement of the audience. Having a break in the music gives the audience the opportunity to reflect.

In the example above: Start indicated with /

Break indicated with +

End indicated with \

Why do you think the example sound cues are in the places that they are?

Reflection point

Think of a devised piece you have recently created. Apply the sound knowledge you have learned in this unit to list the following possible ideas for:

- sound cues
- types of sources you might use
- types of microphone pick-up patterns needed
- Foley effects you could use
- soundscapes you could create, with a list of the sounds layered
- Brechtian approaches with music/song.

4.3 Costume and mask

Big question

- How do costume and mask designers create a design for performance?

Starting point: What do costume and mask designers do?

Costume designers create the designs for characters. They also balance those designs against the textures, colours and other design elements (for example, lighting and set designs) on stage within a scene. Costume designers must ensure the costume:

- enables the actor to move as required
- is durable enough to last for the length of the performance run
- is comfortable
- fits in with the production's visual style
- tells the audience about the character (gender, historical period, socio-economic status, etc.).

The same applies to mask design. In fact, masks need to be even more robust, as they are physical objects that can be removed, put down, possibly damaged or lost. They are also much more difficult to replace, especially if a mask has been made specifically for a particular performer.

500 BCE: The ancient Greek playwright Aeschylus created specific costumes for actors to wear to perform his tragedies; the happy and sad mask faces, often used as a symbol of the theatre, date from this time, when masks were used to suggest comedy or tragedy.

1200s: In Europe, masks were used in performances for royalty and nobility.

1300s: Japanese Noh theatre was formed and the use of masks for various roles was introduced.

1300–1600: During the Renaissance in Europe, masks resurged professionally for **masques**, ballet and in commedia dell'arte (see page 52) performances for the clown character.

1500–1600: The introduction of stock characters in commedia dell'arte meant that everyone in the audience understood what the characters stood for from their costumes.

1700–1800: A desire for greater detail and accuracy in costume design began to be expressed by both directors and audiences.

1800–1900: The **avant-garde** movement gave new life to the culture of theatre masks.

Key terms

masque: a form of entertainment popular in the 16th and 17th centuries, characterised by acting and dancing by masked players

avant-garde: describing things that are cutting edge or ahead of their time

Spotlight on practitioner:
Caroline Siedle

Caroline Siedle (1867–1907) was one of the first costume designers to be acknowledged in a theatre programme for her designs. She was the first woman to be recognised consistently as a professional designer in the USA. In the late 1800s, costume design was rarely recognised and consequently company managers used to be responsible for selecting costumes, which were often rented. It wasn't until 1936 that costume design was formally recognised as a design speciality.

Explore: Elements to consider in costume and mask design

The key stages of costume and mask design are:

- Analyse: Analyse the script and create a **costume/mask plot**.
- Research: Explore the character hierarchy (who has relationships with who) and location of the action. This will inform the costumes/masks.
- Initial sketch/layout: Create a rough sketch within the chosen colour scheme.
- Final sketch: Sketch out your final design (usually with paints). These can be shown to the actors to help them visualise their character.
- Drawing for cutter/tailor: Provide a working drawing and discuss the details of a cut and fit with a cutter/tailor.
- Source garments/masks: Garments are either **pulled**, rented, shopped (bought) or constructed (made).
- Pattern draping: Take the cloth and shape it on a mannequin to create a 3D representation of the costume, to allow for cutting and pinning.
- Fittings: Actors attend fittings once the costume is pinned; make alterations before sewing begins.
- Technical and dress rehearsals: Ensure costumes and masks are fit for purpose and look as planned on stage.

Key terms

costume/mask plot: an outline of which character is in which scene, when the actors change and what costumes/masks are needed

cutter: a wardrobe craftsperson who creates patterns and constructs the costumes for females (a tailor creates male costumes)

pulled: selected from a stock of costumes

Activity 1

Think about your recent devised work, then copy and complete the table below to create a costume plot. The first one is an example.

Actor's name	Character	Costume	Entrance	Change	Notes
Holly	Thespis	A white robe with a gold belt. Bare feet.	Page 4	Exits stage page 5 and the gold belt needs to be removed.	No dresser needed; actor can change themselves.

Trestle is a professional theatre company that specialises in mask. The company applies the following rules to using masks in performance:

- Never let the audience see you putting the mask on.
- Never speak through a full-face mask.
- Aim to face the audience when wearing a mask.
- Do not put your hands on or near the mask.

When working as a mask designer and applying Trestle's rules, you need to ensure these rules are not broken.

 Activity 2

Imagine you are a mask designer on the same devised piece as in Activity 1.

- If your actors needed to talk, which set of Trestle masks below would you use?
- Complete the table below showing your understanding of which health and safety risks could arise with a masked actor and why?

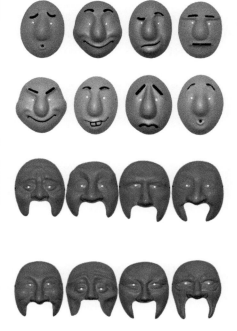

Health and safety consideration	Risk to: actor, crew or audience	Why?
Scene changes with darkness and moving scenery	Crew, masked actor and possible front row auidience	
Skin infections, spread of illness		the removal of masks, which contain sweat and germs

Develop: Relating your costume and mask knowledge to a play

Read Text 4 below – an extract from the ancient Greek tragedy *Antigone*, written by Sophocles in around 441 BCE. (See page 40 for the features of Greek tragedy.)

Plot summary

The opening scene shows Antigone telling Ismene (her sister) that she plans to bury their brother (Polynices) who has died at war. This is against the orders of Creon (the king), who has said that Polynices must remain unburied as punishment for his treason. Antigone is determined to give her brother a proper burial.

Text 4

ANTIGONE: My own flesh and blood – dear sister, dear Ismene, […] an emergency decree, they say, the Commander has just now declared for all of Thebes. What, haven't you heard? Don't you see? The doom reserved for enemies marches on the ones we love the most.

ISMENE: Not I, I haven't heard a word, Antigone. Nothing of loved ones, […] not since the two of us were robbed of our two brothers, […]

ANTIGONE: I thought so. That's why I brought you out here, past the gates, so you could hear in private.

ISMENE: What's the matter? […]

ANTIGONE: …Our own brothers' burial! Hasn't Creon graced one with all the rites, disgraced the other? Eteocles, they say, has been given full military honors […] But the body of Polynices […] He's to be left unwept, unburied, a lovely treasure for birds that scan the field and feast to their heart's content. […]
There you have it. You'll soon show what you are, worth your breeding, Ismene, or a coward – for all your royal blood. […]

ISMENE: …what good am I to you?

ANTIGONE: Decide. Will you share the labor, share the work?

ISMENE: What work, what's the risk? […]

ANTIGONE: Will you lift up his body with these bare hands and lower it with me?

From *Antigone* by Sophocles, Act 1, Scene 1

Activity 3

Copy and complete the table below with ideas for costumes for Antigone and Ismene in this scene.

Character	Personality/characteristics to consider	Appropriate colours (related to character traits)	Movement and blocking to consider
Antigone	Brave, devoted, hasty		
Ismene	Cowardly, innocent, someone who complies with rules or accepted behaviours		

Activity 4

Draw several masks showing different sets of facial expressions that could suit either Antigone or Ismene in the extract above.

Apply: Using costume and mask in the style of a practitioner

Spotlight on practitioner:
Steven Berkoff (b. 1937)

Berkoff is an English director and playwright with an unusual approach to the visual elements of his productions. His approach to design is minimalistic and often includes mask. Berkoff is influenced by classical Greek, Noh and Kabuki theatre (see page 24), which is evident in his extensive use of make-up and mask. In his productions, Berkoff uses mask to create eerie effects to make characters look completely unnaturalistic. His main intention is to dehumanise (take away the character's human features and qualities). To achieve this in choral work, he creates a sense of commonality rather than individuality.

Berkoff's passion for non-naturalism is influenced by Brecht, who wanted his audience to question society, and would often break the **fourth wall** by making backstage elements visible on stage (for example, a costume rail). Asking actors to make costume changes on stage both distanced and shocked the audience further. Brecht would not use traditional costumes and clothing would be used to simply state/resemble a character (for example, an apron for a housewife). Brecht was known for using labels on actors (signs worn round the actor's neck) to point out information (for example, 'I am a school boy').

Activity 5

As a costume/mask designer, consider how you would include the following practitioner elements into your design for a devised piece influenced by Berkoff and Brecht:

- dehumanised facial features (for example, misaligned eyes, a misshapen mouth)
- a half-mask with extensive non-naturalistic makeup
- a design that allows costume changes to happen in front of the audience
- a symbolic element of the costume to stereotype
- a label/sign worn by a character to give further information, for example, 'Innocent younger sister'

Key term

fourth wall: an invisible/imagined wall that separates the actors and the audience

Reflection point

Thinking of your devised work, look at the image showing different measurements taken for costume-making. Choose an actor and consider which measurements you would need for your design. Not all measurements are needed for all costumes. For example, a short-sleeved blouse will not require measurement H.

You may want to create a table of measurements needed for particular clothes to be made for an actor:

Item of clothing/ costume:	Measurements needed:	Design ideas:
Trousers	B, C, L–M, K–M, R	
Jacket/blazer	E, B, O, H, F, G	

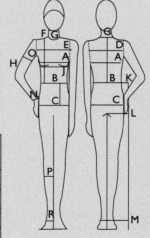

Bust	A
Waist	B
Hips	C
Back Width	D
Front Chest	E
Shoulder	F
Neck Size	G
SLeeve	H
Under Bust	J
Wrist	N
Upper Arm	O
Calf	P
Ankle	R
Nape to Waist	G-B
Waist to Hip	B-C
Front Shoulder to Waist	F-B
Outside Leg	K-M
Inside Leg	L-M

4.4 Set and props

Big question

- How do set designers create a design for performance?

Starting point: What does a set designer do?

A set designer works with the director and other members of the creative team to establish the overall visual concept of a production. They are responsible for all the set drawings, a scale model box and overseeing the set construction. They also work closely with the carpenters, scenic artists and props master.

Activity 1

A set designer must produce the following drawings:

- basic ground plan
- composite ground plan
- sections of the stage space
- front and side elevations of every scenic element and any additional sections as required.

Research what each of these plans looks like and decide in which order the drawings would be created.

532 BCE: The ancient Greeks began performing outdoors in an amphitheatre space; they invented the **skene**.

700–1500: The rear wall of the theatre was used only as scenery; important information about a location was given through character's lines.

1600s: Using their knowledge of architecture and perspective, the Italians developed **flats**, solid **backdrops**, **raked stages** and **wings**.

1700s: The 'curtain' began to be lowered for scene changes and the **scrim** began to be used for effects; the stage was framed with a proscenium arch.

1800s: Scenery started to become more accurate; the model box was developed and there was a revolt against the 2D world of painted canvas. More complicated works began being produced, which meant the need for a wooden stage floor to provide effects in the form of traps, slots and elevators.

Key terms

skene: a 3D structure like a tent or hut – made of fabric or light wood, placed at the back of the stage, in front of which performances took place

flats: upright, light, flat pieces of scenery that can be painted or covered with cloth

backdrop: cloth hung at the back of the stage

raked stage: a sloped stage that slants upwards away from the audience

wings: the sides of the stage, out of sight of the audience

scrim: a very light, translucent fabric used extensively in theatre, sometimes referred to as gauze

Explore: Working from a bare stage

The key stages of set design are outlined below.

- Pre-design: Read the play and do preliminary research. Meet with the director to discuss story, character and themes.
- Conceptual design: Sketch out ideas, deciding on the stage/audience formation; think about the logistics of different settings/locations.
- Physical design: Take the sketches and focus on the size, placement and angles of the set – this can be hand drawn or created using **CAD**. The 2D drawing is turned into a 3D model in the form of a **white card model** or by using software such as **SketchUp**.
- Final design: Once approved by the director, the final design is created. You can research and add detail such as décor, furniture, props, colour, and so on. Then the model box can be created and shown to the cast and production team.
- Finalised plans: Floor plans, elevations and sections are finalised and detailed; specific details are shared with the building team to ensure accuracy.

Activity 2

Copy and complete the table below by researching some of the different formations of stage layout and audience placement.

Staging	Definition	Advantages	Disadvantages
End on	Audience sits on one side only		
In the round			Flats and background drapes can't be used as it will prevent the audience from seeing all of the action on stage.
Thrust	Audience on three sides, with an extension of the staging 'thrusting' into the audience		
Traverse		Either end of the stage will be clear entrances and exits to/ from the stage.	

Activity 3

Draw a ground plan for a devised performance you recently created. Decide if you would use the following features of design and, if so, where you would place them.

- wings
- curtains
- gauze/scrim
- flats
- platforms/**rostra**

Develop: Relating ideas to a play

The Changeling was one of the most popular revenge tragedies of the English Renaissance. First performed in 1622, it is set in 17th-century Spain. The play's themes are treachery, sin and a person's downfall. The play has two plots that run in parallel, a main plot and a sub-plot. The main plot is set in the town of Alicante and is the tragedy storyline. The sub-plot takes place in the madhouse and this is the comedic storyline. There is a lot of rapid switching between these two plots, so fast scene changes are necessary. As there is so much to consider and interpret, and so many different creative perspectives, no two productions of the play would be designed the same.

Activity 4

Look at these photos from three different productions of *The Changeling*, in 1988, 2006 and 2012.

National Theatre, 1988

Cheek by Jowl, 2006

Young Vic, 2012

As a set designer for a production of *The Changeling*, you begin your research by looking at these past production images. What ideas do they give you with regard to the following:

- the use of a **fly gallery** for quick location changes
- the potential for a **revolve**
- the use of the wings
- the use of projections to indicate settings.

Key terms

fly gallery: an area above the stage where scenery can be stored and then 'flown' in and out with the use of ropes

revolve: a mechanically controlled section of the stage that rotates to help speed up the changing of a scene

Theatrical properties, or 'props', are objects on stage. Unlike scenery, props are moveable and portable. The table below outlines the different categories.

Prop	Description
Hand props	Anything handled or carried by an actor
Personal props	Props worn or carried by an actor and issued to them, rather than stored on the props table
Set props	Mainly referring to furniture; these are objects that add to the look of the setting, with which the actor interacts
Set dressing	Furniture sourced to 'dress' the stage and not handled by actors.
Practicals	Props such as lamps that work on stage like they do in real life
Breakaways	Props that are designed to break on cue, such as bottles

Read another extract from *The Changeling*.

> **Text 5**
>
> **DEFLORES:** Yes, here are all the keys: I was afraid, my lord,
> I'd wanted for the **postern** – this is it.
> I've all, I've all, my lord – this for the **sconce**.
>
> **ALONZO:** 'Tis a most spacious and **impregnable** fort.
>
> **DEFLORES:** You'll tell me more, my lord. This descent
> Is somewhat narrow, we shall never pass
> Well with our weapons, they'll but trouble us.
>
> [*Takes off his sword …*]
>
> **DEFLORES:** Do you question
> A work of secrecy? I must silence you.
>
> [*Stabs him …*]
>
> **DEFLORES:** I must silence you. [*Kills him*]
> … Ha! what's that
> Threw sparkles in my eye? – Oh, 'tis a diamond
> He wears upon his finger. It was well found:
> This will approve the work. What, so fast on?
> Not part in death? I'll take a speedy course then:
> Finger and all shall off. So, now I'll clear
> The passages from all suspect or fear.
>
> *Exit with the body*
>
> *The Changeling* by Thomas Middleton and William Rowley, Act 3, Scene 1

Apply: Using set and props in the style of a practitioner

Sally Jacobs was the Set Designer for Peter Brook's 1970 production of *A Midsummer Night's Dream* by the Royal Shakespeare Company. Within the design, Jacobs had to ensure the set created an illusion for the audience. (There are many images of this production available to view online.) The production used large metal coils as the woodland, a spinning plate on a rod representing a flower. They used the fly gallery by having a character descend on to stage using a trapeze. Brook's intention was to move away from realism and create a production of **metaphor**. For example, the metal coils represented the characters of the Mechanicals (a group of Athenian tradesmen who are rehearsing a play within the forest). The white box design had no **masking**, so everything could be seen, including the structures supporting the trapezes. The audience could see the actors playing the fairies as they walked across the fly floor and watched the parts of the play they did not appear in.

Spotlight on practitioner:
Peter Brook (b. 1925)

Through his highly original productions, director Peter Brook forces his audiences to use their imagination by stripping the stage bare, rather than representing naturalistic settings. His idea of this 'empty space' is designed to encourage the audience to try and see what is not there. Brook's work has been influenced by Antonin Artaud's Theatre of Cruelty – an approach to theatre that 'assaults' the audience's senses (see page 198).

Plot summary

Alonzo (brother of a noble lord and the suitor to Beatrice) asks Deflores (a servant to Vermandero who is the governor of the castle) for a tour of the castle. Deflores says he will show him around later and hides a sword in his cloak. As they enter a narrow passage, Deflores advises Alonzo to leave his sword behind.

Vocabulary

postern: a back door or gate
sconce: a small fort designed to defend a castle gate
impregnable: describing a building or other place that cannot be broken into

Activity 5

Reread the summary of the scene and the extract itself. Then create a props list and note what type each prop is, using the information from the table opposite.

Key terms

metaphor: a phrase to describe an object that is not literally true but it helps to explain an idea or make a comparison.
masking: scenery used to conceal part of the stage or backstage from the audience

Activity 6

Brook put a new spin on a classic play. Think of a production you have studied or seen. List the changes you would introduce to make the production less realistic and more metaphorical.

Spotlight on practitioner:
Adolphe Appia (1862–1928)

At the end of the 19th century, Adolphe Appia and Edward Gordon Craig were both theatre practitioners who revolted against the traditional approaches to set design. They did not want to see an actor standing on a flat floor surrounded by realistic painted canvas or backdrops. They both wanted 3D sets that included steps, columns, ramps and platforms, and the use of directional light to intensify the atmosphere and mood of a production. Their ideas became the foundation of a style now known as 'New Stagecraft'.

Activity 7

Look at this image, which is similar to the type of set designs that Adolphe Appia would have created in the early 1900s, with the use of steps, ramps and platforms.

Select a scene from a play you have read recently. Imagine that it was going to be staged on this set and answer the following questions:

- How would the actors enter and exit the stage?
- What is the furthest upstage and downstage point they would use?
- Where would you position the audience?
- Would the stage be raked?
- Would you add colour to this set?

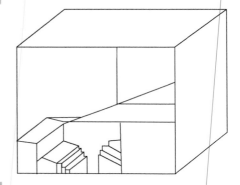

Antonin Artaud's set and staging were characterised by the following features:

- He experimented with the actor–audience relationship, always wanting the audience to be 'inside the drama'.
- He liked the actors to surround the audience to add to that sensory experience.
- Audience members would often sit on swivel chairs to allow them to easily follow the action.
- He often used raised platforms or galleries so the actors had an aerial view of the audience, again making them feel trapped in the drama.

Activity 8

Using the information about Artaud, think of your most recent devised piece of work and re-draw the set design/acting space to try to include/enhance the performance in an Artaudian style.

Reflection point

Think of a devised piece of work you have recently created, and apply the set and props knowledge from this unit.

- Create a props list (with category of prop) and **props plot**.
- Decide whether you could use revolves, traps or the fly gallery to improve the performance.

Key term

props plot: a document that lists the movement of each prop for a production, where it starts and ends and which actor/member of crew has responsibility for it

4.5 Developing a design portfolio

Big question
- How do you present your design for others?

Starting point: Undertaking research and clarifying intentions

A design portfolio needs to clearly demonstrate:

- clear artistic intentions
- consultation with all members of the creative company
- consideration of the style, practitioner, influence or tradition of the piece.

A portfolio should contain:

- notes from rehearsals
- annotations of scripts or ideas as they develop
- sketches
- diagrams
- photographs of rehearsals, technical rehearsals and elements that are created and made during the process. It can be good to annotate/label these too, to add further clarity.

It is important as a designer that you consider the rest of the group and the work they are creating. They will carry on rehearsing when you are researching, so you must ensure that you review their work regularly in case changes to the staging affect your design. You should all have a consistent approach to the genre or theatre style in which you are working. You may need to find a way of communicating the development of your design. An acting company might also report to designers through **rehearsal reports** written by the Deputy Stage Manager and then passed to all design and technical staff.

Activity 1

In groups, brainstorm and clarify the intentions of the devised work you are creating. Make sure that the group allows you to be innovative and clear with your design, to fully support the style of work being created. Make notes on: Who? What? Where? When? Why? and How?

Key term

rehearsal report: a form completed in rehearsal to record notes that affect other production departments; given to all heads of departments (costume, lighting, props, set) straight after the rehearsal

Explore: Theatre spaces/layout and audience construction

The layout of the space in which a performance takes place has a significant impact on designers across all technical disciplines.

Key term

apron: any part of the stage that extends past the proscenium arch towards the audience

Activity 2

Look at each of the stage layouts below. Consider how they could impact your design for a devised work in one of the roles below. Use the table to record your ideas.

- Set designer
- Lighting designer
- Sound designer
- Costume designer

Four types of stage

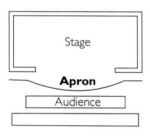

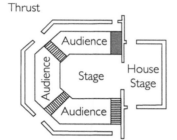

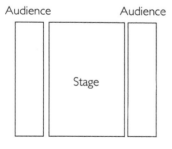

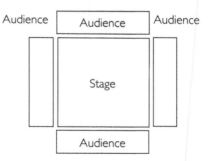

For each type of stage, copy and complete a table like the one below.

Designer role	Type of stage	Positives	Negatives
Set	Proscenium arch		
Lighting	Proscenium arch	Can use on stage and over audience lighting bars with ease, as well as lighting from the wings.	
Sound	Proscenium arch		
Costume	Proscenium arch		

Now work with your actors to stage/block the work in the best configuration for your design. Ensure that you are able to support the creative intentions of the piece whilst being inventive with your design.

Develop: Creating sketches

Most technical disciplines require you to create sketches.

Lighting:

- Draw where the lighting bars are in relation to the performance space.
- Identify the plug socket locations.
- Using a lighting lantern stencil, add the different lanterns you intend to use and the direction/angle they will point towards the stage when rigged.
- Label any gel colours and their numbers, as well as any gobos.
- Label the areas of the stage they are lighting.

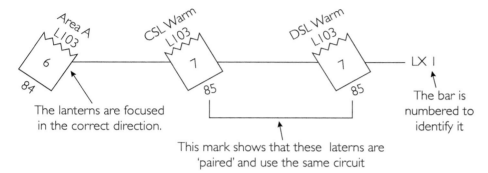

The lanterns are focused in the correct direction.

This mark shows that these laterns are 'paired' and use the same circuit

The bar is numbered to identify it

Sound:

- Create a sound schematic (like a flowchart of the SMASH diagram on page 111).
- Draw on the ground plan the location of your speakers and the direction they are pointing.

Costume:

- Sketch the designs from front, side and back.
- Annotate the sketches with colour, texture and any accessories needed.
- Take measurements from the actors and annotate the design with them.

Set:

- the ground plan, drawn to scale (1:25).
- a side elevation, if necessary, to explain your artistic intentions more clearly.
- a model box, made to 1:25 scale.

Tools you may need for designing:

- scale ruler
- lantern template for lighting
- template of scaled people for perspective
- craft knife and art materials for the model box.

Activity 3

Consider all of the above information, then a create a **risk assessment** like the example shown on page 130 (which should be added to your portfolio). Complete it for your design in performance.

Key term

risk assessment: a form completed after identifying and assessing risks, potential hazards and the probability of something negative happening; these risks are then documented and the plan would be updated if anything should change

| Date of Assessment: | | | Production: | | | Company Manager: |

| Dates of Performances/Rehearsals: | | | Duration of Performances/Rehearsals |

| Assesor: | | | Job Title: |

Activity/show element: [e.g. Smoke on stage, inexperienced crew, props, moving set …]	Hazard involve: [e.g. Slips, trips falls from set, fire hazards, injury from props, electric shock …]	Persons in danger: [e.g. Cast & crew, public et.c]	Likelihood of injury: (I = Unlikely 5 = Likely)	Severity of injury: (I = Not severe 5 = severe)	Total Risk Score	What measures are in place to minimise risk of injury?

| Is the production adequately controlled to reduce risk of injury?   Yes/No |

| Further actions required: |

| Signed: .... |

Apply: Presenting the final designs

Ensure that all documents are collated from the creative process, and produce a contents page so that you have a clear structure and coherence in your portfolio. Regardless of whether (as a designer) you have created work in the style of a practitioner, a particular style of theatre or from a tradition, you must ensure that you have looked at productions in that style, tradition or from that particular practitioner. This will enable you to analyse the production photos, archived recordings or reviews of the work and include them in your portfolio.

Keep a rehearsal diary that shows the development of ideas – you can add design ideas to it and begin to formulate your plans. Insert extracts into the portfolio to show the development of the work and annotate these extracts where necessary to aid understanding. Always remember that others will need to read your portfolio and, if it isn't clear, then your intentions might be misunderstood.

Activity 4

Look at this example of a rehearsal diary from a director of a production.

In the middle of rehearsing a scene, Alfie (an actor) has an idea and turns to Nathan (the sound designer) and requests some music for the scene. Nathan quickly responds with a live musical option and talks to the musical director (Jemilla) who quickly improvises an upbeat piece of music. All the actors in the scene remark on how much it helps them and it certainly adds to the atmosphere. Alfie says the sound is good, but is too repetitive – like 'a heartbeat' – and the deputy stage manager (Helen) is concerned about cueing this in at the same time as giving a visual cue to the fly floor. Jemilla experiments with different options and says she can take her own cue from the actor.

Create your own diary entry for the last rehearsal you attended. Include photos, sketches and details that will be helpful to look on and reflect on.

4.6 Evaluating your designs

Big question

- What features do you need to evaluate as a designer?

Starting point: Why evaluate?

Theatre is a public spectacle. It is created to be watched. By its very nature, audience members will either like or dislike the content, the way a certain actor portrays a character, the way it has been directed and the way it has been designed. People have written reviews of theatre productions for centuries. When professional theatre is reviewed, it includes all aspects of the performance. When you evaluate your work, you need to achieve both depth and breadth in covering all aspects of your work.

When you evaluate as a designer you are being self-critical, which is different from generic theatre evaluation. It is important to know the difference between the two skills of evaluating and analysing.

- To evaluate is to judge, calculate or form an idea on the quality, importance or value of something.
- To analyse is to study or examine something in detail to discover more about it in order to explain/interpret it.

Activity 1

Read these snippets from theatre reviews and decide if the comments are evaluating or analysing.

Snippet	Evaluating (✓)	Analysing (✓)
'…the billowing curtains set the scene and were an effective recurring scenic motif.'		
'…the play helps to confirm that what makes a difference is having the tools, networks and friends and/or family to help us through the maze.'		
'…the play's ability to combine comedy and tragedy, great songs with a searching examination of both the nature-vs-nurture debate and the malign role of class in society strikes me as remarkable.'		

Explore: Feedback

As a designer, you can receive feedback in the following ways:

- from actors
- from designers of the same art form
- from designers in another design area that were affected by your design (for example, how the lighting design affected you as a set designer)
- from audience members
- by watching the performance live yourself
- by watching footage
- by looking at production photos.

Activity 2

Create a questionnaire for your audience, to gather their feedback on your production. Include questions about the elements of your design that you want to ensure have been interpreted correctly and understood.

Develop: Process, review and make changes

When you are working on your design individually, remember to intermittently return to the actors in your group to review the work and ensure any changes being made are not going to impact your design. The rehearsal process allows you to observe, question and challenge ideas, as well as offer ideas to support the creative process.

The purpose of a technical rehearsal is for the operators and crew to try out the process, and for the director and design team to agree that the lighting, sound and technical elements are running satisfactorily. As a design student, you will probably be operating as well as designing, and you may take on the role of the director.

If you have made changes as a designer and you want to see how this affects the performance, you might want to run the performance **cue-to-cue**.

A dress rehearsal offers a chance to review how your changes look without stopping the run of the performance, unless essential adjustments are needed to be made. The dress run happens with actors in full costume and all technical elements operating.

> ### Key term
>
> **cue-to-cue:** from one essential cue to the next, with actors jumping ahead as required, also known as doing a 'top and tail'

Apply: Reflecting and moving forward

When reflecting on your design work, consider these key questions:

- What would you do as a designer if you had more time in the rehearsal and development process?
- Do you feel things were underdeveloped by the actors, which meant that you were restricted in what you could add?
- If you had a crew (see table to the right), what more could you have added to your design and operation during performance?
- If you had a larger budget, what other elements would you have added to your design?
- If you had the freedom to choose a different performance space or configuration, where would you set your performance?
- As a student, you only have one design element to consider. If you were in a professional production, you would have to think about how your design affects others.
- What would you do to consider the impact on others? For example, if you are devising a scene which takes place in a shoe shop and the set designer wants to have a raked stage, this would make the design/choices of shoes harder for the costume designer because health and safety would need to be considered for the actors moving on stage.

Design area	Crew roles
Lighting	Production electrician
	Lighting operator
Sound	Sound operator
Costume	Cutters/tailors
	Assistant designer
	Dressers
Set and props	Assistant designer
	Props master
	Props assistant/buyer

Activity 3

Think about a piece of recent theatre you have watched (either professional or the work of your peers). Pick a particular design aspect and write a brief paragraph on each of the following:

- What changes would you make to that design, given what you interpreted from the script?
- What would you do if the performance took place in a different configuration (for example, in the round)?
- If there were no budget restrictions, what would you add to the performance?

4.7 Apply your skills

Big question

- How can you apply your skills in other contexts?

Starting point: Designing for different genres and styles of theatre

As a designer, it is important to understand the difference between genre and style (see pages 40–44) and appreciate how the type of theatre you are working in, and the way in which a director wishes to stage it, affects a designer.

The table below outlines some examples of the genres and styles of theatre.

Genre	Style
Physical theatre: performance that tells a story through physical movement and gestures.	Naturalism/realism: portraying real life on stage with realistic set and staging.
Absurdist theatre: performance that abandons convention form to show the human struggle in a senseless world.	Epic theatre: As created by Brecht, forces the audience to constantly question and challenge what they are observing, rather than become emotionally attached.
Commedia dell'arte: a form of theatre with sketches, scenarios and masked characters based on stock characters from society.	Melodramatic: Performance that is exaggerated through the use of stereotypes.
Musical theatre: Theatre that combines music, song, dance and dialogue.	Immersive: Focusing on the audience members as individuals, concentrating on their personal opinions, emotions and immersing them in the world of the play by placing them within the performance itself (like Forum Theatre).

Activity 1

Research the following plays, then copy out this table and decide which genre of theatre they belong to.

Play	Playwright	Genre
London Road	Alecky Blythe	
Rosencrantz and Guildenstern are Dead	Tom Stoppard	
Top Girls	Caryl Churchill	

Which style of theatre do you think would most suit these genres when performed and why? For example, Come From Away, a musical written by Irene Sankoff and David Hein, is based on the true story of a small town called Gander in Newfoundland, Canada. The town housed, supported and fed 7000 stranded passengers following the closure of air space on 9/11. Its genre is musical theatre and it is performed in a minimalistic Brechtian style. The story is based on real events, so it could be argued that an immersive approach could work and include the audience in the action as members of the community.

Explore: Designing for devised and scripted performance

A devised performance is a theatrical creation where the content originates from collaborative work that is often improvised and then performed by an ensemble (see Chapter 3). A scripted performance means a play written by someone (a playwright) that is performed by others.

As a designer for devised theatre, there is one major advantage of creating original work: the audience has never seen it before so it cannot be compared to other performances of the same content. The biggest disadvantage is that, as a designer, you have to start from nothing, with just a theme or stimulus as a starting point. You will not be able to look at past productions or reviews to gather ideas.

As a designer for a scripted performance, you have been given a set of circumstances by the playwright. This helps you form the basis of your design. The biggest disadvantage is that your design can be compared to other productions and audiences have a preconceived idea of what the performance will be like.

Activity 2

Read these stage directions from Scene 3 of *Mother Courage and Her Children*:

> **Text 6**
>
> *Military camp.*
>
> *Afternoon. A flagpole with the regimental flag. From her cart,* **festooned** *now with all kinds of goods, Mother Courage has stretched a washing line to a large cannon, across which she and Kattrin are folding the washing. She is bargaining at the same time with an armourer over a sack of* **shot***. Swiss Cheese, now wearing a* **pay-master***'s uniform, is looking on.*
>
> *A* **comely** *person, Yvette Pottier, is sewing a… coloured hat… She is in her* **stockinged** *feet, having laid aside her red high-heeled boots.*

Vocabulary

festooned: adorned, decorated
shot: bullets
pay-master: someone in charge of administering wages/salary
comely: attractive
stockinged: wearing tights/stockings with no shoes

Write a list of all the given circumstances you can deduce that would have an impact on you as a designer for a performance of this script.

Develop: Adding multimedia to your design

The use of multimedia in theatre is very different to conventional theatre, with a lot for the audience to take in. With so much to look at on stage, the audience is no longer focusing on one main aspect. As an audience, you could watch a production several times and watch different aspects each time. The creativity of a piece is completely on show. Some audience members may feel this takes away some of the 'magic' of theatre. Others may feel that features, such as a fragmented stage picture or videos within the live construction of a scene, add excitement.

There are many ways to use multimedia, including:

- use of cameras, mobile phones or tablets connected through cable or Wi-Fi to give a live feed of action happening on stage
- the use of projections of live action or projected flashbacks or scenes that aren't scripted
- the use of live sound on stage created by actors.

Activity 3

Look at the image below and list all the multimedia elements you can see. From your list, decide which technical departments (lighting, sound, fly floor, stage crew) would have ownership of them.

Apply: Applying a design with wider consideration of other technical departments

Regardless of what design aspect you choose, you need to consider how the actors and other designers and technicians will be affected. For example:

- As a lighting designer, if you choose to always have blackouts in scene changes what impact does that have on the actors?

- As a sound designer, if you have sound effects that are echoes or repetitions of lines, what would you do if the actors' lines go wrong in performance?

- As a costume designer, if you choose a colour of fabric and don't show this on stage until the dress rehearsal, what would you do when the lighting design alters the colour? Often colours look different under certain lighting and different fabrics absorb light differently.

Activity 4

Choose one of the designs you have created from an activity earlier in this chapter, based on your devising work. Review this design, making a note of any factors that might affect different departments. What, if anything, might you need to change due to these considerations?

Thinking more deeply

Consider this list of some of the most highly regarded designers in the world and think more deeply about why they are so successful and what distinguishes them from their contemporaries. Pick one and undertake some research.

Designer's name	Area of design	Example show(s)	Where in the world
Peter Mumford	Lighting	*King Kong* (The Musical)	Broadway, NY, USA
Stefan Gregory	Sound	*The Resistible Rise of Arturo Ui*	Sydney, Australia
William Ivey Long	Costume	*Hairspray, Nine, The Producers*	Broadway, NY, USA
Bunny Christie	Set	*The Comedy of Errors*, National Theatre *The Wild Duck*, Almeida Theatre	London, UK

What ideas from their work could you use to influence your designs in the future?

Chapter 5

Writing about play texts

In this chapter, you will develop the skills needed to respond in writing to an extract from a play you have studied, with reference to the rest of the play. This includes identifying key elements, explaining your ideas thoughtfully, and structuring a longer written response. You will build on the skills from Chapter 2, considering the process of moving from page to stage.

5.1 Exploring an extract from a play

Big question
- How do you make sense of a given extract from a play?

Starting point: Finding a focus

In this unit, you are going to explore ways of responding to an extract from a known play. Knowing the play – and the extract – well will help you write confidently and articulately, but the key word here is 'focus'. You may need to focus on a specific character (or characters), ideas or dramatic moments and explain how you would convey a particular effect as actor, director or designer.

Activity 1

Imagine opening one of the plays you are studying and randomly placing your finger on a page. How well do you know this scene? Try it now. Where did your finger land? How familiar were the characters and events on the page? What might you be asked to focus on here?

Explore: Visualising the scene

The following extract comes from a play called *The Jungle*, which draws on real events. The script states that the scene takes place in '*a makeshift Afghan restaurant in the Jungle [...]. It is late at night, freezing cold. The restaurant is restless and busy.*' 'The Jungle' was the informal name given to the camp for refugees and migrants hoping to reach the UK that sprang up in Calais, northern France, in January 2015. The play was first performed after the camp had been demolished.

The Jungle, Joe Murphy and Joe Robertson, a National Theatre and Young Vic co-production with Good Chance Theatre (2018)

Plot summary

This extract occurs near the start of the play. There are rumours that the camp is to be closed down by the French authorities and that everyone will be evicted. The characters in this scene are a mix of volunteer workers from the UK and France, and migrants or refugees from various parts of the world. Derek and Paula (both in their 50s) and Sam (man, 18) are charity workers/helpers from the UK. The other characters here are Boxer (man in his 40s, UK), Amal (a six-year-old Syrian child), Mohammed (35, from Sudan), Salar (32, from Afghanistan) and Henri (French, in his 20s). They are speaking in the restaurant.

Text 1

Paula:	Look after Amal. (*To Amal.*) I'll be back soon, love. Stay with Uncle Boxer.
Boxer:	**Howay**, pet.
Paula:	Don't let her out of your sight. (*Handing the **census** to Derek.*) Derek, finish this off. A boy's been killed on the motorway.
Derek:	I heard.
Salar:	Who?
Paula:	I'm going to identify the body. (*She leaves. Mohammed is filling in a form for Salar.*)
Mohammed:	Salar, how many people come here?
Salar:	Everyone.
Mohammed:	What service do you provide?
Salar:	Have you tasted my rice and beans?
Mohammed:	Why is your restaurant vital to life in the Jungle?
Salar:	(*taking a framed review off the wall*) Give them that.
Mohammed:	We need to do this, Salar.
Salar:	Jungle finished. We have said it for months. Now it's true.
Henri (*to Sam*)**:**	Let's speak honestly. As friends. There isn't any more you can do here. I know you built houses. I know you helped. Now they will be destroyed and that's difficult for you, I understand.
Sam:	No more evictions. You promised me.
Henri:	Come on, you can't have thought it would last forever. Go home and rest. Be with your family. And then do something great with your life
Sam:	The Judge will rule in our favour.
Henri:	Here is the contact of my successor.
Sam:	You're leaving?
Henri:	For Paris. I would be very sad if our relationship were to end this way.

From *The Jungle* by Joe Robertson and Joe Murphy, Act 1

Vocabulary

Howay: a dialect word from the north-east of England that means 'come here', 'come on' or 'OK'

census: an official collection of people's names, where they 'live', their occupation, etc.

Activity 2

Reread the extract, considering these questions:

- Imagine the scene on stage. What sort of staging or design do you visualise? Sketch some ideas for the use of space and a possible set.
- Regardless of what you might know of the rest of the play, what do you learn about the characters or relationships from the extract? Make some notes.

Develop: Using your knowledge of the play

You need to focus on the specifics of the extract, but this will also be informed by your knowledge of a play as a whole. For example, you could draw on the play's:

- genre, style and context – how it falls within (or sits outside) particular traditions or conventions (see pages 38–45)

- design(s) – as indicated in the script, developed in production or implied by the text

- production history – when it was first staged, the critical reception it received, later productions (if relevant)

- sequence and organisation – where the scene 'sits' within the play (what has happened before and after it), and how it fits the overall **narrative arc** or **chronology** of the play

- characters – where does this scene fit as part of their journey? What relationships are being developed or exposed, broken or fixed?

Key terms

narrative arc: the rise and fall of the play's dramatic action
chronology: the time sequence of the play (time-ordered, disrupted with flashbacks, etc., over what time period)

Activity 3

Consider the style and genre of *The Jungle*, based on Text 1. Copy the grid below and tick the boxes that you feel describe the play. Use the blank boxes to add your own terms to describe it, if you can think of any. Remember that the play you study will contain clues about its genre and style, but you should consider how you might develop an interpretation from the themes and ideas in the text. For example, the extract you are responding to may not seem to draw on traditions of physical theatre, but you might still choose to emphasise physical elements in your own interpretation.

Realistic	Naturalistic	Political	Classical
Physical	Stylised	Docu-drama	Modern/contemporary
Poetic	Colloquial	Historical	Symbolic
Epic			

Activity 4

What evidence in the extract makes you select the terms you ticked and/ or added in Activity 3? Here, two students discuss the play:

Ajay

This is a political drama which draws on traditions of epic or political plays from Brecht onwards. It is based on real events, decisions made by governments or authorities that affect ordinary people. Like, the references to the 'census', 'Judge' and the conflict between those who have nothing and those in power.

Maria

I get that, but I think this is a character-driven, naturalistic drama too. There's evidence of a relationship betrayed between Sam and Henri, isn't there? 'You promised me', he says.

Do you agree with Ajay or Maria? Can both be right? Is it possible to draw out one or the other in the way the dialogue is played? Discuss this in pairs, making sure you explain your ideas clearly.

You might be asked to explain how you would perform a specific role in order to convey your interpretation of that character. Remember, to do this you need to:

- decide on your interpretation of that character
- work out how you could convey this.

Activity 5

Work with a partner to rehearse the lines between Henri (a government worker) and Sam (a young, affluent student from the UK, who helps organise the building of temporary homes in 'the jungle'). How would you draw out the personal relationship between the two men? Consider the following:

- What particular ways of speaking or tones would you use? Would they speak in the same way?

- What gestures or movements could you introduce? How could you use space/proxemics? For example, might Sam turn away, or come close to Henri?

- What interpretation of each character does this lead to? For example, could you play Henri as cold and distant and Sam as feeling betrayed? Or could Henri be presented as a brotherly figure and Sam as a younger, wayward child? What other ideas do you have?

Make some notes in response to these questions. You could sketch out the use of space in this scene, perhaps showing how or where characters stand or move at various points.

Apply: Staging the scene

This scene is rich with potential for staging, directing or acting. You will need to feel confident in exploring your own approaches in one of these areas.

Activity 6

Look at this photograph from the first production of *The Jungle*. What does the staging, design and overall style (note one of the actors is sitting eating alongside the audience) suggest about the approach the director wanted to convey in this production? Would you take the same approach? Why or why not? Write 75–100 words, noting down how you might stage the scene.

The Jungle, Joe Murphy and Joe Robertson, a National Theatre and Young Vic co-production with Good Chance Theatre (2018)

Reflection point

The Jungle was written after the camp was dismantled in 2016 and the migrants and refugees living there moved to centres around France. How would knowledge of the real outcome affect how this early scene of the play is viewed by audiences? To what extent are any of the plays you are studying dependent or changed by the audience knowing the broad outcome – either because the events are based on real ones, or because the playwright has signposted what will happen?

5.2 Responding to the extract

Big question

- How do you explain your intentions when writing about an extract?

Starting point: What is 'intention'?

'Intention' refers to your purpose – what you set out to achieve through the way you perform, direct or design a dramatic piece. For example, you might say, 'I want this moment to shock the audience' or 'I wish to change the mood from one of despair to hope'. From studying your own play, you should already have an overall **conceptualisation** of it, but when focusing on an extract, you will need to pinpoint exactly how it will be achieved. One common conceptualisation of plays is to see them as the struggle of an individual against the forces of Fate – as in a classical tragedy (see page 40). This might foreground the psychological motivations of a specific character. A contrasting vision would foreground more general ideas – for example, the suffering of a whole community – or challenge an audience to consider issues from the past or present, such as the causes of war or the role of women in society.

(see page 40)

Key term

conceptualisation: a vision of how the whole play should be interpreted on stage, drawing out particular themes or ideas

---

Activity 1

Think about the play you are studying. Are you exploring a particular conceptualisation? Make brief notes and share ideas in pairs or groups. How might this conceptualisation affect how you write about a particular scene?

Explore: Encountering an extract

You are now going to read a further extract from *The Jungle*. This extract is from the end of Act 1 and the beginning of Act 2. It starts just as the violent destruction of the refugee camp has begun. The setting continues to be the restaurant.

Plot summary

The Jungle opens with an aid worker telling some of the inhabitants of the camp, who have gathered in a makeshift restaurant, that the French authorities are going to evict them. Initially, the eviction is intended to be a 'soft' one (no bulldozers) but by this scene, it has become clear that force will be used. A sub-plot is also developing: a teenage migrant, known by many of the camp members, has died trying to reach Britain. Sam and Beth are two young students from the UK who have been helping at the camp. Safi is a refugee.

Case study:
Interpreting political topics

Plays like *The Jungle*, which are based on a specific political or cultural moment, vary in their form and approach. For example, Gillian Slovo's *The Riots*, about violent disturbances and protests in London in 2011, interweaves spoken evidence from trials and inquiries to create a narrative. The speakers are actors, but the words are those of real people, including some well-known politicians. David Hare's play *The Permanent Way* (2003), about UK government policy with regard to the railways, does a similar thing. Going back further, Wole Soyinka's play *Death and the King's Horseman* (1975) is based on a real incident that took place during British colonial rule in the 19th century, while in Aeschlyus's *The Persians* (472 BCE), the focus of the drama is the defeat of Xerxes's navy at Salamis in around 480 BCE. You will consider the features of political theatre in more detail in Chapter 6.

Activity 2

As you read, consider the following questions:

- As an actor, how would you perform the role of Safi here, in order to convey your interpretation of his character to the audience?

- As a director, how would you direct the actors in these related scenes? What effects would you wish to create?

- As a designer, how would you use one or more design elements to create a setting which would convey your ideas/intentions?

Text 2

Sam:	Beth, come on!
Beth:	I can't.
Sam:	We have to go now!

*A **CRS** Officer enters in full riot gear, stares at them both.*

CRS Officer:	**Bouges-toi!**
Beth:	I won't move.
CRS Officer:	Don't understand you, girl.
Beth:	I'm not leaving him here. I can't leave, I'll never leave.
CRS Officer:	You are in France, you speak French!

Beth stands and faces him.

Beth:	Look at yourself! This is not France!

*The Officer aims a pepper spray canister into her eyes. Safi walks calmly into the **pandemonium**.*

Safi:	Stop.

Vocabulary

CRS: Compagnies Républicaines de Sécurité, specialist French riot police
Bouges-toi!: Move yourself!
pandemonium: wild or noisy confusion

TWO: THE BIRTH (continued from page 143)

In peace and quiet, he addresses everyone.

Safi:	They warned us in Libya. The smugglers. They advised us about safe passage. How to stay hidden, avoid arrest. And one thing they say to me, again and again, I remember…
	'Beware the French. They have absolutely no manners.'
	My name is Safi Al-Hussain, thirty-five years young. Former student of English literature and languages in my home town, Aleppo, so I know a little bit about telling stories.
	Another quotation for you. 'If you open me up when I am dead, you will find Calais engraved upon my heart.'
	One of your queens said that. Is it true for you? Maybe because your armies fought over Calais for so many centuries, which is bizarre to me – have you ever been there?! Or maybe, if you like history, it is because you know Julius Caesar invaded you from Calais in 54 BC. […]
	Open me up. You'll find it there, engraved upon my heart. Like many before me, I lived there to get here. And it takes pain to live side by side. If you are born in the same country as another person this is true. If you are born in a different country, a different continent, even more. Some people will tell you it is easy, but you mustn't trust them. These are difficult things, my friends. I do not pretend we did not make mistakes.
	And many more will be made in the telling of this story, I am sure. March 2015 is the date of birth.

Salar and Mohammed meet. They are cleaner, more awake, looking years younger.

Mohammed:	What a dump.
Safi:	Mohammed Abboud. From Darfur.
Mohammed:	This is the worst place in Europe.
Salar:	Tonight we will be free.
Mohammed:	If we live that long.
Salar:	They said this land is ours to use. We can build here!
Safi:	Salar Malikzai. From Karz, near Kandahar.

More people enter, carrying bags, tents and sleeping bags.

Mohammed:	Let's count the things that kill us. Chemicals, snakes, the filthy land, all rubbish –
Salar:	Is better than bombs, Mohammed.
Mohammed:	Cold, wind, rain –

From *The Jungle* by Joe Robertson and Joe Murphy, Acts 1–2

Vocabulary

One of your queens: a reference to Mary I who, on her deathbed in 1558, is said to have lamented the loss of Calais, previously governed by the English

Develop: Exploring intentions

A student has made these initial notes about Safi in planning a response.

> **Safi – role and voice**
>
> - like a narrator? He introduces Salar and Mohammed
> - goes back to earlier time when camp was started
> - 'freezes the action' in order to tell the story of the past
> - monologue – directed at audience 'for you' – breaks fourth wall by speaking directly to the audience
> - like a traditional prologue? (even though this scene occurs after the opening scene in which we find out the 'Jungle' is to be demolished)

Key term

mode of speech: a particular form or style of speaking (reflective, narrative, questioning, etc.)

Activity 3

In small groups, prepare a short performance of the scene. Focus on three key elements:

- Safi's initial entrance: What effect do you wish to create? How does he speak? Who is he addressing 'Stop' to? (Just the actors? Or is it a wider comment about the action on stage – if so, what else might be going on?) What happens when he says 'Stop'? Do actors freeze? Leave the stage?
- Safi's monologue: Is his intention the same here? Or are you looking to create new effects? What different **modes of speech** does he use? Is his speech all of one tone and style or might it change? (For example, there is his own history – who he is, where he comes from; then there is the section about British history and Calais; finally, there is the sense of regret, of looking back.)
- Safi as chorus/narrator, going back in time, introducing Mohammed and Salar: How might the delivery of his lines here be different? For new effect(s), or in order to confirm the way the audience have seen him so far?

You could discuss these issues before you begin working on the scene. Or, try staging the scene to see what arises, then discuss how it could be adapted or altered to bring out various ideas about Safi and the effects you wish to create.

Activity 4

Once you have worked through the performance, note down the interpretation you feel works best. As before, you might wish to sketch out any supporting details about movements, or annotate a copy of the script with your ideas. Think about the following:

- What vocabulary could you use to describe your interpretation of Safi's performance?

- Which, if any, of the words in the box below could you apply to different words, phrases or parts of the performance of the actor playing Safi? For example: 'Safi walks calmly into the pandemonium' – the stage direction might suggest Safi is omniscient (all-knowing), as if he is able to stop time and look at things with hindsight and experience.

- Are there others you could add?

still	jokey	passionate	energised	reflective	cynical	knowing
distant	observing	omniscient	passive	challenging	disturbing	
plain-speaking	mysterious	engaging	collaborative	aggressive		

After you have made notes about the particular aspect in the extract, you will need to organise your thoughts into a clear response. One way of structuring a response about Safi in the extract would be to follow the order you worked on when rehearsing the scene:

- paragraph 1: locating the scene – general information about where the scene falls in the play, and about Safi's overall role.
- paragraphs 2–3: Safi's initial entrance – what you are trying to convey?
- paragraphs 4–5: Safi's monologue – developing this idea or shifting to a new aspect.
- paragraphs 6–7: Safi's role as chorus/narrator – further development or confirmation of your overall conceptualisation of Safi, or a new aspect you wish to bring out.

Reflection point

Consider how you might situate this moment in Safi's overall journey in the play. Where does it stand in terms of what we learn about him and what will be revealed as the play progresses?

Now think about the play you are studying. Choose a scene at random and pick one of the main characters in it. Where does this moment come in that character's development across the play? Are they in a moment of crisis, of revelation, of rising or descending status, of self-awareness, or something else?

Apply: Structuring an explanation of dramatic intention

A student has begun a response to the extract from a performance perspective, explaining their intentions. This might be part of Paragraph 2 from the plan above.

> Safi's performance begins with a moment of high drama as he steps in to halt a violent act of oppression. In 'freezing' the drama, he sets himself apart. Although he will be a participant in the events, here he acts as a kind of omniscient, traditional Chorus – stepping outside time and action to comment on events, informing the audience he will be 'telling […] this story'. By taking centre stage – using an upright, firm posture and standing perhaps between the CRS officer and Beth – he should demand our attention as the narrative voice in a modern tragedy. In this way, the extract can be seen to move from a realistic mode to a more stylised one, a switch which occurs at other points in the drama

understanding of the dramatic action on stage

reference to dramatic tradition and desired intention

supporting reference from passage

reference to use of space and body shape

understanding of intention and play at this point

comment on an overall conceptualisation

Activity 5

Using a similar structure, write the fourth paragraph of the response. Focus on how Safi might speak as he delivers his monologue. Continue this paragraph from this point.

Start with a point about how Safi speaks as the monologue begins:

Safi's first line, 'They warned us in Libya'…

Continue with an explanation of how this might link to where he stands:

As an actor, I would position myself…

Give a reason for this:

Because I want my posture to suggest…

Add the effect you would hope to create (the intention):

The effect should be to…

And add something about how this might be enhanced by how the rest of the ensemble stand or move:

The rest of the ensemble should be…

For example, the CRS officer and Beth might…

Finish with a concluding sentence about the style you hope to create:

Conceptually, the feel of the monologue at this point should be…

5.3 Generating ideas for sections from a whole play

Big question
- How do you demonstrate your understanding of a play as a whole?

Starting point: Knowing a play's action, tone and context

You need to know the play you are studying extremely well so that when you write about it you can draw on your knowledge quickly and accurately. Some understanding of the play will be relatively basic – what happens to whom, and at what point, for example, or why someone changes the way they behave at different points. However, you will need to build a fuller picture than this. How do different scenes or acts vary in location or setting? How might one scene contrast with the next? Are you aware of a particular change in tone or mood as the play progresses – for example, from optimism to despair or from order to chaos?

Activity 1

Quickly select two scenes from the play you are studying that:
- mirror each other in some way (for example, scenes between parents and children or with similar forms – a negotiation, interrogation, etc.) *or*
- feature the same character/s but in contrasting circumstances.

In pairs, discuss the two scenes you have selected and the links/contrasts between them. Say what effect or intention the playwright might have had in the two scenes.

Dialogue can often be categorised into a number of different types or styles, regardless of the situation. For example, one character in a relationship might interrogate the other about their feelings, or a court might question someone accused of a crime about their motives. Equally, a negotiation might take place between the two people in a relationship about what one might gain by being with the other. Plays might also feature inserted narratives or recounts – a character telling a story about the past or characters summarising what has happened, as Safi does in *The Jungle*.

Activity 2

Working in pairs, improvise two short scenes, lasting no more than a minute, where one person visits another in a hospital. The first should take the form of an interrogation (this does not mean it has to be a criminal interrogation – it could be 'What were you doing skiing in the dark?', for example). The second should be a negotiation (for example, 'I want to leave hospital now'/'You can't').

Explore: Exploring how to perform a role

You may be asked to consider fairly open questions about the play you are studying. For example:

- As a director, how would you direct your ensemble in two or three linked or separate sections of the play in order to achieve your intended effects for the audience?

- As a set designer, how would you use design elements to create an appropriate setting for the action of *The Jungle*?

However, some questions might specify a particular effect or aspect to highlight:

- How would you perform the role of Safi in two separate sections from the play in order to engage the sympathies of your audience?

The following two extracts have been chosen by a student who is studying Anton Chekhov's classic naturalist play *The Cherry Orchard*. The student is exploring a question about how someone would perform the role of Madame Ranevsky to engage the sympathies of the audience. Read the first extract carefully on your own.

Plot summary

The play begins on a spring morning in the so-called 'nursery' of Madame Lyubov Ranevsky's ancestral home, in Russia just at the beginning of the 20th century. She has been living with a lover in France for five years, ever since her young son drowned. Having tried to kill herself, she has been brought home by her 17-year-old daughter Anya and her governess. Yasha, her valet in France, has returned with her. They have been met at the station by Gayev (Mme Ranevsky's brother), Varya (Madame Ranevsky's adopted daughter), who has been running the estate, and Firs, the old butler/servant at the house. Madame Ranevsky has returned because of the family's debts. The estate is to be sold at auction unless a solution can be found.

Spotlight on practitioner: **Anton Chekhov 1860–1904**

Anton Chekhov was a highly-influential Russian dramatist who also wrote short stories. His plays often dramatise the clash of Tsarist 'Old Russia', with its ordered system of nobility and serfs, with new, young emerging ideas and the growing middle class. His most famous works include *The Seagull* (1896), *Three Sisters* (1901) and the play you will explore in this chapter, *The Cherry Orchard* (1904).

Extract A

In this scene, Madame Ranevsky has returned from Moscow to the family house. The family face huge debts and a solution is needed.

Varya: I ought to check the luggage is all there. (*Leaves*)

Mme Ranevsky: Is this really me, sitting here like this? (*Excited*) Oh, I feel like… dancing, I feel like dancing! If it's a dream, don't waken me. Because… I love this place. I love it so much I couldn't see it properly from the train. For tears. (*Pause*) Coffee. (*She drains the cup.*) Thank you, Firs, thank you, dear old man. It's good you still live.

Firs: Not yesterday. Day before.

Gayev: But deaf.
FIRS mumbles his way to the coffee table.

Lopakhin: (*Checking watch.*) I have to catch a train to Kharkov in an hour. Pity. I wanted a good look at you. And a talk. (*Pause*) You're as magnificent as ever.

Pischik: And even more beautiful. ***A la mode***, is it? I swear my heart's not stopped pounding like a race horse's since she arrived.

Lopakhin: (*Slight awkwardness.*) Your brother here, Leon, says I'm a **boor**, a **kulak**, but it doesn't hurt me. He's welcome to his opinion. All I ask is that you trust me as before, hold me in the same regard as before. My father was **serf** to yours and to his father, too. But you've done so much for me, you've helped me forget all that… history… and love you as my own sister. More, perhaps.

MME RANEVSKY stands, cup in hands, crosses to the table, where FIRS laboriously pours another cup of coffee.

Mme Ranevsky: I can't sit still, forgive me. (*Paces room a little, touching things. Laughs suddenly.*) This happiness is insufferable. Laugh if you like, I know it's silly. (*She presses the bookcase with her cheek.*) My own bookcase. (*Strokes table.*) My own table. (*Kisses it.*)

Gayev: Nurse died while you were away.

Mme Ranevsky: Yes, I know. May she rest in God's arms. They wrote me.
Crosses to her seat, coffee in hands.

Gayev: Anastasi died too. Oh, and Peter… erm… the one with the squint… handed in his notice. He's joined the police force.
Takes a box of sweets from his pocket, removes one, sucks it.

Plot summary

Pischik is a friend of Madame Ranevsky's – an elderly nobleman who is constantly in debt. Lopakhin is a successful businessman, but he is conscious of his lower social class, and that his family once worked for the Ranevskys. Varya is said to have come from 'simple people', so one can assume her parents were once serfs, like Lopakhin's, so her social status is probably more like that of a governess, rather than a 'real' aristocratic daughter.

Vocabulary

A la mode: fashionable
boor: a thug or brute
kulak: a prosperous farmer
serf: a labourer, bound to their master's estate

Pischik:	My daughter… Dashenka… sends her… regards.
Lopakhin:	Mme Ranevsky is right, this is no time for gloom. Let me cheer you up with this. (*Checking watch.*) There isn't time for a full discussion – I can't miss my train – but here it is in essence. The cherry orchard is down to be sold by auction to pay off your debts. This much you know. Now, the date of the auction has been set for August the twenty-second. (*MME RANEVSKY puts down her cup suddenly.*)
	But you can go to your bed tonight and dream pleasant dreams, because there's a way out. Now listen. Your land is less than twenty miles from town and near the railway, right? If the orchard and the land by the river were to be parcelled up into plots and leased out for weekend cottages, you'd have a per annum yield of twenty-five or even thirty thousand. What about that!
Gayev:	Bloody nonsense. Absolute bloody… (*He internalises his thought suddenly.*)
Mme Ranevsky:	I'm not sure I understand… what you're saying, Mr…

From Trevor Griffiths' adaptation of *The Cherry Orchard* by Anton Chekhov, Act 1

The Cherry Orchard, directed by Neil Austin, National Theatre (2011)

Vocabulary

ballroom: a grand room designed for a ball – a large party with dancing
Eschew: avoid or reject

Plot summary

Extract B takes place in Act 3 towards the end of the play during a party at the house with music, dancing and magic tricks. Trofimov had been teasing Varya about her non-relationship with Lopakhin, and denying his own with Anya, Madame Ranevsky's 17-year-old daughter. Varya has left, and they now await the arrival of Gayev and Lopakhin with news about the sale of the estate. Note that 'Liuba' is Mme Ranevsky.

Activity 3

Why might a student have chosen this scene as one that was suitable for portraying Madame Ranevsky as a sympathetic figure?

Now read the second extract the student chose. Is Madame Ranevsky presented equally sympathetically here? What specific lines or phrases might an audience respond to?

Extract B

In this scene, Trofimov, an idealistic young man who was tutor to Madame Ranevsky's son, is trying to reassure her about the sale of the house and orchard. They are in a room adjacent to the **ballroom** *where a party is taking place.*

Mme Ranevsky:	Where's Leon! All I want to know is: have I been sold or not? I suppose all… disasters are incomprehensible; I don't know what to think, I seem… lost somehow. I feel like screaming or something even more banal and stupid. (*Turning to TROFIMOV.*) Help me. Say something. Please.

She's distraught, under the effort of control. TROFIMOV takes her by the arm, restores her to her chair, squats beside her.

Trofimov:	(*Distinctly*): Liuba. It doesn't matter. Sold or not sold, it has no meaning now. That's all in the past; finished with long ago. The fields have reclaimed the thin road you travelled. Be easy now. **Eschew**… self-deceptions. For perhaps the first time in your life, you're allowed to stare truth frankly in the face.

continued

Mme Ranevsky: Truth? What's that? Perhaps you can see it, your eyes are young. I look and I see nothing. Such confidence you have, Peter – is there a problem in the world you can't solve? But think about it: isn't it only that none of the problems you solve has ever really touched you; hurt you. When you look so… bravely to the future, isn't it only that you haven't had experience to make you fearful. You're braver, deeper, honester than any of us, but you lack… generosity, you lack consideration. Just think a little more about *us*, Peter, just a little, mm? I was born here, and my father, and his father before him. I love it, this place, house, orchard; without them, there's no meaning to my life. I'd sooner be sold *with* them than left without them.

She takes TROFIMOV's head in her hands, kisses him on the forehead.

It's where my son was drowned. Here. Give me some pity, dear, loving friend.

Trofimov: I sympathise deeply, you know that.

Mme Ranevsky: (*Pushing him away rather violently.*) Then why can't you say it differently? Differently!

From Trevor Griffiths' adaptation of *The Cherry Orchard* by Anton Chekhov, Act 3

Case study:
Productions of *The Cherry Orchard*

For most of the 20th century, Chekhov's work was perceived as a sort of nostalgia for a Russia that disappeared, and the dilemmas facing the new middle classes with their 'new money'. The first production, directed by Stanislavski (see page 47) in 1904, approached the play as a tragedy. But Chekhov was unhappy at this portrayal, feeling it ignored farcical and comic elements, and the fierce strength of several characters. Trevor Griffiths, whose adaptation of the play you are reading here, does not present the play as a universal experience (one in which the audience and characters share the same plight). He suggests it needs to be seen as a political play of its time. You will need to decide your own interpretation of it.

Activity 4

Read both scenes carefully again – this time in small groups. Discuss how you might perform this to highlight Madame Ranevsky as a sympathetic character. Consider:

- how she speaks and moves; any specific gestures she makes; how she reacts and responds to others
- how this links to the intended effect: 'sympathies' – feelings of understanding, sadness, pity – on the audience.

In order to generate specific ideas, start with any obvious clues or information the playwright gives. For example, the same student has noted some references from the first scene:

Aspects of performance	Extract A	Extract B
Voice	(i) Is this really me, sitting here like this? (*Excited*) (ii) Thank you, Firs, thank you, dear old man.	(i) I seem… lost somehow.
Body, movement, space	(i) (*Paces room a little, touching things.*) (ii) (*She presses the bookcase with her cheek.*)	

Activity 5

Copy and complete the table, adding further references. Use your learning from Chapter 2 about how an actor uses physical and vocal skills to develop a role.

- From Extract A, add evidence you could use to develop ideas about how to perform the role of Madame Ranevsky. Remember: you are looking for any clues the playwright has given about how she might act.

- Then look closely at Extract B. The table already mentions her response to Trofimov, who has urged her to seek the truth. What other clues can you find that might help portray her sympathetically? (Think about what she says about her son, the orchard, and how she interacts physically with Trofimov.)

The Cherry Orchard, directed by Tim Mitchell, Birmingham Repertory Theatre (2010)

Develop: Broadening your ideas

You could build a response just around the references you have identified, but it is better to develop ideas around the rest of the scene you have selected. The text you are studying may not give any of the clues that Chekhov provides in *The Cherry Orchard*, so your response might be entirely based on your own knowledge and ideas. As you have seen, these performance possibilities fall into two broad categories (what Madame Ranevsky says and how she behaves), but within those two categories are many further possibilities. Look again at Chapter 2, on performance skills, and consider the more detailed opportunities. These might include:

Voice: What is her tone, pace of delivery? Does she leave pauses, or hesitate? What emphasis does she give certain words or phrases? How quickly does she respond to what others say? Does she leave silences or spaces before speaking? If so, where?	**Body:** What posture does she adopt? How does she use her mouth and eyes? Where or at whom does she look and for how long? Does she address any lines directly to the audience or to individual characters? Does she smile, grimace, purse her lips?
Movement: Does she move quickly or slowly around the stage? Does her movement change between lines or scenes (for example, one scene, anxiously moving about, and in the other still and focused)? How does she use her hands?	**Space:** Where does she stand in relation to other characters (her proximity to others)? How does she use personal space? She clearly comes close up to Trofimov when she takes his head in her hands. However at other points, does she stand close to him, or on the other side of the room?

Activity 6

What other aspects can you add to the table?

Here, a student has made some notes around one of Madame Ranevsky's lines.

Quotation

- 'This happiness is insufferable. Laugh if you like, I know it's silly.'

Interpretation or intention

- She says she is happy, but conversely states it is 'insufferable', which suggests she is in pain. The happiness arises from returning to her family home but is tainted with the knowledge that it cannot last.

- She says they (the family) can 'laugh' if they want to, but perhaps she feels mocked? Is this someone who is teetering on the edge of a nervous breakdown? Or is it simply that she is the only one who feels so profoundly about the house?

Performance possibility

- She does not smile when she says she is 'happy'. Instead, her face creases as if wincing, perhaps placing her hand on her heart as if to control the pain. The word 'insufferable' should be emphasised, drawn out as if the word itself is painful.

- When she says, 'Laugh if you like', she stares at the others, slightly accusingly, challenging them to find her amusing. She stands with her back to the bookcase, as if defending it.

Activity 7

Now do the same for one of the references you have included in your table.

- Select the reference.
- Decide on an interpretation for Madame Ranevsky. This could be to continue the idea of her as depressive or anxious (as suggested in the example above), or as simply sad and mournful, or some other characterisation.
- Suggest some performance ideas to accompany the reference, drawing on the details listed.

Case study:
The Taming of the Shrew, Royal Shakespeare Company, 1995

Some companies employ movement specialists who work with a cast to explore a role through body shaping, dance patterns, and so on. In the Royal Shakespeare Company's production of *The Taming of the Shrew* in 1995, movement director Emma Rice worked with the actor playing Petruchio to develop the idea of him as a 'trickster' – someone who couldn't be trusted, a slippery, manipulative figure. One idea was to have him stand side-on, thus denying the audience a full view of him, as if to suggest you could never get the complete picture of him as a person. (Production images are available online.)

Apply: Generating ideas from two scenes

Reread Extracts A and B and note down five key ideas in each extract about how you would perform the role of Madame Ranevsky to engage the audience's sympathies. You can reuse some of the ideas you have identified that arise from the clues given by Chekhov, but try to include two or three ideas that do not come from 'obvious' evidence in the text.

You could record these ideas in several ways. One would be to create two spider diagrams, like the examples below.

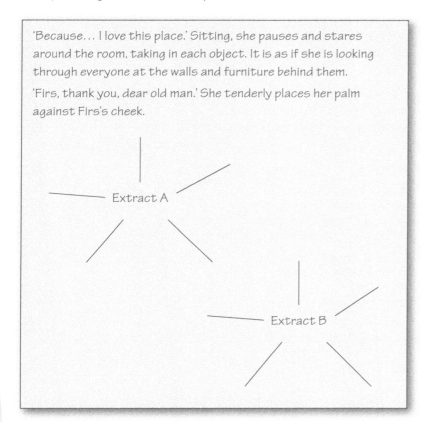

'Because... I love this place.' Sitting, she pauses and stares around the room, taking in each object. It is as if she is looking through everyone at the walls and furniture behind them.

'Firs, thank you, dear old man.' She tenderly places her palm against Firs's cheek.

Extract A

Extract B

Once you have your two diagrams of ideas (or lists, if you prefer) try to identify any common ideas in the way you present Madame Ranevsky. Can the tenderness of the first scene for Firs be carried through to her treatment of Trofimov in Extract B?

Finish by writing a sentence or two about your portrayal of Madame Ranevsky that could form a theme on which to base your ideas. For example, you might see her as someone damaged and on the verge of a breakdown, or as stronger but blind to the realities of the situation.

Reflection point

Select any main character from one of the plays you are studying. Choose two sections of the play in which your character shows either weakness or strength. Create your own spider diagrams, each with five points about how that character could be performed to show one of these two character traits.

5.4 Structure and analysis

Big question

- How do you turn your ideas into a structured analysis?

Starting point: Revisiting your ideas

In this unit, you will organise the ideas you developed in Unit 5.3, to create a coherent response to a task that asks you about a whole play.

Activity 1

In terms of a written response, 'structure' can refer to the order and sequence in which you present your ideas, but it can also refer to *how* you link your ideas within or between paragraphs. With a partner, discuss which aspects of structuring an essay you think are particularly challenging, and which you feel confident about.

Explore: Different ways of structuring a response

You may be asked to respond to a whole text, or write about two or three sections you have chosen or that have been chosen for you. Whatever the style of question, you may need to select specific moments to illustrate your ideas. An effective structure of such a response requires:

- reasonably equal coverage of your two or three selected scenes
- evidence that you have addressed the different aspects of the task
- supporting references and selected quotations.

One structure would be to tackle each scene in turn. For example:

- introduction
- part 1 of response: *The Cherry Orchard*, Act 1 – Madame Ranevsky, Lopakhin and rest of cast
- part 2 of response: *The Cherry Orchard*, Act 3 – Madame Ranevsky and Trofimov
- conclusion.

The advantages of this are that it is clear what you are writing about and when. You are also more likely to give equal attention to the two parts.

Activity 2

What *disadvantages* to this approach can you think of? You could consider:

- links and connections between the scenes
- contrasts or changing dynamics.

An alternative approach would be to deal with aspects of Madame Ranevsky's performance and consider how these might apply across both scenes. For example:

- introduction
- part 1a of response: use of voice
- part 1b of response: use of body
- part 2a of response: movement and gesture
- part 2b of response: space and proxemics, etc.
- conclusion.

The advantages of this are it ensures you focus on the performance aspects and you are likely to cover a wide ranges of approaches.

However, you may end up 'jumping' between scenes or sections, which might confuse a reader unless you can clarify your reasons for doing so.

Develop: Developing from a basic structure

Using the first structure, you might organise your points as follows.

Introduction:

- How the two scenes show Madame Ranevsky at different points in the action (firstly, her arrival at the house; secondly, awaiting news about the auction) and how this might affect your interpretation of her role.

Main paragraphs:

First half

- Act 1: Madame Ranevsky's initial appearance: how she emphasises particular words or phrases – 'dancing', 'love'; how she interacts with Firs.

- Act 1: how she responds to Lopakhin – when she '*stands*' and '*crosses to the table*' – perhaps using gesture to acknowledge his kind words, establishing eye contact.

- Act 1: when she moves around the room; how her affection for the room is conveyed – her timing, energy; the architecture of the space and how she responds to it.

- Act 1: her response to the suggestion to cut down the cherry orchard, when she says, 'I'm not sure I understand...' How the shock registers in her facial expression, her tone, speech volume, and so on.

Second half

- Act 3: the anxiety she demonstrates while waiting for the auction results; how she moves as she says 'I seem… lost somehow'; how spatial levels change when she is physically collapsing.

- Act 3: how she responds to Trofimov's words – about the house/ orchard having 'no meaning', perhaps shrinking back, change in breathing, use of pauses, realising she does not want to 'stare truth frankly in the face'.

- Act 3: her long speech to Trofimov; the gloom or despondency of her tone of voice; the vehement emphasis when she says about the house/orchard that she would 'sooner be sold *with* them'. How her stance or posture might draw attention to the drowning of her son.

- Act 3: how the audience can be made to sympathise when she pushes Trofimov away.

Conclusion:

- The overall intention about Madame Ranevsky you wish to convey.

Activity 3

Fill in your own ideas using the second structure, choosing moments in one or both scenes to exemplify how Madame Ranevsky should be played. You might want to look back over any notes you made in the previous unit.

- introduction: The general impression you wish to make with your performance

- paragraphs 1–2: use of voice (selected examples across both scenes)

- paragraphs 3–4: use of body and gesture (selected examples across both scenes)

- paragraphs 5–6: movement (selected examples across both scenes)

- paragraphs 7–8: space and proxemics, and so on (selected examples across both scenes)

- conclusion: summing up how these contribute to the sympathy you wish to evoke.

Another key aspect of structure is how you shape specific points within paragraphs in order to analyse in detail. You need to ensure you:

- make your core ideas or points clear

- support them with reference to the extract or extracts you have selected

- analyse the reference and how it might shape your performance idea

- link or develop the analysis to fit with the overall interpretation or intention you wish to convey.

Look at this analytical paragraph from a student writing about the opening to Extract A from *The Cherry Orchard*.

I would try to engage the audience's sympathies from my first appearance in Act 1 as I sit in the chair sipping the coffee brought to me by Firs. I think the words, 'Is this really me, sitting here like this?' should not be spoken to anyone in particular, but as if to herself, the emphasis falling on the word, 'me' to stress the disbelief that she is home. Additionally, I think Madame Ranevsky's posture would be to sit back in the chair, as if relishing the comfort and embrace of her own furniture; she might even run her hands up and down the sides of the armchair as if questioning whether it is real or not.

(annotations)

- establishes the exact moment in the scene
- apt reference selected
- analysis leads to performance idea
- connective indicating linked idea to come
- suggested performance idea
- explains intention
- further linked performance idea

Activity 4

Write the next paragraph from the same response. You do not need to add three performance ideas, as in the model above, but try to begin with one idea and add one more linked point to show you are thinking about the overall effect you wish to create. Use the following reference and at least two of the listed performance ideas below.

Point in scene:

• Madame Ranevsky has stood up and is moving around the room.

Reference:

• 'This happiness is insufferable. Laugh if you like, I know it's silly.'

Performance ideas:

• She makes a gesture of some sort to accompany these words.

• Her facial expression indicates either her suffering or her happiness.

• Her ensemble awareness – the way she moves or responds to others' movements (or stillness).

• Her tone and breathing indicate her state of mind.

Overall interpretation/intention:

• To show her happy? Sad? Regretful? Excited?

For example, you could consider how a repeated gesture could become a **motif** for a character. What repeated gesture could Madame Ranevsky make, both in this scene and the second, which would emphasise an aspect of her character? Could she dab her brow with a handkerchief or fan herself at moments of intense feeling?

Now write your paragraph. Begin:

When Madame Ranevsky has finished her coffee, and has stood up, she…

> ### Key term
> **motif:** a recurring idea in a play

Apply: Crafting your own response

Now draft a response using your own ideas.

Activity 5

Look at these three quotations from *The Cherry Orchard*:

• '(*Turning to TROFIMOV.*) Help me. Say something. Please.'
• 'I love it, this place, house, orchard; without them, there's no meaning to my life. I'd sooner be sold *with* them than left without them.'
• 'It's where my son was drowned. Here. Give me some pity, dear, loving friend.'

Choose one of the quotations and craft a paragraph drawing on your own ideas about how the role should be performed. These all come from Extract B, so you could begin with a connective to create a link with the first extract. Begin:

In a similar way/In contrast/We can also see how, the audience's sympathies are engaged in Extract B when…

> ### Reflection point
> Although Madame Ranevsky is not a character you are studying from your own play, think about the ideas you have had. Are there any that are transferable to your characters? Any gestures, ways of speaking, and so on?

5.5 Apply your skills

Big question

- How do you plan and write a response to an extract from a play?

Understand the task

You may come across a range of tasks on the extract from the play you have studied. Here are some examples of tasks based on *The Jungle* extract from earlier in the unit (Text 2, pages 143–144).

> *What effects would you wish to create for the audience through your direction of the actors at selected moments from the extract? Explain how you will achieve your intentions.*

> *As a designer, how would you use design elements to create an appropriate setting for the action of the extract? Refer to one or more of the following design elements in your answer: set, lighting, sound.*

> *How would you perform the role of Safi in the extract, in order to create sympathy in the audience?*

> *What effects would you wish to create for the audience through your direction of the actors at selected moments from the extract? Explain how you will achieve your intentions.*

> *The original production of The Jungle was a piece of immersive theatre. As a director, how would you use selected moments from the extract to immerse the audience in the play's action?*

Reread Text 2 on pages 139–140, then look at this example of an extract-style question:

> How would you perform the role of Safi, in the extract, in order to convey your interpretation of his character to the audience?

You are being asked to:

- focus on performance skills
- write about the character of Safi
- focus on the extract (though you might bring in supporting detail from the rest of the play)
- write about your own ideas (how you see his character)
- comment on the effect of your performance on the audience.

yellow:	particular skills to explore
green:	who you are focusing on, and what you have to do – interpret
blue:	the specific part of the play
purple:	additional aspect – the effect

Gather ideas and evidence

Annotate a copy of the text, with some initial ideas.

- Safi's initial entrance (from 'Beth: Look at yourself! This is not France!' to 'Safi: Stop').
- First part of Safi's monologue (from 'They warned us in Libya…' to '… about telling stories').
- Second part of monologue (from 'Another quotation for you…' to 'March 2015 is the date of birth').
- Third part – Safi as narrator (from 'Salar and Mohammed enter' to 'Cold, wind, rain').

Remember to select key lines, phrases or stage directions to support your points.

Plan your response

Below are three ideas for structuring your response:

- A: Use the sequence above, which works through the extract in chronological order, selecting examples/words/phrases as they occur to comment on your interpretation of Safi.
- B: Select particular ideas about Safi's role and explore these in turn, such as his role as commentator on the action or as narrator, telling the audience about what is happening, or as a figure in his own right within the play.
- C: Focus on performance skills or areas and deal with each in turn. For example, Safi's:
    - voice: pitch, pace, pause, projection, volume, articulation, tone, cueing, inflection, accent, breathing, repetition, emphasis
    - body: posture, gesture, facial expression, eye contact
    - movement: timing, direction, energy, ensemble awareness, pathways, repetition
    - use of space: levels, personal/general space, proximity.

Choose one of these structures and note down the points you would make. Remember that you will not have space to address every performance skill, so be selective – for example, you may decide that Safi's use of space between him and the ensemble is especially important but that repeating gestures or movements is not. (NB. Performance skills in Structure C will need to be referenced in the other two structures.)

Write your response

Write your response to the task.

- How would you perform the role of Safi, in the extract, in order to convey your interpretation of his character to the audience?

Evaluate your response

Read the following extract from a response to the task. Think about:

- what this student has done well
- what they might need to do to improve the response.

Safi, in lots of ways, is the central character of the play so I think this centrality should be reflected in how he speaks and moves. This is his first appearance in the play, which has been characterised so far with conflict and disagreement. I think I would play him as someone who will bring a moment of calm when he enters. The script states that he walks 'calmly' onto the stage, so I'd make his walk steady and purposeful. The ensemble should begin to slowly go into suspended animation with the CRS officer lowering his gun, and eventually freeze on the word 'Stop!' At this point, Safi should be directly facing the front. Then, I'd get him to walk slowly to downstage right and then downstage left, making eye contact with members of the audience some way back. This is to further establish an idea of authority.

— overall conceptualisation of Safi, if rather basic

— reference to movement

— useful performance ideas

— clear intention

Then when he starts talking about what has happened, he should have returned to centre stage, but still face the audience. The line 'They warned us in Libya' should be stated without smiling. When he gets to stating his name, he should do so proudly, sounding out each part of his name clearly. Next, when he gets to the section where he says, 'If you open me up when I am dead, you will find Calais engraved upon my heart,' I think he should place his palm, fingers spread on his own heart, and keep it there for the duration of the line.

another suggested performance idea, but what is the intention?

use of gesture

It would be a good idea for the frozen ensemble to slowly move off the stage at this point.

reference to use of space, proximity – but not really explained

During the next part, he should focus his eye contact on more specific members of the audience – especially when he says, 'Have you ever been there?' about Calais. How this line might be said will vary on where the play is performed. Its original production was first performed in the UK in London so the line would be ironic, as most, if not many, of the audience would have been there.

draws on production history, but to what end?

Just before Mohammed and Salar enter, Safi should move to the side of the stage, perhaps downstage right again, and face inwards. The signal for their entrance should be his words, 'March 2015 is the date of my birth'. Although the attention of the audience should now shift to them, Safi is still the voice of authority, so his mention of their names should be stated firmly but flatly without emotion. Here, the intention should be for him to be a narrator who is all-seeing – which he is because he is looking back at events that have already happened.

further movement reference

useful explanation of role and intention

You could almost say he is like a traditional Chorus figure at this point.

opens up new idea but undeveloped

Commentary

This response works through the extract and picks out some useful performance ideas arising from the script. However, a number of ideas are undeveloped or not relevant, and occasionally the student loses sight of the intended effect.

Now, read this extract from a second response to the same scene. Assess how this is a better response than the first. What criteria are you using?

The defining idea of Safi's performance here should be to establish an authoritative but challenging relationship with the audience. The production history of *The Jungle* is such that it was intended as a piece of immersive theatre in which the fourth wall between audience and actors was not just broken, but entirely shattered. For example, in the Playhouse production in 2018, the audience became visitors to Salar's restaurant. Thus, Safi's performance should be tailored to an intimate sharing of an experience.

— over-arching idea of the intended effects

— knowledge of play's production history

— over-arching idea of the intended effects

However, I would also draw attention to the theatricality, to ask the audience to engage with these powerful political ideas. So, when Safi walks on stage and says, 'Stop!', the audience – even if eating – should stop, too, to listen. Safi's tone must be authoritative. The actors on stage (Beth, police, and so on) should freeze. To add to the sense of impending violence, the officer should still have the canister raised.

— interesting contrasting intention

— comment on the ensemble reactions

In 'freezing' the drama, Safi sets himself apart. Although he will is also a participant, here he acts as a kind of omniscient, traditional chorus – stepping outside time and action to comment on events. I would also play Safi at this point as a sort of Master of Ceremonies. He should take up a position centre stage, and then extend both arms to the side, palms to the floor, and dismiss the ensemble. They should drop their arms, turn and move silently and swiftly away.

— drawing on theatrical traditions and conventions, though could be developed

— linked gesture

At this point, I think Safi should sit down on the edge of one of the restaurant tables – making it clear he is about to tell a story. He now assumes a new role – that of narrator – but one who is also a protagonist. He should emphasise the words 'warned' and 'advised' to stress that their meaning was different to the reality – that nothing could have really prepared the refugees. Then, I think when he is about to state his own name, he should stand up, and establish a different sort of status, moving towards even more intimacy with the audience. He should state his name slowly, perhaps even pausing between each element – 'Safi [pause] Al [pause] Hussain' or repeating it – to emphasise how his name, and his life, means something.

— movement and linked effect

— vocal performance

— useful mention of change in status due to levels

— pace

I think posture will be very important at this point, too. He should be upright, shoulders back. The words 'thirty-five years young' should be said clearly, and he should emphasise the word 'I' in 'I know a little bit about telling stories' – again, stressing his authority, the need for the audience to listen to him. There should be a sense of urgency here, for the audience to understand what happened, which should link to the political roots of the play, which treads the line between community theatre and perhaps 'agit-prop'.

— moving on to new area – posture

— links the performance to genre aspects

Commentary

This response provides a clear vision or conceptualisation of Safi's role and how it can be interpreted. It makes relevant use of contextual information, but is precise and detailed on the performance possibilities, along with apt references to the script.

Big question

- How do you write about the whole play?

What will the task involve?

You will have to answer **one question** from a **choice of two** on a play you have studied. You might be asked to write about an aspect of the play **as a whole** or select **two or more sections** from it to write about. Below are some examples.

> How would you perform the role of Lopakhin in two or more sections in the play in order to reveal his status as an outsider?

> How would you perform the role of Madame Ranevsky in **two separate** sections of the play, in order to convey your interpretation of her character?

> As a director, how would you emphasise the tragic elements of the play in two or more sections?

> As a costume designer, outline your designs for two or three characters in the play. Explain how these designs would be appropriate to your interpretation of *The Cherry Orchard*.

> As a director, how would you direct your ensemble in **two separate sections** of the play to create dramatic impact for the audience?

Decoding a task

Look at this annotated exam task:

> How would you perform the role of Madame Ranevsky in **two separate** sections of the play, in order to convey your interpretation of her character?

you, not anyone else

focus on performance skills, not design

this character – not others

I need to decide the two sections I will write about

get across my view based on the script

the sort of person she is

Choose one of the other tasks and decode it in the same way.

Generating ideas and planning

Here are some possible ways of approaching the Madame Ranevsky task above.

Interpretation of character	Romantic, out of touch with reality, perhaps slightly unstable.
Possible sections of the play I could refer to	Entrance and response to Lopakhin's proposal to cut down the orchard, Act 1.
	Varya, Gayev and her standing at the window, remembering the past; later in the same scene, Act 1. 'Varya: Look, Mama, the trees…'
	Speech in Act 2 talking about her past to Lopakhin and the others about the mistakes she's made. 'I'm terrified something will happen…'
	Conversation with Trofimov (Act 3) starting, 'Where's Leon?'
	End of the play as she hears news of the auction (Act 3), from 'Well, then? The auction, what happened?'

You could comment on the following areas:

- physical appearance and costume
- delivery style
- movement, gesture, posture, energy, stance
- vocal, facial and physical expression
- pace, pitch, pause, accent, emphasis in specific lines

- physical contact, eye-contact, eye-line
- non-verbal communication
- use of space
- use of props and accessories
- interaction with other characters.

You will also need to draw on Chekhov's key ideas:

- her memories and the symbolic nature of the cherry orchard to the family
- the death of her son
- her past and her love affairs
- her relationship with Lopakhin, who has the means to 'save' the house/orchard.

Where appropriate, you could also refer to:

- naturalistic performance conventions (see pages 18 and 133)
- theatrical/cultural/historical context of the play
- language and stage imagery
- genre and style
- performance history.

Structure your response

Look again at the guidance on pages 156–157 and select a structure.

- Decide on your own interpretation of Madame Ranevsky.
- Plan your points once you have generated your ideas and selected relevant evidence.
- Now write your response.

Evaluate your response

Read this opening to a response to the task. How could it be improved?

When Gayev, Varya and Madame Ranevsky stare out of the window at the orchard in Act 1, it is clear she does not want to escape the past and cannot face the present. It is like she is a child again. 'My bed was… here… by the window.' I would look down and perhaps even crouch and place the palm of my hand on the floor. Then, I would stand slowly and maybe place my hand on Gayev's arm to steady myself. This unsteadiness would be something which could recur, maybe in her voice too. So, when she says, 'I could see the orchard from it', I think her voice should waver and sound hoarse. Although the Chekhovian style may be naturalistic, I think she should create a sort of romantic, almost fairytale like feel here with her memories. I think the idea of unsteadiness in voice and movement could also be seen when she talks with Trofimov at the start of Act 3. The stage directions state that 'Trofimov takes her by the arm, restores her to her chair'. It is interesting that when she first arrives at the house, she is offered a chair. In this scene though it is the worry of waiting to hear news of the auction that is driving her mad. So, I would get her to hold her head in two hands as if trying to block out the world.

Commentary

This opening is rather jumbled and crams in too many different ideas about Madame Ranevsky's performance across the two chosen scenes. There needs to be greater clarity about the different scenes, and greater focus on individual elements. Some of these might be better in later sections of the response. There is also insufficient attention to the effects, or to explaining ideas around naturalism.

Thinking more deeply

Character metaphors or analogies

One key way in which actors sometimes 'get inside' a role is to settle on a coherent centralising idea for a character. This could be seen as the broader conceptualisation of a character, or just a way to explore their potential speech and gesture. For example, here are a number of possible ways of approaching the role of Madame Ranevsky. Note the word 'approaching' – the idea may not be literally interpreted, but used as a way into understanding how she might act.

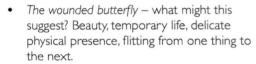

- *The wounded butterfly* – what might this suggest? Beauty, temporary life, delicate physical presence, flitting from one thing to the next.

- *The queen bee* – what might this suggest? Core importance and controlling power; a sense of less important figures 'buzzing' around her; the power to hurt, sting – but also give sweetness, nourish, and so on.

- *The 'madwoman in the attic'* – what might this suggest? The disintegrating figure who has been broken by the world but at the same time speaks truths that others might not be able to face.

- *The mother hen* – what might this suggest? The matriarch who gathers everyone to their bosom and offers comfort and nourishment; not glamorous but steady and reliable.

- Can you think of any other analogies you could make?

Look again at the two scenes (Extract A and Extract B) on pages 150–152.

- Do any of these interpretations seem to fit how you see Madame Ranevsky? It may be possible that a combination of these elements works – or none at all.

- If any do, how would these approaches affect or drive the way you played the character?

Write a paragraph explaining how one of the interpretations above (or one of your own) could inform your performance of Madame Ranevsky. Include at least two references to the extracts to support your ideas. Begin:

I see Madame Ranevsky as a sort of… in the play. For example, in the first scene she could…

As a student of AS and A Level Drama, it is important that you develop a strong understanding of the skills required to be an effective academic researcher. At this level, you need to demonstrate your understanding of dramatic text, genres and of theatre-making traditions, styles and practices. The skills required to successfully investigate a genre, practitioner or production include:

- identifying an appropriate research focus
- identifying a series of key research questions
- reviewing the field of literature on a specific subject
- identifying appropriate research sources
- identifying appropriate research methods
- creating a research plan, including detailed milestones
- keeping and organising detailed notes
- evaluating the reliability of your sources.

In this chapter, you will consider the stages of the research process by exploring a series of case studies and considering examples of research materials. You will develop the skills of analysis and evaluation and consider a range of methods for presenting the outcomes of your research.

6.1 Becoming an effective researcher

Big question

- How can you identify a suitable topic for your research?

Starting point: Choosing a topic for a case study

The first task in planning a research investigation is choosing your topic. You might decide to explore a particular theatrical genre, playwright or period of theatre history. More specifically, you might look at the production history of a set of plays that characterise a theatrical genre. One of the most useful ways of focusing your research is to come up with ideas for a case study. Case studies involve detailed examination of a particular subject. The research is focused on a defined period of time and a particular place (for example, a country). Case studies may use quantitative methods (analysis of numerical data) and qualitative methods (analysis of non-numerical data). Before you decide on the finer focus of your topic, you should read relevant literature, such as plays written by a playwright you are thinking of studying, or recent reviews of a play in production.

All good research begins with a key question, which should be closely aligned with your choice of subject. It should lead to a number of other questions and form a framework for the research. For example, look at the following research question written by a student who is interested in exploring the way in which Fugard reflected the political context of South Africa in the 1960s and 1970s:

> Athol Fugard's aim to 'shatter white complacency and its conspiracy of silence' informs his style of theatre. How is this shown in his plays *Sizwe Bansi is Dead* and *The Island?*

This overarching question could lead to a number of other 'How' questions:

- How did Fugard's political message change over time in his plays?
- How did audiences respond to his messages?
- How successful were his plays?
- How did Fugard use theatrical methods to communicate with the audience and who were they?
- How did Fugard's plays contribute to the ending of apartheid?

These questions might then provide the structure for a case study. An investigation of the research question above might therefore include study of Fugard's political themes, the socio-historical context of his plays, characters and settings, production history and critical reception. The research question will also determine the choice of research methods.

Activity 1

Copy and complete the following table to consider the strengths and weaknesses of different research methods.

Research method	Strengths	Weaknesses
Literature review (for example, books, articles)	Covers a range of areas	Depending on source of publication, could be biased
Spectatorship (viewing of live or digital performance)		
Secondary research (review of archive material or data sets, for example, collections of related information)		
Scrutiny of performance documentation, including programmes, photographs, director's copies		
Practice as research (performance workshops and laboratories)		
Quantitative review of data (for example, ticket sales information)		

Explore: Creating a research plan and identifying appropriate sources

Once you have evaluated and selected your research methods, you need to create a research plan. This should identify the research sources you intend to use and include a timeline for each stage of the research. You should also assess what problems you might face in finding out what you need to know. For example, is material out of print or difficult to source? Are the tickets to a performance you need to attend sold out?

Research sources might include:

- production photographs
- archive recordings
- interviews with practitioners
- reviews of productions
- newspaper articles
- transcripts from events, such as speeches made by directors or actors
- famous speeches
- personal diaries or journal entries
- production artefacts, including costumes or props
- diagrams and sketches showing the design concept for a production
- secondary source material on the specific context of the period, e.g. an extract from a book on World War I
- manifestoes.

Once you have identified relevant sources, you need to analyse and evaluate them. It can be helpful to ask yourself:

- Who is the author and what was their purpose in writing?
- When was the source created?
- What was the critical reaction to the piece?
- Why does the writer highlight…?

Imagine that one of your sources is performance documentation surrounding the original production of Fugard's *The Island* in 1973. You find some reviews from the period and realise that the most negative reviews are located in newspapers operated by the South African apartheid government, and you are therefore able to detect the presence of **bias**. This might lead you to decide that it is important to write about the critical reception of Fugard's plays, so you will add further research to your plan. At every stage of your research, it is essential to critically reflect on the success of your chosen sources.

Key term

bias: prejudice against a person or group that is considered unfair

169

Develop: Engaging with primary and secondary research material

When planning and conducting your research, you will need to read a broad range of literature, including books, articles, critical reviews and commentaries. Some of this information may be found in your school library, but it is likely you will need to broaden your research to public libraries or online sources. Whether you are conducting research with an ensemble as part of the devising process or undertaking a detailed individual investigation, you will need to identify the field of literature (the material most relevant to your task). Creating a comprehensive formal bibliography (a list of written sources) is also an important part of your research. It is best to compile the bibliography as you work through your research plan. Present it in a recognised style, such as the Harvard system, and ensure that all sources are referenced fully and consistently. (Full details of how to use this reference system are available online.)

The sources that you use in your research may be primary or secondary.

- Primary sources are first-hand accounts of a topic, written by people who had a direct connection with it. Primary sources include original documents such as newspaper reports, letters and diary extracts.
- Secondary sources are one step removed from the time/subject, and present information originally found elsewhere. Examples include textbooks, critical articles and analyses of speeches.

When reviewing the literature surrounding a practitioner, theatre tradition or style, you could consider:

- socio-historical context in which the tradition or style emerged, or in which the practitioner's work was first developed
- cultural and artistic purpose of the drama
- political intentions of the drama
- working methods
- preferred theatrical space and actor–**audience configuration**
- role of the director, actor and designer in the work.

For example, if you were reviewing literature about Fugard's plays, you might follow these steps:

1. Begin by identifying the main writers who have written about Fugard. Find their key texts – books and articles.

2. Search the bibliographies in these texts to get ideas about where else to look for information to help direct your next steps.

3. Look closely at the dates of publication of the most significant books and articles, and then try and find additional sources that go beyond these dates, such as articles or reviews written earlier or later than your initial sources.

4. Identify key terms in the literature and use those to help generate further lines of enquiry.

> ### Key term
>
> **audience configuration:** the placing of the audience in relation to the performing space

Imagine you were conducting a literature review as part of a case study on the use of symbolism in two of Lorca's plays – *Blood Wedding* (1933) and *Yerma* (1934). Your starting point could be:

- the production history of *Blood Wedding and Yerma*
- key words associated with the research focus – 'Lorca', 'symbolism', 'marriage', 'blood'
- the context in which the plays were written – Spanish society between 1920 and 1936
- Lorca as political activist.

If you chose to start with the production history of the two plays, you would probably identify theatre reviews, academic books and articles on the plays which reference productions, and newspaper coverage of their opening performances.

You might be answering the following research question:

> How have different directors responded to the symbolism in Lorca's plays *Blood Wedding* and *Yerma*?

Read the following review of a modern-dress production of *Blood Wedding*.

Blood Wedding, 9 March 2015, Graeae Theatre Company, Dundee Rep

Graeae is famous for its globally acclaimed work with disabled performers; and David Ireland's brave and thrilling adaptation of the text, set in a roughly contemporary UK full of Scottish, Irish and estuary voices, noises up a series of issues around inclusion, exclusion and prejudice. So the bride, Olivia, played with terrific presence and humour by Amy Conachan, has no legs, although she reassures her future mother-in-law that everything else is in working order; her fiancé Edward is black, although, as her auntie Shirley observes, not very black. Leonardo, whom she adores with a fatal passion, is much blacker; although her father is clear that that's not why he doesn't like him. And Edward's mother, Agnes, is profoundly deaf; although that doesn't stop her from being prejudiced against people with no legs.

The result – on Lisa Sangster's brilliantly-lit function-suite set – is a riot of dark observational comedy shading fiercely into tragedy, featuring a rogue's gallery of memorable performances from an ensemble that includes Ann Louise Ross as Aunt Shirley, and Gerard McDermott as Olivia's **stuffed-shirt** father. At the play's core, though, are the twin performances of Ricci McLeod as Edward, a good man appalled by the violence of his fate; and EJ Raymond as his mother, an ancient and yet ominously modern figure of tribal hatred and revenge, biding her time, but finally telling the last of her menfolk exactly where to plunge the knife, and how hard.

From a review by Joyce McMillan in *The Scotsman*

Vocabulary

stuffed shirt: a conventional, pompous person

Activity 2

Make some notes on the following questions:

- How might the director of the 21st-century production have been influenced by their socio-cultural context?
- What were the key features of the performances of the actors playing the lead roles in the two productions?
- Which of the plays' themes did the designer seem to focus on and why?

Having looked at several modern productions of the plays, you might then turn to the available source material on the original productions. Lorca directed the first production of *Blood Wedding* at the Teatro Beatriz in Madrid in 1933. The performance included a minimalistic stage design, carefully co-ordinated speech, music and movement, and perfectly timed delivery of the text. Lorca based the play on real events, so the context of life in rural Andalucia in Spain was key to the staging of the play, including the use of a flamenco guitar and harsh, bright lighting to simulate the hot sun. *Yerma* premiered in late 1934 at another theatre in Madrid, the Teatro Español. By this point in this career, Lorca was being criticised for his outspoken Republican sympathies. Critics said the play was immoral, especially in its portrayal of a wife murdering her husband. In performance, the painted backdrop to the production was bold in colour and design. The highly physical movement style enabled Lorca to draw out the symbolism of his language.

In order to build a comparative framework for analysis, you should consider similar aspects of each production. In the example here, you might focus in particular on the different responses to the productions of *Blood Wedding* – the outrage critics expressed after the original production and the modern audience's enjoyment of the vibrancy and challenge the play presented. You could organise your ideas in a table like the one below.

Production element	Original production	21st-century case study production: Graeae, 2015
Performance style	Choreographed movement and stylised gestures; actors work together to create a choral effect.	Actors with physical impairments create a comic style by drawing attention to the contrast between them and able-bodied members of the cast.
Set and use of space		
Costume and props		
Lighting, including multimedia		
Sound		
Audience response		
Critical reception (newspaper critics and academics)		

You might extend this exploration of the production history by looking more closely at some critical discussion of the plays. The collection of three plays published by Nick Hern Books (2017) recommends a specific biography – alongside an academic introduction to the plays by Gwynne Edwards – that was published in 1989.

When considering the production history of a play, you will also need to explore visual sources, including production photos, design sketches and diagrams and images contained in the programme. The photograph here is from a critically acclaimed production of *Yerma* at the National Theatre in 2016.

Now consider the costume sketches for a production designed by Simon Higlett for the Royal Exchange in Manchester in 2003. Higlett explained that he was struck by a sense of the setting, of barren earth surrounded by water. He describes how he was drawn to the universality of the themes and a sense that this play could happen anywhere. The designer describes the research process he went through when planning the costumes, including looking closely at images of Spain during the Civil War in the 1930s. The peasant clothing of the period has clearly informed the shapes and styles of the costumes. At the end of the play, he introduced a series of masks painted in the colours of the landscape and included objects, such as skulls, to suggest the twinned ideas of growth and decay.

Yerma, Simon Stone, National Theatre (2016)

Activity 3

Create a spider diagram of the ideas from the plays that you can see in these images. How has the director ensured that the production speaks to a modern audience?

Apply: Creating a research plan

How might you use the information in this section to help you develop a research plan for either your work with your group or your individual investigation? What will be the timeframe for the plan and how will you measure progress?

Activity 4

Use the following template that shows the first four weeks of an eight-week investigation to help structure a plan. (This example uses the research task on page 171)

Week	Research question	Research activity	Research method
1	What are the main sources of symbolism in the two plays?	Reread the plays and annotate moments of symbolism; identify books and articles that respond to Lorca's use of symbolism.	Close analysis of the text; note-making.
2	How did the director of the original production of *Blood Wedding* reflect the symbolism in the play?	Identify reviews, photos and notes of original productions.	
3	How did the director of the original production of *Yerma* reflect the symbolism in the play?		
4			

6.2 Researching theatre genre

Big question

- How can you identify the key features of a genre in a text?

Starting point: Identifying key features of the absurd genre in a text

A case study about a specific genre must first consider the context in which it arose. In this unit, you will explore the Theatre of the Absurd as an example of the study of a genre. Absurdism emerged in the years between the two world wars (1918–39) and was concerned with the futility and brutality of human behaviour.

Imagine that you have decided to investigate the key features of the Theatre of the Absurd. You have come up with the following research focus:

> How did the playwrights of absurd drama communicate their key themes and ideas to an audience? Discuss this question with reference to the plays of Samuel Beckett and Eugène Ionesco.

You might begin to answer this question by reading some of the articles and essays written by the two playwrights. In an essay written in 1957, the playwright Eugène Ionesco defined the absurd as 'that which is devoid of purpose'. For Ionesco, if a person is separated from their context, their actions become 'senseless, absurd, useless'. The central theme of plays in this genre is the absurdity of the human condition. The playwrights often present associated ideas, such as the freedom to act, the boundary between waking and dreaming, and the corrupting nature of power. Absurdist plays tend to include:

- poetic or nonsensical language
- lengthy monologues
- absence of a clear storyline
- stark, simplistic staging – a single object or symbolic prop
- use of blackouts to signify the passing of time, and stark, simplistic, lighting
- the appearance of random characters
- fatalistic cyclical structure – nothing has changed by the end of the play
- powerful visual images, including violent or brutal images.

Spotlight on practitioner: **Eugène Ionesco (1909–94)**

Ionesco wrote his plays in French but studied English, and was very interested in what happens to language during translation. His earliest plays, including *The Bald Prima Donna*, were received as comic farces, although the features of absurdism can be seen in the rejection of conventional plotline and the use of repetition in dialogue. In these plays, his characters appear not to be fully human and are puppet-like, with barely concealed dislike developing into expressions of contempt. *Rhinoceros* (1959) is considered the most expressive of the genre. In it, a man is forced to watch his friends turn into rhinoceroses as they conform to the machine-like existence of modern society.

Absurdist playwrights, including Samuel Beckett, Jean Genet, Jean-Paul Sartre and Ionesco himself, were particularly interested in using language to express the pointlessness of the human condition. Their theatrical texts were rich with symbolic images and metaphors. It is perhaps no surprise that they then chose the visual medium of the theatre to bring the imagery in their language to life and to present characters and situations which were symbolic of the absurd.

Explore: Absurdist conventions in Ionesco's plays

The extract below is from the opening of Ionesco's absurdist play *The Chairs*. The play has only two characters – the old man and the old woman – who appear to live alone in a grand old apartment. They prepare for a fictional party by setting out a series of chairs for guests who will not arrive. In this scene, the Old Man and the Old Woman are looking at the view from their window.

Text 1

SET: *Circular walls, with a recess at the rear of the stage. The stage is very bare [...] The accompanying sketch makes the plan clearer. Centre, down-stage, there are two chairs, side by side. A gas-lamp is suspended from the ceiling.*
The curtain rises. Semi-darkness. The OLD MAN *is standing on the stool leaning out of the left-hand window. The* OLD WOMAN *is lighting the gas-lamp. A green light. She goes and pulls the Old Man's sleeve.*

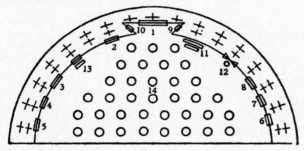

OLD WOMAN: Hurry up, dear, and close the window. I don't like the smell of stagnant water, and the mosquitoes are coming in, too.

OLD MAN: Don't fuss!

OLD WOMAN: Come along now, dear, come and sit down. Don't lean out like that, you might fall in. You know what happened to Francis I. You must be careful.

OLD MAN: Another of your historical allusions! I'm tired of French history, my love. I want to look. The boats in the sunshine are like specks on the water.

OLD WOMAN: You can't see them, it's night-time, my pet, there is no sun.

OLD MAN: It's still casting shadows, anyway. [*He leans right out.*]

OLD WOMAN: [*pulling him back with all her might*]: Ah! ... You're frightening me, my dear ... come and sit down, you won't see them coming. It's no use trying. It's dark ... [*The Old Man reluctantly lets her pull him away.*]

Abridged from *The Chairs* by Eugène Ionesco, Part 1

Activity 1

One of the most useful ways of understanding the key features of a genre or style is to practically explore the text. In small groups, follow the instructions to set up the stage as Ionesco describes. Then discuss the following questions:

- Who are the old couple waiting for?
- Where are the old couple? How long have they been in this place?
- How could a designer suggest the futility of the chairs and of the act of waiting?
- Which of the conventions of absurdism can you identify here?

Focusing specifically on lighting, sound and costume, create some sketches and diagrams for staging the text. You could use some furniture to set up the stage and improvise the props using other objects.

Develop: Past productions – exploring critical reception

One of the most effective research methods for exploring the features of a theatre genre in a particular play is to examine its production history, including critical reviews. *The Chairs* was originally staged in 1952 and was labelled a 'tragic farce'. The actors themselves financed the production and suffered significant losses when they played to a near-empty auditorium. Ionesco's belief that 'the theatre cannot be epic because it is dramatic' seemed to confuse audiences, who were disappointed with the sight of an old couple conducting a series of mundane preparations for an event which exists only in their own minds. The increasing number of chairs represents the emptiness and futility of the lives of the old couple. When a third character of the 'orator' is finally introduced, he is deaf and dumb, and can only offer a series of inarticulate grunts. In the original production, the orator looked, according to Ionesco's stage direction, 'like the typical painter or poet of the last century' with 'a smug, pretentious look'.

Over the last 70 years, the play has been performed on a number of occasions with different interpretations of this mysterious third character. In 1997, the play was revived by the physical theatre company Théâtre de Complicité (see page 50). The set design for this production emphasised the claustrophobia of the couple's relationship with tall wood-panelled stage flats and a series of doors surrounding the stage in a semi-circular shape.

Shafts of light were focused across the stage, creating a series of eerie shadows. As the old woman, the actor Geraldine McEwan was critically admired for using her high pitch and volume to indicate the increasing level of frenzy in her delusions. In contrast, the orator appeared as a silent conductor of proceedings. (Production photos are available online.)

In 2010, in a production staged in Bath, UK, the chairs were hung above the heads of the audience. Reviews suggest that the characterisation of the old couple was designed to highlight the theme of aging. In 2016, the play was given an innovative staging by the visually impaired theatre company Extant. The old couple appear to have retreated to an underground bunker and are surrounded by rotting machinery. The orator is dressed in a white anti-radiation suit. The striking red stockings of the old woman appear to reflect the play's message that we seek to hold onto our youth even as the ageing process weighs upon us.

The Chairs, Maria Oshodi, Extant (2016) (Additional production photos are available online.)

Activity 2

Review the information above in light of the research question on page 174. Identify the theatrical style which the company Extant were demonstrating. Conduct some further research on modern productions of Ionesco's plays to explore the different ways in which companies have approached his absurdist style.

Information about past productions drawn from analysis of secondary sources helps a researcher to understand how different directors have interpreted the play for their specific audience. By comparing and contrasting the use of different production methods, including set, lighting, sound and performance style, you can identify the influence of particular contextual circumstances (and themes and ideas) on a company.

Now read another extract, from later in the play.

Text 2

OLD WOMAN: So it's really true, they're going to come this evening? You won't want to cry any more. When we've got scientists and property-owners, we don't need daddies and mummies. [*Silence.*] We couldn't put the meeting off now. I hope it doesn't make us too tired! [*The excitement is mounting. The OLD MAN has already started trotting round the Old Woman, with short, uncertain steps, like a child's or a very old man's. He has already succeeded in taking a few steps towards one of the doors, but has come back to go round her again.*]

OLD MAN: You really think we shall find it tiring?

OLD WOMAN: You have got a bit of a cold.

OLD MAN: How could we postpone it?

OLD WOMAN: Let's invite them for another evening. You could telephone them.

OLD MAN: Don't be silly. I can't, it's too late. They must be on the boats by now!

OLD WOMAN: You oughtn't to have been so rash. [*A boat can be heard slipping through the water.*]

OLD MAN: I believe that's someone already … [*The noise gets louder.*] …
Yes, someone's coming! … [*The OLD WOMAN gets up too and hobbles about.*]

OLD WOMAN: Perhaps it's the Orator.

OLD MAN: He wouldn't be in such a hurry. It must be someone else. [*A bell rings.*] Ah!

OLD WOMAN: Ah! [*Nervously the OLD COUPLE make for the concealed door back-stage right. As they move, they go on talking.*]

OLD MAN: Come along …

OLD WOMAN: I haven't combed my hair … wait a moment … [*She tidies her hair and straightens her dress as she hobbles along, pulling up her thick red stockings.*]

OLD MAN: You ought to have got ready before … you had plenty of time.

OLD WOMAN: What a sight I look … such an old frock on, all creased up …

OLD MAN: You'd only got to iron it … hurry up! You're keeping people waiting. [*The OLD MAN reaches the door in the recess, followed by the grumbling OLD WOMAN; for a moment they disappear from sight; they can be heard opening the door and then shutting it again, as they let someone in.*]

From *The Chairs* by Eugène Ionesco

Activity 3

Instead of focusing on the broader features of a genre, you might decide to focus instead on a specific playwright and the characteristics of the genre in their work. Conduct some further research into the playwrights of the Theatre of the Absurd. Create a research question which would enable you to explore the Theatre of the Absurd specifically through an investigation of the plays of one particular playwright.

Apply: Planning an investigation of the features of a genre

Imagine that you have decided to conduct a comparative investigation into the absurdist plays of Eugène Ionesco and Samuel Beckett, using the question on page 174. To begin with, you would need to establish a framework for comparative analysis. You might choose to compare:

* staging and position of the audience
* character types
* stage directions for use of space
* design requirements
* language.

Consider character types as an example. In *The Chairs*, an audience would see the comedy of an old couple constructing an imaginary world in which they greet visitors from a social elite. The scene includes a number of elements that set up the contrast between fiction and reality, including the clothing of the old couple, their infirmity and their use of vocal affectations as they greet their visitors.

In Beckett's play *Waiting for Godot*, a pair of old men, probably vagrants, claim to be waiting for someone called Godot, who never arrives. While waiting, they engage in a number of conversations and meet a few other characters.. They are dressed in ill-fitting clothing apparently for the outdoors, which is also quite formal in style. The two characters argue and engage in a series of pointless activities. The dramatic scenario created by Beckett could be directly compared with Ionesco's bleak 'moral disaster', in which Beckett himself described the theme of the play as 'nothingness'.

In order to identify and examine the hallmarks of absurdism in these plays, you could take the following steps:

1. Identify a couple of key scenes – including the scene in Text 2 – and conduct some research into the original production style. Find relevant documentary material, including programme notes, photographs and reviews, as well as comments made by the playwrights themselves in interviews.

2. Compare the original production with more recent interpretations – identify one modern production of each play, and analyse and evaluate the use of production methods.

3. Identify critical discussions of the genre – articles, books and manifestoes created by artists who have aligned themselves with the movement.

4. Explore the influence of the absurdists on contemporary theatre practitioners – examine visual and documentary evidence.

Activity 4

Consider the impact of absurdism on contemporary theatre by undertaking the exploration activity outlined as step 4 above. Create a list of the sources of evidence that you will need to examine. See if you can answer the following question:

What does absurdism look like in the contemporary theatre?

Waiting for Godot, Andrew Upton, Barbican Theatre (2015)

6.3 Researching theatre practitioners

Big question
- How can you identify the hallmarks of a practitioner across their body of work?

Starting point: Features of Greek tragedy

When exploring the work of a particular practitioner, a key question is the extent to which performance style has been influenced by the practitioner's choice of text. For example, in a career spanning 40 years, the director Yukio Ninagawa had directed a number of Greek tragedies. Imagine you were researching Ninagawa's work through the following question:

> What are the hallmarks of Ninagawa's theatrical style? Discuss with specific reference to his staging of Greek tragedy.

Look at the example below, which shows some information a student has gathered about Greek tragedy.

The most prolific period for the ancient tragedians was the 5th century BCE. The plays consisted of five elements: the prologue (introductory speech), parados (entry of the characters), episode (stages in storytelling), stasimon (choral interludes) and exodus — staging? (conclusion). The earliest tragedies were related by one actor, but Aeschylus and Sophocles added a second and third, and, later, a chorus. Later within the Greek period, Euripides introduced greater technical experimentation and emphasis on realism. In his famous — genre? study of the genre, the *Poetics*, the philosopher Aristotle introduces the concepts of mimesis (imitation) and catharsis (emotional cleansing) alongside the three 'unities' of time, place and action in which the play does not seek to represent events taking place beyond one place and one day.

The spectators of the tragic theatre of ancient Greece would find — venue choice? themselves seated in large outdoor amphitheatres (seating up to 17 000 people) facing the throne of the priest of Dionysus, who would oversee the drama. At the centre of the amphitheatre was the playing area – the orchestra. To the right and left of the theatre were the parados, used for the entrances and exits of both actors and audience. Behind the orchestra was the skene or scenic house, fronted by a raised platform known as the proskenion. Greek — design? actors often wore masks as a symbol of the Dionysiac ritual. The development of comedy included innovations in the development of costume and props including moulded body parts.

Activity 1

Read the notes and use the annotations to come up with a series of further research questions. These questions could be used to shape the research plan.

Explore: Ninagawa's directorial style

Spotlight on practitioner: **Yukio Ninagawa (1935–2016)**

Ninagawa was born in Kawaguchi in the eastern region of Japan's South island. He was 32 when he established his first theatre company. In 1974, he was invited to direct his first Shakespeare play in a large-scale venue. This began a longstanding relationship with Shakespeare's works and, in 1988, a decision to direct the playwright's entire body of work. The director has spoken about his interest in the genre of tragedy and this has influenced his work on both Greek and Shakespearean tragedies. In 1983, Ninagawa undertook his first international tour with Euripides's *Medea*. After this, he was invited to collaborate with a number of prestigious producing houses, including the Royal Shakespeare Company, with whom he presented *King Lear* in 2000. With the Ninagawa Company, he won a number of awards for his innovative visual and highly stylised production style. At the 1985 Edinburgh Festival he directed a Samurai-style Macbeth in which the actors performed in Samurai kimonos around a giant Buddha. Ninagawa was also committed to the use of classical Japanese theatre forms including Kabuki and Noh (see page 24), and in 2005, produced a Kabuki version of Shakespeare's *Twelfth Night*. In 2006, he founded a theatre company specifically for people over the age of 55, the Saitama Gold Theater.

Macbeth, Yukio Ninagawa, Barbican Theatre (2017)

Ninagawa's production style included:

- use of non-traditional large theatre spaces – empty warehouses and conference centres
- symbolic minimalism – for example, a single tree to represent a forest, a pile of earth to represent a mountain
- Japanese design – painted backdrops, kimonos, etc.
- vibrant colour schemes – groups all dressed in the same colour
- classical music, particularly requiem pieces which support funeral processions
- large-scale chorus – *Oedipus* contained a chorus of 160
- elements of pop culture – settings included video game shops and karaoke
- use of vertical space – objects floating in space, actors lifted into the air in chariots.

Ninagawa's performers were expected to be highly disciplined. The performance style is pared down (reduced to its simplest form) so that every gesture and encounter is meaningful. His performers also use choreographed movement to express heightened emotions.

Activity 2

Working with a partner, undertake some research into Ninagawa's productions of Shakespeare's plays, focusing on the cross-cultural references. Make some notes on the director's approach to characterisation.

Ninagawa staged Sophocles's play *Oedipus Rex* four times between 1976 and 2004. The 2004 production was staged in an amphitheatre outside Athens and set in medieval Japan. At the back of the stage, in the position of the Greek skene, were a series of tall black flowers on giant stems. As a background track, the audience could hear the sound of traditional Japanese instruments called Sho. The 20-strong, all-male chorus of Theban citizens (Oedipus is the King of Thebes) dressed in scarlet provided striking contrast with the monochrome set. The movement of the chorus created its own spectacle. At times, the chorus moved ritualistically around the stage, resembling a number of monks at prayer. At other times, the chorus separated as it narrated the terrible acts experienced by the characters.

Even the publicity poster for the production played a role in communicating the themes to the audience. The central image contained the two principal actors set against a white background with drops of blood floating past as if through space. Oedipus and Jocasta (his queen) have their hands joined but Jocasta's nails are unnaturally long, suggesting the violence to come.

After his many stagings of *Oedipus*, Ninagawa also produced two of Euripides's most famous plays, *Orestes* and *Medea*. In the 2006 production of *Orestes*, the playwright's focus was on the torment of the central character, caused by the pursuit of the Furies (demons) after he has killed his mother in revenge for her murdering his father. The play is built around a series of conflicts, including that between living a life of torment and death and the tension between responsibility to one's mother and that owed to the father. Ninagawa's stylistic hallmarks were evident in the use of a vast minimalistic stage and with basic cloths covering the main characters, in contrast to a female chorus dressed in flowing black dresses. The production ended with a rainfall of paper — representing the decrees of the Gods falling onto the audience.

Activity 3

How might you develop a case study focused on the exploration of *spectacle* in Ninagawa's productions? What kind of research questions could you devise? Try to draft a suitable research question.

Develop: Focus on design aspects of Ninagawa's productions

Ninagawa used mask alongside makeup and costume to project the extreme emotional life of the characters in his Greek productions. Set designer Tsukasa Nakagoshi worked with Ninagawa's company from 1987. He describes the experience of working with Ninagawa as being very visual, with discussions of ideas for colours and shapes that incorporate different cultural images. The set design for *Oedipus* consisted of a large concrete fortress-like structure, including a staircase which led to the centre of the stage. In contrast to the sand-coloured columns, the actors were clad in bright robes. In this production, the masks of the chorus, with pained facial expressions, provided a visual reference to the downfall of the central character.

Like *Orestes*, *Medea* tells the story of the destruction of an aristocratic family. Pushed aside by her warrior husband, Jason, for another woman, Medea exacts her revenge by murdering Jason's new wife. In Ninagawa's 2005 production, the floor of the stage was covered in a blanket of brightly lit artificial lotus flowers set in a pool of water. When he first staged the play in Japan in 1978, the director used an all-male cast, dressing Medea in a traditional kimono. In 2005, the actress playing Medea was seen moving frantically between the flowers, splashing through the water and spotlight at the top of a staircase leading up to a room of horror. At the end of the performance, the audience was treated to the spectacle of a horse-drawn chariot taking Medea off into the afterlife. Use of stylised masks covered in jewels in the 1978 production was replaced with a chorus of women of different ages covered in red robes. Intense lighting effects were a feature of both productions, with a clear focus on the use of coloured gels (see page 104) to create changes in atmosphere.

Activity 4

Conduct some further research into Ninagawa's approach to theatre design. There are numerous production photos available online. You might like to focus on the widely documented productions of *Macbeth* or *Hamlet*. Organise your notes in a table like the one below.

Feature	Design features
Use of space	
Set	
Lighting	
Sound	
Costume and makeup	

The director Peter's Hall's analysis of the original Greek masked chorus suggests that 'all the masks create the line that only one voice utters... it not only allows extremes of emotion; it allows the moods of a group to change like lightning'. Throughout his career, Ninagawa experimented with the role of the chorus in communicating with the audience. Often the chorus was presented on an epic scale, but always thoroughly rehearsed and perfectly timed. In Kabuki-inspired productions, the chorus was often stylised in costume and makeup, and precise in its movement. In more hybrid productions, members of the chorus huddle in dark corners of the stage in one moment, then become part of the audience for the unfolding drama, only to appear in shafts of light in another moment, narrating or commentating. Choreographed movement is key to the impact of Ninagawa's chorus. Archive material, including visual images, reveal his commitment to the visual spectacle and underpins his interest in geometric shapes.

Use of Peter Hall's commentary on Greek theatre as a secondary source helps the researcher to understand the importance of mask in the genre and then to apply this understanding to reading of reviews of Ninagawa's productions. If you were answering the question set out at the beginning of this unit, for example, you would want to examine a range of sources that consider the use of mask in the theatre, in order to decide on the extent to which Ninagawa drew from theatrical traditions to inform his own style.

Activity 5

How might you undertake structured research into the different uses of mask in theatre from the Greek period to the Restoration? Try the following research exercise with a partner.

- One person undertakes research into the use of the mask in Greek theatre by identifying articles and books on Greek theatre.
- The other person conducts similar research into the use of mask in the theatre of commedia dell'arte in the 16th century (see page 52).

Compare notes on your findings and, using the information given above, identify any influences on Ninagawa's work.

Apply: Planning a written response to an investigation of a practitioner

Having looked closely at the hallmarks of Ninagawa's style, you are in a position to think about how to approach a discussion of this body of work. Imagine you were responding to this case study question:

How did Ninagawa approach ancient Greek tragedy? How did his staging ideas change over time and how have they influenced modern theatre-makers?

Consider the following suggested framework for the investigation.

Introduction: brief biography of Ninagawa and his origins in the visual arts (100 words)

⬇

Rationale for choice of subject and defining features of his work (200 words)

⬇

Outline of research methods and evaluation of approach: value of documentary analysis including visual resources (200 words)

⬇

Discussion of Ninagawa's broad body of work – identification of hallmarks of his style and transitions in his production style (600 words)

⬇

Discussion of case study production 1 – earlier production – discussion of performance style, design elements, use of Noh and Kabuki theatre forms (600 words)

⬇

Discussion of case study production 2 – later production – site-specific theatre, use of digital technology (600 words)

⬇

Discussion of Ninagawa's influence on the contemporary theatre – critical response, use of his hybrid approach to theatre-making by companies such as Robert Lepage (600 words)

⬇

Conclusion: summary of main points (1000 words)

⬇

Bibliography

Activity 6

How might this approach help you to plan your own investigation of a practitioner? Look back at the notes you have made during this section and plan a similar investigation. Follow the steps below:

- Step 1: Identify the hallmarks of the practitioner's style.
- Step 2: Identify key productions/periods in their career.
- Step 3: Create an overarching research question.
- Step 4: Identify the range of possible primary (including the play texts for the productions) and secondary sources.
- Step 5: Create a research plan which has a clear time frame and is risk-assessed for any potential barriers to success.

6.4 Researching theatre texts

Big question

- How can you investigate different aspects of a text in performance?

Starting point: Exploring the social, cultural, historical and political context of a text

Another key area of research for an essay is the production history of a particular text through time. This unit uses Arthur Miller's play *A View from the Bridge*, first staged in 1955, as an example. Imagine you are investigating the following question:

> How have directors of Arthur Miller's *A View from the Bridge* treated the character of the flawed anti-hero? Discuss this question with reference to three key productions of the play.

In order to answer this question and identify the key characteristics of the anti-hero, you would need to explore the context of the play.

A View from the Bridge was influenced by Miller's experiences of working with the dockworkers in Brooklyn Harbor, many of whom were immigrants like his own parents. The plot is based on a true story told to him by a young lawyer friend and was also influenced by his interest in the form and structure of Greek tragedy. The story revolves around the Carbone family, headed by dockworker Eddie. The play explores how Eddie's tragic flaw of jealousy leads him to betray the cousins who are illegally lodging with him.

Activity 1

Consider a play you are studying. Undertake some research and make brief notes on the period in which it was written. Divide them into four categories of context: social, cultural, historical and political. Understanding the context will enable you to identify how it influenced the play's plot, setting and characters.

Social	Historical
The civil rights movement gained momentum with the fight against the segregation of African Americans entering mainstream society. 1950s New York was gender-segregated with most men in the workplace and most women looking after the home.	Morocco declares its independence from France. Fidel Castro lands in Cuba.
Cultural	**Political**
Elvis Presley enters the US charts for the first time with 'Heartbreak Hotel' Post-WW2 culture emphasised opportunities to re-fashion society.	Egypt nationalises the Suez Canal, sparking an international conflict. The Soviet Union invades Hungary

Spotlight on practitioner: Arthur Miller (1915–2005)

Miller was born in New York to immigrant parents. His family owned a large clothing manufacturing business but during the Wall Street Crash in 1929 they lost everything and had to move from wealthy Manhattan to working-class Brooklyn. Growing up, the young Miller witnessed first-hand the hardship of the Great Depression that followed the Crash. Many of his plays explore the human impact of living in a capitalist society and the pressure to try to achieve the 'American Dream' of success and prosperity. In 1956, he testified in front of the House Un-American Activities Committee in relation to his alleged involvement with communist sympathisers. At this time, he was associated with other artists who had been accused of being sympathetic to the communist regime of Soviet Russia, the self-declared enemy of the USA. Miller's experiences during this period informed his writing of *The Crucible* in 1953, a play based on the witch-hunts that took place in the American Midwest in the 17th century. In the 1960s, Miller's plays were banned in the Soviet Union. Miller campaigned for the rest of his life for freedom of speech for writers across all genres.

Explore: Theatrical approaches to creating Miller's characters

The Carbone's family home in a Brooklyn tenement block is at the heart of the action of the play and is described in detail in the stage directions. The outside world is represented by a set of ramps which run across the stage and are critical in establishing the context of the neighbourhood in the play. In the following extract from Act 1 of the play, we are introduced to Eddie and his wife Beatrice's niece Catherine, whom they adopted following the death of her mother, Beatrice's sister. Here we begin to see that Eddie's protective feelings towards Catherine are significant and stronger than they should be.

Vocabulary

the willies: a feeling of discomfort

Text 3

CATHERINE	Hi, Eddie!
	EDDIE *is pleased and therefore shy about it; he hangs up his cap and jacket.*
EDDIE	Where you goin' all dressed up?
CATHERINE	(*running her hands over her skirt*) I just got it. You like it?
EDDIE	Yeah, it's nice. And what happened to your hair?
CATHERINE	You like it? I fixed it different. (*Calling to kitchen*) He's here, B.!
EDDIE	Beautiful. Turn around, lemme see in the back. (*She turns for him.*) Oh, if your mother was alive to see you now! She wouldn't believe it [...]
CATHERINE	(*She sits on her heels beside him.*) Guess how much we paid for the skirt.
EDDIE	I think it's too short, ain't it?
CATHERINE	(*standing*) No! Not when I stand up.
EDDIE	Yeah, but you gotta sit down sometimes.
CATHERINE	Eddie, it's the style now. (*She walks to show him.*) I mean, if you see me walkin' down the street –
EDDIE	Listen, you been givin' me **the willies** the way you walk down the street, I mean it.
CATHERINE	Why?
EDDIE	Catherine, I don't want to be a pest, but I'm tellin' you you're walkin' wavy.
CATHERINE	I'm walkin' wavy?
EDDIE	Now don't aggravate me, Katie, you are walkin' wavy! I don't like the looks they're givin' you in the candy store. And with them new high heels on the sidewalk – clack, clack, clack. The heads are turnin' like windmills.
CATHERINE	But those guys look at all the girls, you know that.
EDDIE	You ain't 'all the girls'.
CATHERINE	(*almost in tears because he disapproves*) What do you want me to do? You want me to –
EDDIE	Now don't get mad, kid.
CATHERINE	Well, I don't know what you want from me.
EDDIE	Katie, I promised your mother on her deathbed. I'm responsible for you. You're a baby, you don't understand these things.

From *A View from the Bridge* by Arthur Miller, Act 1

This scene reveals the beginnings of Eddie's overprotective behaviour towards Catherine. The character of the family man who is presented as well-meaning but ultimately defeated by his own fatal flaws is one that appears in several of Miller's plays. In the original London production in 1956, Anthony Quayle's performance as Eddie was described as 'memorable,' full of 'stumbling, inarticulate passion and envy'. On opening night, Miller was accompanied by his new wife, Marilyn Monroe, who was said to have commented that Eddie's line 'you're walking wavy' was a reference to her preference for tight clothes. In 2015, the National Theatre production in London starred Mark Strong as Eddie and set the play in a blank space, which some critics felt resembled a prison. Throughout the performance, Strong's characterisation was marked by great intensity and stillness as Eddie struggled with the reality of his feelings towards Catherine.

Activity 2

Read the scene in small groups. Come up with a series of questions you can use to explore the relationship between the two characters in this scene. Then put volunteers in the hot seat and ask them the questions, which they must answer in character. Make notes on what you discover about the background and inner life of the characters.

In Alan Ayckbourn's acclaimed 1987 revival of the play at the National Theatre in London, Michael Gambon interpreted the character naturalistically. A variety of facial expressions and an increasingly slouched posture suggested the weariness caused by his growing feelings of loss, as his niece announces her plans to marry and leave the family home. Reviews of Gambon's performance suggest that it was the small physical details that were particularly effective. On learning later in the play that Catherine has a job, Eddie stabbed the tablecloth angrily. As Catherine becomes romantically involved with his lodger Rodolpho, Eddie gazed intensely at his newspaper. His pent-up anger was later released as he hurled a table against the wall. The performance was also marked by sensitivity as, after making a call to report his illegal lodgers to the authorities, his knees sagged and he fell to the ground in recognition of the consequences of betraying his people.

Reflection point

How could you use what you have learned from the information and activity on this page to help you examine how various actors have approached the character in performance?

Develop: Production history – focus on design elements

One way of understanding the presentation of character is to explore the use of design. In the stage directions, Miller describes the Carbone house as entirely 'skeletal'. The flat is 'clean, sparse, homely' with only the dining room visible, and doors leading into the kitchen and bedrooms. Eddie's world is therefore shown as simple and reflects his low-income status.

Downstage right is a desk that serves as the lawyer Alfieri's office. Alfieri, a 'portly, good-humoured' lawyer, acts as a kind of Greek chorus, speaking directly to the audience at the start and end of the play.

Read the following extract. Eddie has come to see Alfieri to discuss his concerns that Rodolpho's desire to marry Catherine might be motivated by his need for legal residency in the USA. Alfieri tries to force Eddie to reflect on his own feelings for Catherine and the importance of letting her move away from home.

Text 4

ALFIERI Eddie, I want you to listen to me. (*Pause*) You know, sometimes God mixes up the people. We all love somebody, the wife, the kids – every man's got somebody that he loves, heh? But sometimes… there's too much. You know? There's too much, and it goes where it musn't. A man works hard, he brings up a child, sometimes it's a niece, sometimes even a daughter, and he never realises it, but through the years – there is too much love for the daughter, there is too much love for the niece. Do you understand what I'm saying to you?

EDDIE (*sardonically*) What do you mean, I shouldn't look out for her good?

ALFIERI Yes, but these things have to end, Eddie, that's all. The child has to grow up and go away, and the man has to learn to forget. Because after all, Eddie – what other way can it end? (*Pause*) Let her go. That's my advice. You did your job, now it's her life; wish her luck, and let her go. (*Pause*) Will you do that? Because there's no law, Eddie; make up your mind to it; the law is not interested in this.

EDDIE You mean to tell me, even if he's a **punk**? If he's –

ALFIERI There's nothing you can do.

EDDIE *stands.*

EDDIE Well, all right, thanks. Thanks very much.

ALFIERI What are you going to do?

EDDIE (*with a helpless but ironic gesture*) What can I do? I'm a patsy, what can a **patsy** do? I worked like a dog twenty years so a punk could have her, so that's what I done.

From A View from the Bridge by Arthur Miller, Act 1

Vocabulary

sardonically: critically but humorously
punk: a contemptible person
patsy: someone stupid or easily fooled

Alfieri's warnings to Eddie contribute towards the rising tension in the play. The use of theatrical space in this scene is key to its impact. Eddie has stepped out of a domain where he is king and into another, more formal, environment in which he is forced to confront the reality of his feelings for Catherine. In staging this scene, it is important that the audience is able to focus on the intensity of Eddie's growing frustration. The feelings that he has for Catherine ultimately define his status as an anti-hero.

It is useful in research like this to examine how directors have highlighted Eddie's conflicting emotions. In the 2009 production of the play directed by Lindsay Posner, the scene was enclosed in a small area of light, with Eddie's shadow cast up against the forbidding black walls of the enormous tenement block. The stylised nature of the setting contrasted with the naturalistic space inside Carbone's flat, and every detail of the interior decoration was carefully considered. A few months later, in spring 2010, another revival on Broadway, directed by Greg Mosher, focused on the period detail of 1950s dress and used a revolving set to suggest that the play is full of hidden corners and unspoken thoughts. In contrast, the minimalistic design of the 2015 production directed by Ivo van Hove created a claustrophobic space, with the audience on three sides. Stark white lighting ensured that every twitch of every muscle could be seen, with the final violent moments of the play symbolically enhanced by a shower of blood. The *Guardian* critic Lyn Gardner suggested that, by stripping away the tenement block, the director had returned the focus onto the universal nature of the themes:

> This is not just somebody else's family tragedy. It speaks directly to us and suggests that there is an Eddie Carbone lurking in all of us.

Activity 3

Consider the options for designing this scene. Working in pairs, create a spider diagram that captures your ideas for the various production elements. Compare your ideas with the staging devices used in the productions outlined above.

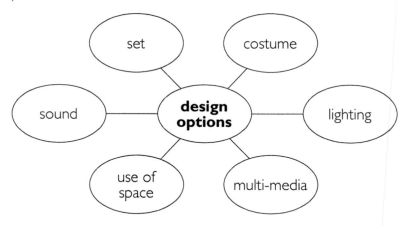

Apply: Writing an introduction to a research question on a text in performance

When analysing the artistic decisions of theatre-makers in bringing a text from page to stage, you need to support your ideas with evidence. When investigating the production history of a text in performance, you might demonstrate breadth of research by using the following sources to discover how the play was staged and the critical response:

* production photos
* reviews
* academic articles on the play
* books about the playwright
* articles written by the playwright.

Below is an example opening paragraph of an essay answering the following question:

> How does the production history of Arthur Miller's plays reflect the social and historical context in which they are performed? Discuss with reference to two plays in performance.

When designing this question, the student read a number of secondary sources about Arthur Miller, as well as a number of his plays. They eventually decided to focus on the tragic nature of the plays.

Arthur Miller is arguably one of the most influential figures in modern theatre history. His depictions of the tragic fall of the anti-hero have provided audiences with much to reflect upon. In this essay, I will be discussing particular interpretations of two of Miller's plays – *All My Sons*, first staged in 1947, and *A View from the Bridge*, first staged in 1956. Since the time of the original productions, social changes have inevitably made some impact on audiences' response to the drama. However, I will argue that the universal nature of Miller's themes and the everyman quality of his characters have enabled directors to transcend the values and attitudes of their time. With a particular focus on the decisions made by directors and designers, I will refer to a wide range of research materials to analyse and evaluate the impact of context on production style.

first three sentences set the scene for the reader and introduce the focus of the essay.

establishes a clear argument for the essay.

notes the importance of comprehensive research and key skills.

Reflection point

How could you use the approach provided here to help you write an introduction to your own investigation? How can you convince the reader that you have established a clear focus for your investigation? Remember to provide clear reasons for your choice of topic.

6.5 Examining practice as research

Big question

• What are the key features of practice as research?

Starting point: Key concepts in practice as research

Practice-based research is a form of research that incorporates an element of disciplinary practice in the research methodology. In this form of research in drama, you would investigate the methods of professional practice through practical work. The project may or may not result in a performance. Artist-researchers who choose this kind of methodology believe that making art is an important means of understanding art and can generate new insights and perspectives on a subject. Practice-based researchers tend to focus on a range of social or cultural questions including those focused on an exploration of identity, community, storytelling and environment. The focus is on the creation of new knowledge using experiential means. However, researchers will usually capture the process and their findings in a written format.

There are some elements of practice as research which can be summarised as follows:

• in-depth enquiry into the subject
• reflection in action
• application of theory
• improvisation
• deconstruction – unpicking of meaning in a text.

There is also a subtle difference between practice-based and practice-led research. In practice-based research, the investigation of the question is highly practical and is likely to include workshops. In practice-led research, the research must lead to new understanding about the practice itself. For example, whether a workshop led by the researcher is the best way of finding the answers to a question or whether the question is better answered through a series of exercises led by members of a company.

The process of conducting practice-based research involves engagement with a range of different types of documentation. Researchers distinguish between integral and external documentation as follows:

• Integral documentation includes the materials created by the practice process and could include script drafts and annotations, costume designs, set designs, choreographic notation.
• External documentation includes material that documents the 'performance encounters' in a way that references the possible contents of the performance as research – for example, photographs, final scripts, video footage.

Activity I

Imagine you have decided to pursue the following question using a practice-based research approach. What sort of workshop activities might you plan to explore this theme? How would you present your findings in a written format? What kind of visual evidence might you include?

> How does Arthur Miller present the theme of community honour in *A View from a Bridge?*

Explore and develop: Practice-led research exploration of the themes in *A View from the Bridge*

The ideas and activities that follow are an indication of how a researcher might use practice as a form of research for a written essay. Practice-based research is one of several research methods and you should consider using more than one method as the basis for a written essay.

Read the following extract from Act 1 of the play. In this scene, Eddie tries to explain to Catherine the importance of maintaining silence when the immigration status of a member of the community is questioned.

Vocabulary

stool pigeons: people who listen out for information that they can use to their advantage by relaying it for money, or other favours, to those in power

Text 5

EDDIE	...Now lemme say it once and for all, because you're makin' me nervous again, both of you. I don't care if somebody comes in the house and sees them sleepin' on the floor, it never comes out of your mouth who they are or what they're doin' here.
BEATRICE	Yeah, but my mother'll know –
EDDIE	Sure she'll know, but just don't be the one who told her, that's all. This is the United States government you're playing with now, this is the Immigration Bureau. If you said it you knew it, if you didn't say it you didn't know it.
CATHERINE	Yeah, but Eddie, suppose somebody –
EDDIE	I don't care what question it is. You – don't – know – nothin'. They got **stool pigeons** all over this neighborhood they're payin' them every week for information, and you don't know who they are. It could be your best friend, you hear? (To BEATRICE) Like Vinny Bolzano, remember Vinny?
BEATRICE	Oh, yeah. God forbid.
EDDIE	Tell her about Vinny. (*To* CATHERINE) You think I'm blowin' steam here? (*To* BEATRICE) Go ahead, tell her. (*To* CATHERINE) You was a baby then. There was a family lived next door to her mother, he was about sixteen –
BEATRICE	No, he was no more than fourteen, cause I was to his confirmation in Saint Agnes. But the family had an uncle that they were hidin' in the house, and he snitched to the Immigration.
CATHERINE	The kid snitched?
EDDIE	On his own uncle!
CATHERINE	What, was he crazy?
EDDIE	He was crazy after, I tell you that, boy.
BEATRICE	Oh, it was terrible. He had five brothers and the old father. And they grabbed him in the kitchen and pulled him down the stairs – three flights his head was bouncin' like a coconut. And they spit on him in the street, his own father and his brothers. The whole neighborhood was cryin'.
CATHERINE	Ts! So what happened to him?
BEATRICE	I think he went away. (*To* EDDIE) I never seen him again, did you?
EDDIE	(*rises during this, taking out his watch*) Him? You'll never see him no more, a guy do a thing like that? How's he gonna show his face? (*To* CATHERINE, *as he gets up uneasily*) Just remember, kid, you can quicker get back a million dollars that was stole than a word that you gave away.

From *A View from the Bridge* by Arthur Miller, Act 1

Activity 2

Imagine that you have been asked to participate in a workshop designed to explore the theme of community and identity. Follow these practical stages in the exploration of the text:

- Working in small groups, improvise the events in the story of Vinny Bolzano, including the moment where he makes the telephone call to the authorities. Take photos or a short film to document the process.
- Discuss the possible consequences of Vinny's actions – create a short script for the scene where the immigration officers come to arrest his uncle. Consider the different types of language that the characters might use.
- Now explore the tension between Catherine, Eddie and Beatrice. Nominate roles and place all three actors at the back of the stage. Begin to read the dialogue. Every time a character takes status, ask them to take one step forward. At the end of the piece, make notes on what you have decided or discovered about the relationships between the characters. If possible, video the session and record a commentary.

One of the key features of practice-based research is immersing yourself in the genre, form and/or style of the subject. One of the leading practitioners is Phillip Zarrilli, whose practice-based research into the use of Asian performance practices has included professional training in a range of disciplines, including martial arts, Noh and Kathakali. His interest in the use of physical performance methods has led him to engage in a series of collaborative workshops focused on developing an actor's psychological understanding of the character. A practice-based research approach to the exploration of text could therefore also include the application of practitioner-based methods or theatre styles such as physical theatre.

Activity 3

Design your own practical workshop-based exercise designed to explore the specific relationship between Eddie and Beatrice in the scene in Text 5. Try to include the ideas of a specific practitioner such as Stanislavski (see page 47) or Berkoff (see page 121).

Apply: Create a sample plan for practice as research project

Drawing on your experience of practical exploration of the text, imagine you have decided to create a project plan for a practice-based investigation into the theme of community in Miller's plays. You are investigating the following research question:

> How does Arthur Miller explore the theme of community in his plays? Examine the creation of place and identity in *A View from the Bridge* and *All My Sons*.

The investigation will include a series of three exploratory workshops (such as the one you might have created for Activity 2) and will use Stanislavski's methods to examine the possibilities for staging the text. The intended outcomes are as follows:

- Examine the nature of the theme of community through practical exploration of the plays.
- Use Stanislavski's methods to examine the psychology of key characters.
- Explore Miller's commentary on the different identities of the insider and the outsider in Italian-American communities of the post-war period.

Workshop 1

Focus: Explore the role of Eddie through three key extracts

Improvisation, status exercises, animalisation in which the actors choose a specific animal which most closely resembles the character, and develop the physical characteristics of that animal.

Workshop 2

Focus: Explore the nature of the Italian-American community

Contextual research – construction of a montage of information

Verbatim exploration – newspaper reports on the consequences for those who testify against the illegal acts of others.

Workshop 3

Focus: Compare characterisation of leading 'father figure' roles in both plays

Hot-seating, monologue writing, script-based physical work including given circumstances, magic if and circles of attention.

The outcome of the workshops will be documented using rehearsal notes, video footage, interviews with actors, script annotations and sketches. Evaluation will be undertaken using a range of methods including questionnaires, reflective journals completed by the company and video reflections.

Activity 4

How could you use this model to plan a practice-based research investigation into a playwright or series of texts within a specific genre? Create a project plan for your investigation that specifies activity and provides a clear set of reasons for your choices.

6.6 Developing a research proposal for a practitioner-based investigation

In this chapter, you have explored how to conduct research into genres, practitioners and performance texts. In Chapter 1, you were introduced to the work of Jerzy Grotowski, who was particularly interested in the work of Eugène Ionesco. In this section, you will focus more deeply on Grotowski to see how you could create an appropriate focus for an investigation of a practitioner. First, consider the hallmarks of his system of performance training known as the Poor Theatre.

Spotlight on theatre tradition: **Grotowski's Poor Theatre**

After moving his company to the city of Wroclaw in 1965, Grotowski started work on his most famous piece, *The Constant Prince*, based on the story of the martyrdom of a prince who refuses to exchange his land and his people for his freedom. By this stage he had started to define his 'Poor Theatre' approach, with reference to the stripping away of all but the simplest of staging devices. Grotowski worked intensively with the actor playing the lead role of the Prince, to help him master the physical embodiment of the conflict with his aggressors (represented by the chorus). The production design emphasised these conflicts by costuming the chorus in military uniform, while the Prince was covered only in a loin cloth and remained centre stage for much of the performance. Grotowski believed that the 'total act' of communing with the spectator–performer was the 'actor's deepest calling'. His later work was therefore intended to transcend the separation between actor and performer.

Grotowski's work is characterised by the following stylistic features:

• choral movement led by a focus on intense rhythmic movement and the coordination of the breath of the actors
• repetition of movement and sound, which comes from the movement of the body
• symbolic imagery such as the kneeling of the Prince in supplication to the court
• use of religious text and iconography
• contrasting and extreme emotions – laughter in the face of death and pain
• experimentation with a range of forms of vocal expression including chanting, groaning and animal roaring
• reference to ancient texts and myths
• appeal to the 'collective unconscious' of the spectator or the psychology of the audience who are connected during the performance.

Activity 1

Imagine that you have identified a link between Grotowski's focus on the 'total act' of the performer and the physical style of the more experimental theatre companies to emerge in the last few decades. You have decided on this research question:

> Grotowski's commitment to the achievement of a 'total act of theatre' has had a significant influence on the development of contemporary theatre. Discuss with reference to the work of Théâtre de Complicité and Robert Lepage.

Using the information in this chapter, create a research plan to investigate this statement. Use this template to help you. It assumes a six-week research period. The research period does not include any dedicated writing time.

Research sub- question	Research method	Weeks	Success criteria
1. What are the key features in Grotowski's theatre style?	• Examine Grotowski's writings. • Explore critical commentary on his work. • Examine production photos and reviews of his productions. • Examine visual evidence for his productions including design sketches.	1 and 2	• Clear understanding of Grotowski's style and implications for performers and designers. • Identification of transitions in his work.
2. How has Théâtre de Complicité used Grotowski's ideas?		3 and 4	
3. How has Robert Lepage used Grotowski's ideas?		3 and 4	
4. What is Grotowski's legacy in the theatre of the 21st century?		5 and 6	

What other possible research sub-questions are there? How might you represent your findings? What kind of visual evidence might you want to include?

You now have enough information to help you analyse Grotowski's style and evaluate his influence on modern theatre. An essay plan for this question might look like this:

- Section 1: Introduction to focus of research, including rationale for choice of topic.
- Section 2: Outline of research methods and approach, including evaluation of choices.
- Section 3: Outline key hallmarks of Grotowski's style, including examples from his productions.
- Section 4: Outline of impact on Complicité, with examples from production history and reference to reviews of productions.
- Section 5: Outline of impact on Lepage, including production examples and reference to interviews.
- Section 6: Comparison of Complicité and Lepage, and reference to impact of Grotowski on contemporary companies.
- Section 7: Conclusion: Return to focus of question and summarise key points.

Reflection point

How can you use your experience of working on practitioners to help you identify a practitioner whose work you might be interested in exploring? What elements of their practice have you seen represented in live or digital theatre?

Thinking more deeply

Antonin Artaud was one of the key influences on Grotowski. This final example of an investigation combines a focus on a practitioner with an exploration of a genre. A student has decided to explore the following question, researching a wide range of companies:

> How has Artaud's Theatre of Cruelty influenced the development of modern physical theatre?

Spotlight on practitioner: **Antonin Artaud (1896–1948)**

Artaud's membership of the surrealist movement gave him an interest in the non-naturalistic landscape of dreams and ideas. Artaud wrote material for the theatre that would allow him to rouse the audience from what he considered to be the torpor or inertia of the naturalistic theatre of the time. In the Theatre of Cruelty, the audience is confronted with the cruelty of life – things that are complex or painful – using a range of production methods. The audience is usually positioned close to the action, in the round. During the performance, the senses are bombarded with stark images, bright lights and loud clashing sounds. The characters in Artaud's plays express things that the audience might think but do not say. The whole 'total theatre' experience is designed to be relentless and demanding.

Below is an example of a conclusion, which is designed to remind the reader of the key points of the investigation.

> In conclusion, we can see how Artaud's radical approach to theatre-making has left a legacy for contemporary audiences. In moving towards an 'extreme consideration of stage elements', theatre-makers of the 21st century have been inspired by Artaud's interest in the relationship between theatre space and the audience. Artaud's determination that the audience would be woken from sleep by a 'combination of objects, silence, shouts and rhythms' has influenced companies such as Punchdrunk and Frantic Assembly to create dramatic sequences which are episodic and multi-layered. It is clear from the popularity of the work of these companies, and the visual evidence from their productions, that the total theatre hieroglyphics of Artaud's original productions have been refashioned for a new audience hungry for spectacle. Artaud's sounds of fury live on.

How could you weave your conclusions together in a final paragraph? Review your choice of research questions and try to create a set of bullet points which you think might provide a summary of your possible findings (a hypothesis).

Glossary

acting area: the space in which the actor may move in full view of the audience

action: the movement or development of the plot or story in a play; this could be created by passage of time or character motivation

alienation effect: distancing an audience from the action to ensure they do not forget that they are watching a play

amphitheatre: a large semi-circular auditorium set in an outside space

amplification: the process of increasing the volume of sound

antagonist: the opponent of the hero or main character of a drama; someone who competes with another character in a play (usually the protagonist)

apron: any part of the stage that extends past the proscenium arch towards the audience

archetypal: typical of a certain kind of person or thing

arena stage: type of stage without a frame or arch separating the stage from the auditorium, in which the audience surrounds the stage area

aside: a comment directed at the audience that is not supposed to be heard by the other characters

audience configuration: the placing of the audience in relation to the performing space

auditorium: the part of a theatre, concert hall or other space in which the audience sits

avant-garde: describing things that are cutting edge or ahead of their time

backdrop: cloth hung at the back of the stage

barndoors: a metal structure placed on the front of a lantern which enables a designer to shape the light, such as narrowing the beam to create the effect of a 'crack' of light

bias: prejudice against a person or group that is considered unfair

blocking: the path of an actor's movement on stage, including entrances and exits

box set: a set with three walls, leaving the fourth wall to be imagined

CAD: computer aided design; used by designers to improve the quality of designs

canonical text: a text considered to be of significant cultural value as a work of art

carbon arc lamp: the first form of electric light; the light is created by a spark or electric arc with two carbon rods with a gap between for air to pass between

caricature: an imitation of a person in which certain striking images are exaggerated for comic effect

catharsis: the feeling of release felt by the audience at the end of a tragedy; a sense of being set free from the emotions of the play

character: a person portrayed in a scripted or devised play, novel, or other artistic piece

choral movements: simultaneous group movement of the actors

chorus: a group of performers who speak, sing or move in unison; the chorus may also narrate the action

chronology: the time sequence of the play (time-ordered, disrupted with flashbacks, etc., over what time period)

climax: the moment of greatest intensity in a play – often the turning point in the drama

comedy: a play that treats characters and situations in a humorous way

conceptualisation: a vision of how the whole play should be interpreted on stage, drawing out particular themes or ideas

conflict: the internal or external struggle between opposing forces, ideas, or interests that creates dramatic tension

contact improvisation: a system in which movement is initiated by physical contact between two bodies; they may roll, fall, turn, jump while giving support to each other, giving and taking weight

contrast: the dynamic use of opposites or significant differences to create dramatic effect

costume/mask plot: an outline of which character is in which scene, when the actors change and what costumes/masks are needed

cue: the trigger for an action to be carried out at a specific time

cue-to-cue: from one essential cue to the next, with actors jumping ahead as required; also known as doing a 'top and tail'

cue list: a list of lighting states with a brief description

cutter: a wardrobe craftsperson who creates patterns and constructs the costumes for female characters (a tailor creates men's costumes)

cyclical: describing a circular structure where the actions at the beginning of the play are revisited at the end

cyclorama (cyc): a large curtain or wall (often concave) positioned upstage in a theatre

dB: abbreviation of 'decibel', the measurement for sound

dénouement: the final moments in the drama, usually involving an element of either resolution or dramatic climax

design elements: a general term to refer to props, costume, set, lighting and sound

devised drama: drama that is developed through collaboration to create an original piece of work

dialogue: spoken conversation used by two or more characters to express thoughts, feelings and attitudes

director: the person responsible for deciding the artistic interpretation of a performance of a play; they work with actors and designers to bring their vision to the stage

downstage: the section of the stage closest to the audience

dramaturg: someone who interprets, edits and adapts a play text to match a director's vision

dress rehearsal: a full performance, with all costumes, set, lighting, sound, etc., as if it was being performed to an audience

Glossary

end on: traditional audience seating layout where the audience is facing the stage from the same direction

ensemble: the group of performers who come together to make a production

epilogue: a short scene or speech at the end of a play, reflecting on what has happened

episodic: a series of complete scenes, each of which contains a unified story or set of actions

exposition: the part of a play that introduces the theme, main characters and current situation in the story

expressionist: expressionism was an artistic movement which emerged in the early 1900s, which aimed to provoke an emotional response in the audience through more abstract forms; in theatre, scenes could be nightmarish and often episodic

farce: a genre of comedy often characterised by a series of unlikely coincidences, a fast pace and careful comic timing; from the French 'farcir', meaning 'to stuff'

flats: upright, light, flat pieces of scenery that can be painted or covered with cloth

flow: the electricity/power running through the light

fly gallery: an area above the stage where scenery can be stored and then 'flown' in and out with the use of ropes

focus: in acting, the act of concentrating or staying in character; it is also used to refer to the way actors and directors can direct the audience's attention to somebody or something on stage; in lighting, the adjustment of the size and shape of a beam of light and/or the direction in which it is aimed

Foley: the reproduction of everyday sounds, normally used in post-production film editing; in theatre, it is used off stage with a microphone to create live sounds as they happen in real time on stage

follow spot (spotlight): a powerful, moveable lighting instrument which projects a bright beam of light on to the stage/actors

footlights: lights used at floor level at the edge of the stage to provide general up-lighting of actors

form: the way in which a play is constructed

fourth wall: an invisible/imagined wall that separates the actors and the audience

gel: a transparent coloured material placed in a gel frame at the front of a lantern to project colour onto the stage

general wash: a general fill of light/colour evenly spread across the stage

genre: the type, or category, of drama that a play belongs to

German Naturalism: not to be confused with a naturalistic acting style, Naturalism was a genre and movement from around 1880 to 1900 which tackled difficult or taboo subject matter, centering around working-class protagonists; the characters are seen as victims of their socio-economic background, 'controlled' by external forces

gesture: any movement of the actor's body that is used to convey meaning, attitude or feeling

given circumstances: the specific conditions that characters find themselves in

gobo: a stencil placed inside a lantern to cast a pattern or shape of light on stage

group narrative: the story created by the group of performers for the audience

improvisation: the spontaneous and imaginative use of movement and speech to create a character or object in a particular situation and to develop the scene

inflection: a change in pitch or loudness to emphasise specific words in speech

in the round: a staging form in which the audience surrounds the stage on all sides

interaction: the action or relationship between two or more characters

juxtaposition: placing two elements close together or side by side to show similarities or differences

Kathakali: a traditional Indian dance that is perfected during a long period of training

language: in drama, the particular way in which a character speaks

lantern: the name given to a light used in the theatre

layer: to stack two or more sounds together to achieve a sound effect/music track; this is usually done using a computer software package where the tracks can be seen 'stacked' on top of one another

lazzi: stock jokes of commedia dell'arte, involving comic improvisation

levels: divisions of the vertical space to create visual interest for an audience

libretto: the words to an opera

lighting plan: a drawing of the lighting design, showing the positions of the lights, lighting bars and further details, such as colours

lighting rig: the structure in which the lanterns (lights) are all placed

limelight: a cylinder of lime that was heated to produce an intense bright white light; used in theatres before the invention of the lightbulb

masking: scenery used to conceal part of the stage or backstage from the audience

masque: a form of entertainment popular in the 16th and 17th centuries, characterised by acting and dancing by masked players

melodramatic: a term first used in the Victorian era to refer to plays interspersed with songs and accompanying orchestral music; melodrama relies heavily on sensationalism and sentimentality, and often takes a strict view of morality

metaphor: a phrase to describe an object that is not literally true but it helps to explain an idea or make a comparison

mime: the art of portraying characters and acting out situations or creating narratives through gesture and body movement without the use of speech

mise en scène: the various elements that make up the staging of a play

mixing desk: a console where sound signals are mixed and then output

mode of speech: a particular form or style of speaking (reflective, narrative, questioning, etc.)

model box: a small-scale three-dimensional model of the stage space

moment: a very brief period of time in which there is a significant change in the drama

monologue: a sustained speech made by a character; can be directed at another character or the audience

montage: a collection of images or words in one visual image

mood: the atmosphere or feeling of a performance, often created by the music, setting or lighting

mood board: a design board that contains lots of visual ideas

motif: a recurring idea in a play

motivation: the reason(s) for a character's behaviour

movement: stage blocking or the physical movements of the actors on-stage during performance; movement also refers to the action of the play as it moves from event to event

moving lights: automated/mechanical lights that can be refocused/repositioned mid-performance (unlike other fixed lanterns)

multi-roling: When an actor performs two or more roles within one play, characterising each one by changes in physicality, voice, costume, etc., while making it plain to the audience that the same performer is playing different parts

narrative arc: the rise and fall of the play's dramatic action

naturalism: a dramatic style that developed in reaction to the artificiality of theatre, which attempts to show reality on stage

non-verbal expression: communicating feelings, responses or attitudes through gesture, physical movement, facial expression or sounds such as sighs or groans

orchestra pit: an area of the theatre where musicians perform, usually located in a lowered area in front of the stage

pace: rate of movement or speed of action, or the vocal delivery of the text

pause: a short period of silence or stillness in a performance when the drama is communicated non-verbally

performers: actors, singers, dancers, stand-up comedians, magicians, musicians are all examples of performers; they are seen by the audience and communicate the piece

physicality: the way in which something is expressed by the position or movement of the body

pick-up: the area around the microphone where sound signals will be in range

pitch: the particular level (high or low) of a voice, instrument or tune

plot: the sequence of events of a play or arrangement of action

poor theatre: a style of theatre which aimed to strip theatre of all non-essentials (for example, a stage, lighting, sound, costume) to focus on the skill of the actors

postmodern: a late 20th century approach in art, architecture, performing arts and literature that typically mixes styles, often in an ironic way

posture: physical alignment of a performer's body, or a physical stance taken by a performer, which conveys information about the character being played

production concept: the overarching idea for a production

production electrician: the person responsible for the electrical design of all practical lighting elements

production element: a feature of the production, such as the set, lighting, sound and costumes

projection: directing the voice out of the body to be heard clearly at a distance

prologue: originating in classical Greek drama, the term means 'before word', and traditionally took the place of a first act, filling in everything that needed to be known before the play proper began

propaganda: information used to promote a cause or present a message, and which may be biased or misleading

props plot: a document that lists the movement of each prop for a production, where it starts and ends and which actor/member of crew has responsibility for it

props: short for 'properties'; anything used in a dramatic production that is not costume or set; props may be personal (such as a pocket watch) or belong to a room or space, such as a chair that a character uses in a physical way

proscenium: an arch or frame separating the stage from the seating area in a theatre, often intended as a picture frame or 'fourth wall' through which the audience views the action

protagonist: the main character in a drama, who often engages with the antagonist to create tension and conflict

proxemics: the physical distance between actors on stage, often used to signify the relationships between characters

pulled: selected from a stock of costumes

raked stage: a sloped stage that slants upwards away from the audience

rehearsal process: the process of bringing a script to life on the stage, after the initial period of exploration by director and cast has been completed; during the rehearsal process, actors learn to work 'off book' (without a script) and focus on achieving complete fluency in the performance

rehearsal report: a form completed in rehearsal to record notes that affect other production departments; given to all heads of departments (costume, lighting, props, set) straight after the rehearsal

repertoire: a body of work attributed to one person

resolution: how the problem or conflict in a drama is solved or concluded

revolve: a mechanically controlled section of the stage that rotates to help speed up the changing of a scene

rhythm: the tempo, pace or regular pattern of the work

Glossary

risk assessment: a form completed after identifying and assessing risks, potential hazards and the probability of something negative happening; these risks are then all documented and the plan updated/modified if anything should change

role: the character portrayed by an actor in a drama

rostrum: a stationary block/platform for actors to sit or stand on (plural 'rostra')

royalties: a sum paid to a composer or writer for each public performance of their work or each copy of it sold

satire: a play in which irony, exaggerated characters and ridicule are used to expose or attack aspects of society, such as social snobbery or hypocrisy; often used in political drama

satyr play: a rude, energetic and boisterous drama that followed on from or commented on heroic tragedies, placing the protagonists in ridiculous situations; the 'satyrs' who appeared in these plays were legendary half-human, half-animal creatures

scale drawing: a drawing that shows the design to scale, for example 1:50

scene: a self-contained unit within a play, with its own structure

scenery: the theatrical equipment used in a dramatic production to communicate environment or represent a real place

scrim: a very light, translucent fabric used extensively in theatre, sometimes referred to as gauze

script: the written document setting out scene descriptions, stage directions and lines to be spoken by performers in a formal way

scroller: a mechanical accessory that goes on the front of a parcan and which 'scrolls' through several colours

set: the physical surroundings visible to the audience, in which the action of the play takes place

set piece: a scene that audiences would recognise as typical of plays in the genre

setting: when and where the action of a play takes place

shoaling: moving together as a group

skene: a 3D structure like a tent or hut, made of fabric or light wood, placed at the back of the stage, in front of which performances took place

SketchUp: 3D modelling software

slapstick: fast-paced comedy including disaster or clumsy mishap, often played out in physical sequences, sometimes with the use of comic violence

soundscape: a collage of sounds used to create or change the atmosphere in a drama

spatial awareness: also referred to as spatial relationships, a traditional term for what is currently referred to as proxemics

stage configuration: The layout of the stage in relation to the audience

stage flats: large pieces of scenery designed to frame the stage picture

staging: a general term for the choices made by directors and actors about using or adapting performance spaces, as in 'staging a play'

status: the power dynamic between two characters

stimulus: the starting point for a new piece of developed performance work; the finished piece can either be directly related to or inspired by the stimulus, or it can provoke a new direction of ideas

structure: the arrangement of and relationship between the scenes and acts within a play or devised piece

style: the distinct way in which a play is performed, often influenced by the specific time and place in which the play is written

super-objective: the purpose which a character works towards during the play

suspense: a feeling of uncertainty as to the outcome, used to build interest and excitement on the part of the audience

symbolism: the use of symbolic language and imagery to represent ideas or qualities or evoke emotions

tableau: a still moment, in which actors position themselves to suggest relationships between characters, highlight an emotion or increase tension

technical rehearsal: a rehearsal that takes place before the dress rehearsal, in which all technical elements (lighting, sound, set, costume, etc.) are brought together and run through to check for any errors or issues

Theatre of the Absurd: a term referring to plays written after 1945 by writers such as Samuel Beckett and Eugène Ionesco, which influenced later playwrights including Harold Pinter; in a time of anxiety caused by the threat of nuclear warfare, and following the horrors of World War II, the plays seem to question the nature of existence or to represent it as meaningless and absurd

theme: the basic idea of a play

through-line: the journey of a character from the start to the end of the play

thrust stage: a stage that extends into the audience area, with seats on three sides of a 'T'-shaped acting space

tragedians: playwrights who write tragedies or actors who perform them

tragedy: a form of drama based on human suffering that stimulates a mixture of sympathy and horror in the audience at the inevitable downfall, usually death, of the protagonist

transcript: an accurate written account of a conversation, which might include speech utterances such as 'Um' or 'Err', as well as pauses and hesitations

transition: movement, passage or change from one act, scene, section, position, state, concept, etc., to another

traverse staging: a form of staging where the audience is on either side of the acting area

troupe: a group of touring actors who perform in different places

upstage: a position further away from the audience on a proscenium arch or end on stage

vocal expression: how an actor uses his or her voice to convey character

voiceover: speech played through the sound system, sometimes without a physical performer

volume: The amount of sound created can be varied to create mood or atmosphere

white card model: a model that is accurate in 1:25 scale, but contains no surface details, so it can be easily changed
wings: the sides of the stage, out of sight of the audience

zanni: the name given to the stock comic characters in commedia dell'arte

Acknowledgements

We are grateful to the following for permission to reproduce copyright material:

Extracts on pp.13-14, 17, from *The Township Plays: No-Good Friday; Nongogo; The Coat; Sizwe Bansi is Dead; The Island* by Athol Fugard, Oxford University Press, copyright © 1972. Reproduced with permission of the Licensor through PLSclear; Extracts on pp.19-23, from *Lorca-Three Plays: Blood Wedding, Yerma, The House of Bernarda Alba*, by Federico García Lorca, translated by Jo Clifford. Reproduced by permission of Nick Hern Books; Extracts on pp.27, 28, from *The World of Extreme Happiness* by Frances Ya-Chu Cowhig, Methuen Plays, copyright © 2014 by Frances Ya-Chu Cowhig, Methuen Drama, an imprint of Bloomsbury Publishing Plc. Reproduced with permission; Extracts on pp.54, 55, 57-58, 62, from *The Servant of Two Masters* by Carlo Goldoni, translated by Edward Joseph Dent, copyright © 1928, 1952 by Cambridge University Press. Reproduced with permission of the Licensor through PLSclear; The poem on p.96, "The Road Not Taken" by Robert Frost from *The Poetry of Robert Frost*, edited by Edward Connery Lathem, copyright © 1916, 1969 by Henry Holt and Company, © 1944 by Robert Frost. Used by permission of Henry Holt and Company. All rights reserved; Extracts on pp.108, 114, 125, from *The Changeling* by Thomas Middleton and William Rowley, edited by Michael Neill, Methuen Drama, an imprint of Bloomsbury Publishing Plc. Reproduced with permission; Extracts on pp.116, 134, from *Mother Courage and Her Children* by Bertolt Brecht, translated by John Willet, copyright © 1980 by Bertolt Brecht, Methuen Drama, an imprint of Bloomsbury Publishing Plc. Reproduced by permission; An extract on p.120, from *The Three Theban Plays* by Sophocles, translated by Robert Fagles, translation copyright © 1982, 1984 by Robert Fagles. Used by permission of Viking Books, an imprint of Penguin Publishing Group, a division of Penguin Random House LLC. All rights reserved; Extracts on pp.139, 143-144, from *The Jungle* by Joe Robertson and Joe Murphy, Faber & Faber Ltd, 2018. Reproduced by permission of the publisher; Extracts on pp.150-152, from *The Cherry Orchard* by Anton Chekhov, translated by Trevor Griffiths/Helen Rappaport, copyright © 1978, 1989 by Trevor Griffiths. Reproduced by permission of United Agents on behalf of Trevor Griffiths; Extract on p.171, from 'Theatre review: Blood Wedding, Dundee' by Joyce McMillan, *The Scotsman*, 9 March 2015, https://www.scotsman.com. Reproduced by permission of the author; Extracts on pp.175, 178, from *The Chairs/Les Chaises* by Eugène Ionesco, translated by Derek Prowse & Donald Watson, copyright © 1954 by Editions Gallimard, Paris. Reproduced with permission; Extracts on pp.187, 189, 193, from *A View from The Bridge* by Arthur Miller, copyright © 1955, 1957, 1960 by Arthur Miller, renewed © 1983, 1985, 1988. Used by permission of The Wylie Agency (UK) Limited and Viking Books, an imprint of Penguin Publishing Group, a division of Penguin Random House LLC. All rights reserved.

Every effort has been made to trace copyright holders and to obtain their permission for the use of copyright material. The publishers will gladly receive any information enabling them to rectify any error or omission at the first opportunity.

The publishers would like to thank the following for permission to reproduce copyright material:

(t = top, b = bottom, c = centre, l = left, r = right)

p7 Kobby Dagan/Shutterstock; p9 Aerial-motion/Shutterstock; p11 © Jan Versweyveld; p12 Wikimedia commons; p14 Luoxi/Shutterstock; p16 Bjoern Wylezich/Shutterstock; p20 Iryna Denysova/Shutterstock; p24t Kobby Dagan/Shutterstock; p24b Posztos/Shutterstock; p25 Photobank/Shutterstock; p26 The Finger Players; p29 TZIDO SUN/Shutterstock; p32 Andrey Burmakin/Shutterstock; p36 Liv Oeian/Shutterstock; p37 ID1974/Shutterstock; p39t Nicku/Shutterstock; p39b Everett - Art/Shutterstock; p40 Markara/Shutterstock; p43 Donald Cooper/Photostage; p44 Donald Cooper/Photostage; p46 Marie Linner/Shutterstock; p47 Wikimedia Commons; p49 photolinc/Shutterstock; p50 Geraint Lewis/Alamy Stock Photo; p53l Eugene Ivanov/Shutterstock; p53r Eugene Ivanov/Shutterstock; p59 Nick Brundle/Shutterstock; p71 Rebekah Beattie; p72 Igor Tichonow/Shutterstock; p77 Hand carved and photographed by Glacial Art Ice Sculptors. www.glacialart.com; p83 Donald Cooper/Photostage; p85 FrameStockFootages/Shutterstock; p88 hansen-hansen.com, 2000; p90 Rebekah Beattie; p91 Voyagerix/Shutterstock; p93 LOVESONG by Morgan; Edward Bennett; Leanne Rowe; Sam Cox; Sian Phillips; Dress Rehearsal by Franctic Assembly; Lyric Hammersmith; London, UK; 2011; Credit: Johan Persson/ArenaPAL; p96 Vulcano/Shutterstock; p101 Featureflash Photo Agency; p103 Chris Cornish/Shutterstock; p106 sketch by Holly Barradell; p109 photo and set design by Roman Tatarowicz; p111l Bohbeh/Shutterstock; p111lc ED Reardon/Shutterstock; p111c Tadaki crew/Shutterstock; p111rc Dimitris Leonidas/Shutterstock; p111r Africa Studio/Shutterstock; p112 The PodCast host; p117 REDPIXEL.PL/Shutterstock; p119 Trestle Theatre Company; p122 Farknot Architect/ Shutterstock; p124l Donald Cooper/Photostage; p124c Donald Cooper/Photostage; p124r Donald Cooper/Photostage; p127 CHALERMPHON SRISANG/Shutterstock; p131 Metamorworks/Shutterstock; p132 Holly Barradell; p133 Gianni Pasquini/Ipa/Shutterstock; p135 Kozlik/Shutterstock; p136 Michael Warwick/Shutterstock; p137 Wavebreakmedia/Shutterstock; p138 National Theatre Archive; p141 National Theatre Archive; p145 HUANG Zheng/Shutterstock; p149 Gorodenkoff/Shutterstock; p151 Donald Cooper/Photostage; p153 Donald Cooper/Photostage; p158 Kongsky/Shutterstock; p166 Robert Paul Laschon/Shutterstock; p167 Jacob Lund/Shutterstock; p173t Johan Persson/ArenaPAL; p173b Costume sketches, Royal Exchange, Manchester, 2003 © Simon Higlett; p177 Image Courtesy of Terry Braun; p179 Vibrant Pictures/Alamy Stock Photo; p181 Donald Cooper/Photostage; p182 *Oedipus Rex*, copyright © 2004, Bunkamura; p184l Panos Karas/Shutterstock; p184r Korolevskaya Nataliya/Shutterstock.